Public Expenditures, Grow

**Other Books Published in Cooperation with
the International Food Policy Research Institute**

IFPRI

From Parastatals to Private Trade: Lessons from Asian Agriculture
Edited by Shahidur Rashid, Ashok Gulati, and Ralph Cummings Jr.

*The Dragon and the Elephant: Agricultural and Rural Reforms
in China and India*
Edited by Ashok Gulati and Shenggen Fan

WTO Negotiations on Agriculture and Developing Countries
Anwarul Hoda and Ashok Gulati

*Transforming the Rural Nonfarm Economy:
Opportunities and Threats in the Developing World*
Edited by Steven Haggblade, Peter B. R. Hazell, and Thomas Reardon

*Agricultural Research, Livelihoods, and Poverty:
Studies of Economic and Social Impacts in Six Countries*
Edited by Michelle Adato and Ruth Meinzen-Dick

*Information and Communication Technologies for Development
and Poverty Reduction: The Potential of Telecommunications*
Edited by Maximo Torero and Joachim von Braun

What's Economics Worth? Valuing Policy Research
Edited by Philip Pardey and Vincent H. Smith

Land and Schooling: Transferring Wealth across Generations
By Agnes R. Quisumbing, Jonna P. Estudillo, and Keijiro Otsuka

*Household Decisions, Gender, and Development:
A Synthesis of Recent Research*
Edited by Agnes R. Quisumbing

Ending Hunger in Our Lifetime: Food Security and Globalization
By C. Ford Runge, Benjamin Senauer, Philip G. Pardey,
and Mark W. Rosegrant

The Triangle of Microfinance: Financial Sustainability, Outreach, and Impact
Edited by Manfred Zeller and Richard L. Meyer

Reforming Agricultural Markets in Africa
By Mylène Kherallah, Christopher Delgado, Eleni Gabre-Madhin,
Nicholas Minot, and Michael Johnson

Public Expenditures, Growth, and Poverty

Lessons from Developing Countries

EDITED BY SHENGGEN FAN

Published for the International Food Policy Research Institute

The Johns Hopkins University Press
Baltimore

The Johns Hopkins University Press
2715 North Charles Street
Baltimore, Maryland 21218-4363
www.press.jhu.edu

International Food Policy Research Institute
2033 K Street, NW
Washington, DC 20006
(202) 862-5600
www.ifpri.org

LIBRARY OF CONGRESS CATALOGING-IN-PUBLICATION DATA

Public expenditures, growth, and poverty in developing countries : lessons from developing
countries / edited by Shenggen Fan ; contributors: David Coady . . . [et al.].
    p.   cm. — (International Food Policy Research Institute)
  Includes bibliographical references and index.
  ISBN-13: 978-0-8018-8858-8 (hardcover : alk. paper)
  ISBN-13: 978-0-8018-8859-5 (pbk. : alk. paper)
  ISBN-10: 0-8018-8858-1 (hardcover : alk. paper)
  ISBN-10: 0-8018-8859-X (pbk. : alk. paper)
  1. Poverty—Developing countries.   2. Poverty—Developing countries—Prevention.
3. Expenditures, Public—Developing countries.   4. Developing countries—Economic conditions
—20th century.   5. Developing countries—Economic policy—2000–   6. Economic
development—Developing countries.   I. Fan, Shenggen.   II. Coady, David.
  HC59.72.P6P83   2008
  339.4′6091724—dc22   2007037843

A catalog record for this book is available from the British Library.

Special discounts are available for bulk purchases of this book. For more information,
please contact Special Sales at 410-516-6936 or specialsales@press.jhu.edu.

Contents

Figures

Tables

Foreword

Despite the recent successes in accelerating economic growth and cutting poverty and hunger in many emerging economies, more than 1 billion people still live on less than one dollar a day and more than 800 million people still suffer from hunger.

National governments and their international development partners clearly need to do more. Public expenditures can play a crucial role in promoting pro-poor economic growth, in providing public services to the poor, and in transferring income directly to the poor. However, public resources are limited, and their competing uses have enormous opportunity costs. In addition, the effects of public expenditures on growth and poverty may vary by sector and subnational region. These effects may also change over time, depending on the stages of economic development, social and economic conditions, and governance structures. Governments therefore require a strategy that will enable them to allocate and manage public expenditures as efficiently as possible while pursuing higher growth and accelerated poverty reduction.

To support public spending that maximizes pro-poor impact, this book presents a synthesis of the issues, state-of-the-art methods, and major findings related to public expenditures, growth, and poverty. Agricultural research, rural infrastructure, and rural education turn out to be the three areas of government spending that have high returns not only in terms of economic growth but also in terms of poverty reduction. Many antipoverty programs, however, do not seem to have significant impact on the poor. Social spending in the form of food, education, and health subsidies can have positive impact on poor people in the short and long runs, but such programs must be carefully designed, monitored, and governed; many of these programs are not well targeted and are inefficient.

In terms of stages of development, most developing countries still need to focus on broad-based growth, and they should do so by allocating more government expenditures to the sectors that can generate income for the majority of the poor. In most African countries and some Latin American and Asian countries where agriculture remains the livelihood of many poor people, for example, governments need to accelerate agricultural growth generally, through public spending on agricultural research, irrigation, and rural infrastructure. For many emerging economies, such as Chile, China, Thailand, and Vietnam, the focus should shift to spending on economic growth, particularly agricultural growth, in regions and communities where the poor are increasingly concentrated. Social protection for poor households should be phased in much earlier than is often the case.

This book will provide researchers, policymakers, and practitioners with important, up-to-date knowledge about how government spending can best benefit poor people while accelerating economic growth.

Joachim von Braun
Director General, IFPRI

Acknowledgments

Most of the chapters in this book are syntheses of studies that the authors and other prominent researchers have conducted. I am most grateful to the chapter authors and their collaborators for their past and present contributions. In particular, I thank David Coady for co-managing the IFPRI synthesis project that ultimately made this book possible.

Connie Chan-Kang, Neetha Rao, Anuja Saurkar, and Annie White provided able research assistance for Chapters 1, 2, 3, and 7. Most of the cross-country data on government expenditures were collected, complied, standardized, and updated by Anuja Saurkar.

I am also grateful to IFPRI's Publications Review Committee, chaired by Ramón Lopez, for coordinating the review of this book. I thank the anonymous reviewers for their comments on the draft.

Funding from IFPRI's synthesis project supported David Coady, Hans Lofgren, and I in writing our chapters. Funding from the World Bank, U.S. Agency for International Development, European Commission, and Department for International Development (U.K.) supported some of the original research drawn upon in the syntheses in several chapters, particularly Chapters 2 and 3. Funding provided to Shenggen Fan by the Natural Science Foundation of China (approval number 70525003) and the Chinese Academy of Agricultural Sciences is also acknowledged.

Public Expenditures, Growth, and Poverty

1 Introduction

DAVID COADY AND SHENGGEN FAN

More than 1 billion people around the globe still live on less than U.S. $1 a day as measured in purchasing power parity in 2001. Over the past 20 years, rapid economic growth in East Asia has reduced the *total* number of poor people from 800 million in 1981 to 270 million in 2001. In South Asia, during the same period the total number of poor people declined only marginally, from 480 million to 430 million. However, poverty rates did not fall in Africa, Latin America, or the Middle East, and the rate of economic growth was far lower during this period than it was 20 years ago. In fact, the number of the poor in Sub-Saharan Africa has almost doubled, from 160 million in 1981 to more than 300 million in 2001 (Chen and Ravallion 2004). Using the poverty line measured at U.S. $2 per day, the world's total poor increased from 2.5 billion in 1981 to more than 2.7 billion in 2001, and the associated poverty rate fell from 67 percent to 53 percent, which represents a much slower rate than the drop in the U.S. $1 per day poverty rate. It is obvious, therefore, that a "business as usual" approach is wholly inadequate. Instead, a more effective poverty alleviation strategy is urgently required in recognition of the fact that persistent poverty and malnutrition result in irreversible costs to human and economic development.

Developing countries and the international development community are intensifying their efforts by increasing and redirecting resources in order to achieve development objectives. September 2000 saw the largest-ever gathering of world leaders at the United Nations (U.N.) Millennium Summit, with some 150 heads of state participating. Out of this summit came the Millennium Development Goals (MDGs), which outline an agenda for reducing poverty and its causes and manifestations.[1] In 2002, at the Monterrey Conference, rich countries renewed their pledge to increase their development assistance to 0.7 percent of their gross domestic product (GDP). More recently, the U.N. Millennium Project, headed by Jeffrey Sachs, called for a "big push" in donor support to meet the MDG challenge. In 2005, the Commission for Africa,

---

1. The eight goals include cutting poverty and hunger by half; improving education, health, and nutrition; and enhancing development partnerships.

chaired by U.K. Prime Minster Tony Blair, called for rich countries to double their aid to Africa and to cancel debts poor countries owe to rich countries.

Many developing countries have also adopted the concept of poverty reduction strategy papers, or an equivalent, to outline strategic plans and to earmark financial resources to achieve their poverty reduction goals. In Africa, New Partnership for Africa's Development was formed by the Assembly of Heads of State and Government in July 2001 in Zambia. The objective is to make an explicit commitment to a new partnership in development by improving their governance through monitoring and evaluation systems implemented by peer reviewers.

If all these resources are in place, the key questions are these: Can these pledged resources achieve the stated objectives of growth and poverty reduction? What types of public spending programs have the largest impact on the poor, and under what conditions? How should these resources be allocated among different sectors, such as agriculture, infrastructure, health, and education? Before we answer these questions, there is a need to understand how these public resources have contributed to development in the past.

Over the past decade, the International Food Policy Research Institute (IFPRI) has engaged in numerous studies related to public spending and its impact on growth and poverty reduction. These studies have addressed different issues, using different methodologies. Specifically, the IFPRI studies have examined different types of public spending, ranging from short-term subsidies and targeted programs to long-term, broad-based investments in rural education, infrastructure, and technology. Some of these studies have led policymakers in many developing countries to rethink their priorities in allocating their public resources and introducing policy reforms to increase the efficiency of public interventions. However, these independent studies were conducted by different researchers and assessed different types of spending without an explicit integrating framework, which limits the potential impact of these studies both academically and in terms of their policy relevance.[2]

The overarching objectives of this book are to synthesize IFPRI's recent studies on public spending by analyzing the issues addressed and the methodologies used and to draw synergies and lessons from these studies. The key policy issues addressed in the book include the following: What should be the role of government, particularly government spending, in promoting growth and poverty reduction? Within public investment or social spending, how should these types of expenditures be allocated to maximize their impacts on growth and poverty reduction? Are there trade-offs between growth and poverty ob-

---

2. In a recent study, Lopez (2007) also showed the importance of setting the right priorities for government spending to achieve social development goals. He found that nonsocial subsidies reduce agricultural GDP and rural per capita income and degrade natural resources by the overuse of agricultural land.

jectives both within and across sectoral expenditures? By integrating past studies and resulting lessons in order to address these contemporary questions, we offer new insights on the linkages between public spending, growth, and poverty.

The Rationale for Government Expenditures

The theoretical framework used in this book is the standard approach used in public economics to determine the appropriate role of government—particularly its role through public spending—in stimulating the development process. Over the past fifty years or so, both the theory and the practice concerning the role of government intervention have fluctuated widely.[3] As many developing countries acquired independence in the 1950s, the general sentiment was one of suspicion toward a free market and its ability to deliver growth. This was particularly true in economies where there was a perception that the manufacturing sector was artificially suppressed. This led to extensive government interventions, directed mainly at promoting industrialization through import substitution strategies.

In spite of a relatively good growth record in the 1960s, both the oil crisis of the late 1970s and the subsequent debt crisis in the early 1980s resulted in substantially lower (or even negative) growth over these decades. This, in turn, led to a backlash against government "interference" in the economy, which was perceived as stifling private initiatives and preventing efficient responses to these shocks (Little 1982; Rodrik 1999). Led by the Bretton Woods institutions and the so-called Washington Consensus, structural adjustment programs in the 1980s and the early 1990s focused on "rolling back the state" and "making markets work."

Over time, however, it became obvious that these reforms were not delivering the expected growth. This was attributed to a failure to recognize the need for effective institutions to implement required changes.[4] As a result, structural adjustment programs began to place more emphasis on governance and "reinvigorating the state's capability" (World Bank 1997, 27). There was also a more explicit recognition that if such programs were to be capable of delivering more broad-based growth, there was a need to develop more effective institutions for providing social safety nets and social insurance. Furthermore, it was widely accepted that in the absence of effective legal, regulatory, and political institu-

---

3. Stern (1989, 621) refers to the former as "unbalanced intellectual growth," which undoubtedly partly reflects the role that ideology, as opposed to economic analysis, has played in dictating the extent and nature of state involvement in society.

4. There is now general agreement that strong and effective government institutions played a key role in stimulating and fostering economic growth in East Asian countries. For example, government policies to promote physical and human capital accumulation, combined with effective macroeconomic management, were crucial in generating broad-based and sustainable growth (World Bank 1993).

tions, structural adjustment programs were likely to have many unintended adverse consequences and therefore less likely to be promoted by the governments and peoples of developing countries. Thus, institutional reform and capacity building were identified as preconditions for the successful implementation of market-based reforms.

This evolution of theoretical and empirical thinking on the development process is reflected in the current development paradigm. Although there is a broad consensus that renewed economic growth is a necessary condition for meeting the MDGs, it is also widely accepted that growth alone is insufficient and that more direct public action is required (World Bank 1990, 1997; Sahn and Stifel 2000; Haddad et al. 2003). In order for growth to become a sufficient condition, three interdependent policy requirements have been identified. First, growth needs to be broad based, that is, more intensive in labor and agriculture so as to benefit the poor. Second, the asset base of poor households (in particular, their access to education and health services) needs to be strengthened so that they can participate in the growth process. And third, short-term public transfers are required to protect and increase the consumption of the poorest households until they participate in benefits from increased growth through more productive employment opportunities.[5]

To achieve these policy conditions, public spending policy, in particular, plays a crucial role.[6] However, it is not just the scale of government spending that matters, but also where and how public expenditures are allocated and used. Where the initial allocation of public spending across sectors is suboptimal, large welfare gains may be possible from reallocating public spending to sectors in which the government has a comparative advantage. Any credible evaluation of the levels and composition of public expenditures must start with a clear understanding of the underlying rationale or motivation for government intervention. The answers to the questions regarding when, where, and how governments should intervene depend sensitively on the perspective from which one approaches the issue. For our purposes, it is useful to separate the existing perspectives into two categories: the *welfarist approach* and the *social justice approach.*

5. Consistent with these objectives, Drèze (1991) has identified two distinct, but interrelated, roles for public policy. First, there is the *promotional* role, focused on eliminating chronic poverty, which refers to a situation in which households remain in poverty over time due to their small asset base. Alleviating chronic (or "structural") poverty requires an enhancement of their asset base. Second, there is the *protective* role, focused on increasing the current consumption of the structurally poor as well as preventing households that are vulnerable to adverse shocks from entering into a spiral of poverty. See also Morduch (1994) and Hoddinott and Baulch (2000a,b) for related discussions.

6. The World Bank (1997) identifies five fundamental tasks of government as (1) establishing a foundation of law, (2) maintaining a nondistortionary policy environment and macroeconomic stability, (3) protecting the environment, (4) investing in basic social services such as education and health, and (5) protecting the vulnerable. See also Stiglitz (2000) for a similar perspective.

Arguably the most influential, the *welfarist approach* identifies two motivations for government intervention. First, governments should intervene to address market failures and bring about a more efficient allocation of scarce resources. And second, governments should intervene to improve the distribution of resources and reduce poverty. The sources of market failure typically identified in the literature are the absence of competitive markets, the existence of positive or negative externalities in consumption and production, the undersupply of public goods by the market, imperfect information on production and consumption opportunities, missing or imperfect markets, and coordination failures (Atkinson and Stiglitz 1980; Stern 1989; Hoff and Stiglitz 2001). Economic theory also provides guidance on the range of policy instruments that could be used to address these market failures and to reduce poverty, as well as on the likely trade-offs between equity and efficiency inherent in each.

But welfarist theory also recognizes that what governments can achieve is limited by information and administrative constraints, both of which must be understood in order to determine whether and how to intervene. For example, where firms or individuals have more information on the costs and benefits of their decisions, theory suggests that decentralized market-based instruments are preferable. This argument is often used by those advocating wider use of environmental charges as opposed to exclusive reliance on more command-and-control quantity-based regulatory approaches. Where governments do not have access to effective direct instruments for income redistribution, they may have to rely on less efficient policy instruments for redistribution. This is how universal food subsidies have often been rationalized.

It is also important to recognize that equity-efficiency trade-offs are not always present. Where market failures are more pervasive among the poor (for example, where the poor are poor because they are disproportionately affected by market failures), "win-win" possibilities arise, where government intervention leads to both a more efficient and a more equitable allocation of resources. Poverty itself may be the source of the market failure, for example, where lack of access to credit and the absence of savings prevent poor households from accumulating income-generating assets. In this case, the poor are caught in a "poverty trap" that gives rise to persistent poverty. Strategies for alleviating poverty that address both the market failure and the resource constraints dimensions of persistent poverty may thus give rise to a self-reinforcing "virtuous cycle" whereby public policy enables the poor to pull themselves out of poverty through their own actions (Hoff 1994; Banerjee 2001; Ravallion 2002). It is important, therefore, to avoid excessive pessimism regarding a negative trade-off between equity and efficiency objectives and recognize the strong synergies that exist by simultaneously addressing growth and distributional issues.

The *social justice approach* involves justifying government intervention based on various concepts of social justice. Two such approaches that have gained prominence over the past three decades are the *basic needs approach* and the *capabilities approach*. Both of these distinguish between income as a "means" or an "end," and they often highlight the lack of correlation between income and other outcomes that enter into one's concept of development. State intervention is therefore often justified by appealing to some concept of a *just society,* defined in terms of people's right to access some basic needs or capabilities. Intervention is justified when market forces fail to ensure such access.[7]

The *basic needs approach* typically focuses on human needs in terms of specific commodities such as health, food, education, water, shelter, and transport (Streeten 1984). Proponents of this approach argue that, because of the public-good characteristics of these (and other) sectors, the private sector will not supply adequately. This is particularly true in areas that are rural or sparsely populated, which are characteristics often synonymous with poverty.[8] The focus on public-good characteristics clearly introduces a strong overlap with the welfarist approach. The *capabilities approach* views income as a means to the purchasing of goods and services that are valued not only for the utility derived directly from their consumption, but also because they expand one's capability to function as a valued member of society (Sen 1985, 1987).What matter are not only one's actual achievements but also one's potential to achieve.

Where market forces do not allow households to satisfy basic needs or achieve some basic capabilities, there is an argument for public action. Therefore, these approaches appeal to the concept of specific egalitarianism, which requires equality in the distribution of access to certain basic goods and services. Existing distributions and policies that influence them are thus valued in relation to the "distance" from equality in the relevant basic needs or capabilities dimensions. However, the issue of trade-offs, which are especially important in the presence of budget constraints, is not directly addressed. In other words, the budget available to achieve these basic needs or capabilities is implicitly assumed to be endogenous in the sense that it is assumed to be adequate to achieve all basic needs or capabilities. This compares to the welfarist approach, where all distributions and outcomes are essentially expressed in terms of a money metric welfare *numeraire* and higher aggregate income (i.e., efficiency) can be traded off against increasing inequality of income (i.e., equity). Also note that under both of the social justice approaches considered the exact form of action required is still an open question and, from this perspective, the insights from the welfarist approach may therefore still be valid.

---

7. The "freedom to choose" is also often considered an important dimension of a just society. Libertarians tend to focus more on preventing the government from restricting free choice than on the equally important role of government in promoting such freedoms. These freedoms constitute an important component of individual "capabilities" (that is, the capability of turning "means," such as income, into "ends," such as health and nutrition status), as discussed by Sen (1992).

8. The inclusion of food in the list of "basic needs" is possibly problematic from this perspective, because it is likely that household consumption is more often than not constrained by income as opposed to inadequate market supplies (Drèze and Sen 1989).

As indicated earlier, it is extremely important that the role of public policy be understood within the existing set of economic, social, and political *institutions*. Even with the minimalist role assigned to it under a laissez-faire economy, there is an implicit assumption that effective legal institutions are required for the establishment and protection of property rights and the enforcement of voluntary contracts between market participants. The establishment of secure and stable property rights has played a crucial role in modern economic growth. The ability to reap rewards from the accumulation of capital and from innovations provided the incentive for such activities, which underpinned this growth process (North and Thomas 1973; North and Weingast 1989). Generally, the coercive authority to establish and enforce property rights is vested in the state or its local representatives. But in many developing countries, formal state law is ineffective (i.e., too costly, slow, or corrupt), so such authority lies de facto within the domain of informal kinship or community organizations, often acquired through tradition and customs (i.e., social norms).

Both the welfarist and the social justice approaches provide motivations for public intervention on both efficiency and equity grounds. In the presence of market failures (often thought to be pervasive in and a key characteristic of developing countries), economic activities generate "external effects" that need to be internalized in private decisions somehow. One can view successful development strategies as those that develop and enhance institutions capable of achieving this end. As already indicated, these institutions can be state or community oriented and formal or informal. Very often, existing informal institutions are an efficient response in a constrained environment, and state interventions will not always be better at overcoming these constraints. Therefore, before superimposing state intervention on communities, it is important that one have a deep understanding of existing informal institutions, their roles (e.g., regarding efficiency and distribution), and incentive mechanisms. In this respect, reforms that build on existing institutional capabilities, and evolve gradually based on these institutional capacities, are likely to be more effective.

Where the development process (or the reform or intervention process) displaces such institutions, it is important that other institutional arrangements be put in place accordingly. There are many examples in which effective community arrangements work better than ineffective public schemes. For example, 70 percent of irrigated area in Nepal falls under farm (or community) management irrigation systems (FMIS). It is estimated that 40 percent of all food is produced in 15,000 FMIS in hill areas and in 1,700 systems in the Tarai of Nepal (Pradhan 2000). An in-depth comparison of farm-managed and publicly managed systems in Nepal shows that a farm-managed irrigation system does better on performance indicators such as agricultural productivity (Lam 1998). Similarly, to the extent that the development process involves a dilution of informal distributive or insurance arrangements, formal arrangements need to be put in place.[9] Platteau (1991) argues that traditional systems are often less effective because of the existence of population pressures, incentive problems, and covariate risks and that an effective system of social security must go beyond an exclusive reliance on traditional institutions without neglecting their potential contribution.

Consistent with all this, in a recent article Rodrik (2000) identified five core categories of market-supporting institutions: (1) institutions to establish secure and stable property rights, (2) institutions to internalize the external effects arising from market failures, (3) institutions to promote macroeconomic stabilization, (4) institutions to provide social insurance or safety nets, and (5) institutions to manage conflicts (in particular, distributional conflicts). Because the appropriate institutional framework depends on the historical evolution of social institutions and on the nature and capacity of existing institutions, the solution is likely to be highly country specific. Also, with respect to market failures, these are likely to be sector specific, and thus so, too, must the appropriate institutional and public policy responses.

It is occasionally useful to view the formulation of public policy from the perspective of a "social planner." However, when evaluating and prescribing public policies in practice, one should be careful to do so within the wider policy environment of that country. The public policies that should be prescribed, and those that are actually implemented, should reflect *administrative, bureaucratic, political, and social feasibility.*[10] The choice of instruments (e.g., reliance on indirect rather than direct taxation) in developing countries is strongly influenced by administrative constraints, and these may change over time. Or they may reflect the vested interests of political and bureaucratic parties and their constituents as much as those of some fictitious social planner. How public policies impact such groups should therefore play a central role in policy design. Some very efficient transfer instruments may be politically less acceptable (e.g., land taxes) or more acceptable (e.g., universal subsidies).[11]

---

9. The development process is often characterized as involving an increase in idiosyncratic risk while simultaneously involving a breakdown of informal relationships that previously provided a social insurance function. Developed countries have developed "welfare states" in response to such problems. In the words of Rodrik (2000, 19): "Social insurance legitimizes a market economy because it renders it compatible with stability and social cohesion." But it is important to allow for a whole range of formal and informal institutional arrangements that could serve this function.

10. Reflecting this, a number of other criteria are often used when evaluating public interventions, many of which are concerned with the process and feasibility of interventions as much as with their consequences (i.e., outcomes), such as transparency, simplicity, administrative feasibility, political feasibility, or social acceptability (Stiglitz 1988).

11. For example, although they appear to have played a very important part in the impressive development performance in Southeast Asia and, more recently, in China, direct transfers of assets such as land are uncommon, and most such attempts at redistribution have failed for political reasons (King 1977; Powelson and Stock 1987). According to Banerjee (2001, 469): "Land reforms . . . have failed more often than they have succeeded. This is hardly surprising, given that the traditionally powerful landlord class has a stake in undermining the reform and that government officials can be bribed or coerced to go along with them."

The theory of political economy also suggests that the nature of bureaucratic constraints is also important. For example, bureaucrats may derive power over a large budget and thus prevent progress to a more effective transfer mechanism that reduces the importance of this budget (Atkinson 1995). So the potential for "government failure" may be just as important as the potential for market failure when designing transfer systems. Social attitudes also matter. For example, the relatively low take-up rate of "means-tested" benefits compared to categorical benefits is often attributed to the social stigma associated with receipt of such benefits. Therefore, because social, political, and administrative factors influence the level, composition, and effectiveness of public expenditures, one needs to explicitly recognize these forces when evaluating, designing, or reforming public expenditures. But this is not to deny that an evaluation of such policies within the conventional welfarist tradition is still extremely insightful, not the least from the perspective of identifying the trade-offs between equity and efficiency involved (e.g., comparing the welfare cost of one set of instruments to that of another) as well as identifying the socioeconomic characteristics of potential gainers and losers.

Clearly, whatever public resources are available must be used efficiently in achieving objectives. This requires appropriate recognition of the existing administrative and institutional constraints in developing countries and the fact that capacity can be built up only gradually, over time. It also emphasizes the need to consider the most effective way of "delivering" these resources and the potential roles for community, nongovernment, and private agents. This again highlights the role of the state in supporting rather than supplanting existing formal and informal institutions. Thus, due regard must be given to ensuring that policies are both operationally and financially feasible and sustainable. Although in this book we place special emphasis on the distributional or poverty reduction outcomes of these expenditures, we simultaneously recognize that incentives are equally important in that resources need to be raised and allocated efficiently. Nor can we lose sight of the political economy considerations, because these can play and have played a crucial role in determining which policies are adopted and how effective they are at achieving their objectives.

A Conceptual Framework: The Effects of Public Expenditures on Growth and Poverty

Because public resources are limited and thus have opportunity costs, specifying priorities is clearly critical.[12] We treat the government as a social planner that determines the optimal allocation by maximizing a weighted social welfare

---

12. Public expenditures, regardless of the benefits and their distribution, impose a cost on society to the extent that they have alternative uses and are financed by distortionary taxes. This cost is measured not just in the resources that are diverted from private use but also in the deadweight loss associated with distortionary taxation (i.e., the "marginal cost of public funds"). For

function, such as per capita income, income distribution, or poverty rate.[13] There are many classifications of government spending. The International Monetary Fund and the World Bank often divide total spending into three broad categories: economic spending, social spending, and other spending. Economic spending covers the sectors of agriculture and infrastructure (energy, transport, tele-communication, and so on), while social spending includes health, education, nutrition, and social safety nets. Social spending can be further classified into spending for social services (such as education and health), social insurance (pensions and unemployment insurance), social assistance (cash and in-kind transfers to the poor or certain social groups), and employment-generating pro-grams. These different types of government spending are designed to achieve different social development objectives. Other types of spending include that for general administration and defense.

Government spending can also be divided into spending that will have a long-term impact on growth and therefore poverty reduction and that with short-run effects. The first type is designed to build human and physical capital that will have a long-term impact on economic growth, and therefore income, in-come distribution, and poverty. This typically includes infrastructure, educa-tion, and technology. This type of investment can also contribute to poverty re-duction in the short run through increased demand for intermediate inputs, labor, and other factors of production. The second type is spending for social safety nets or welfare spending that often has an immediate impact on income and poverty through direct income (or in-kind) transfers. But the latter could also have a long-term impact if the transfer is conditioned on households' or communities' building human and physical capital. The social indicators such as improved health and education can also be regarded as direct outcomes of these types of spending, as mentioned in the previous section. Because the ma-jority of the world poor are concentrated in rural areas, we pay particular at-tention to how public spending affects the rural poor.

Figure 1.1 illustrates the general framework for this book. This framework differs from the frameworks of previous literature in the following aspects. A significant feature in the literature is that most of the previous studies have con-sidered only one type of government spending or investment.[14] For example,

---

example, Walters and Auriol (2005) estimated that each unit of public expenditures raised in Africa had, on average, a social cost of $1.17. If the social return of a project is less than the marginal cost of public funds, it is not worth investing in the project.

13. This is similar to the approach used by Deacon (1978), Dunne and Smith (1984), Hayes and Grosskopf (1984), and Trimidas (2001).

14. Several studies have considered some components of public spending, for example, Van de Walle and Nead (1995) and Lopez and Galinato (2007). But Van de Walle and Nead mainly fo-cused on public spending and its relation to distribution outcomes. The important impact on growth and therefore the poverty reduction impact of broader investment were barely mentioned. On the other hand, Lopez and Galinato analyzed the effects of nonsocial subsidies and concluded that the

Alston et al. (2000) reviewed case studies on the returns to agricultural research and development investments. Almost none of these studies considered other investments, such as those in infrastructure, irrigation, and rural education. Similarly, there is a large amount of empirical evidence that returns to education are large (Schultz 1988; Psacharapoulos 1994) and that there is a strong causal relationship between infrastructure investments and economic growth (Canning and Bennathan 2000). Moreover, many developing countries have implemented different antipoverty programs or targeted income or in-kind transfer programs. When assessing the effects of these programs, the opportunity costs (e.g., the government could invest these resources in productive sectors) are often not considered (Dev and Zhang 2004). Failing to include other investments will not only lead to biased estimates of included investment, but also make it difficult to compare returns to different types of investment.

Second, until very recently, the direct impact of productive investments such as those on infrastructure was not perceived as a means of poverty reduction, and the literature often ignored the effect of government spending on poverty through multiple channels. For example, many scholars have demonstrated relationships between economic growth and government spending in general and infrastructure investment in particular (Aschauer 1989; Barro 1990; Kessides 1993; Tanzi and Zee 1997; Canning and Bennathan 2000), and only a few have linked investment to poverty reduction (e.g., Jacoby 2000; Van de Walle 2003; Torero and von Braun 2006).[15] Public investment affects poverty through many channels. Public investment in agricultural research, rural education, and infrastructure increases farmers' income and reduces rural poverty by increasing agricultural productivity. These investments also promote rural wages, nonfarm employment, and migration, thereby reducing rural poverty. Very seldom in the literature have these different effects been assessed together using an integrated framework. Understanding these different effects will provide useful policy insights for improving the effectiveness of national poverty reduction strategies. In addition, it will avoid underestimation of the effects on poverty reduction.

Third, public investment imposes a cost on society and involves a deadweight loss associated with distortionary taxes. Therefore, the effects of public investment have to be linked to its overall social cost using a general equilibrium framework (Bourguignon 1991; Piggott and Whalley 1991; Walters and Auriol 2005).

---

share of subsidies relative to that of private goods (or, equivalently, increasing the share of public goods) in the government's budget has, ceteris paribus, a large and significant positive impact on rural per capita income, reduces certain undesirable environmental effects associated with output expansion, and contributes to poverty reduction.

15. Other studies (Howe 1984; Binswanger, Khandker, and Rosenzweig 1993; Goldstein 1993; Jimenez 1995; Lipton and Ravallion 1995; Van de Walle 1996; Lebo and Schelling 2001) have also tried to link infrastructure investment to poverty reduction and income distribution. But empirical analyses of infrastructure investment and its poverty reduction effects have been few.

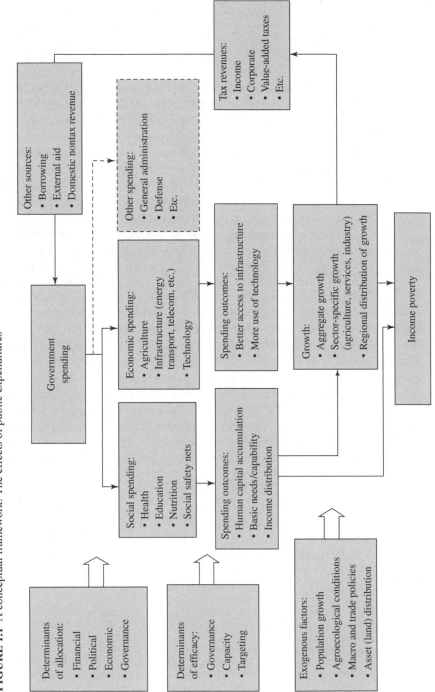

FIGURE 1.1 A conceptual framework: The effects of public expenditures

IFPRI has been working on these related issues, but has not been able to integrate these separate studies using the framework shown earlier. This book is designed to address the resulting knowledge gaps by synthesizing evidence from IFPRI case studies and general literature.

The book starts by first reviewing the trend and composition of government expenditures in developing countries as well as an empirical analysis of the determinants of the spending pattern and their impact. But cross-country analysis is limited by comparability of the data among countries and the difficulty in controlling for institutional, governance, and other socioeconomic, historical, and geographic factors. There is thus a need to conduct country case studies to empirically analyze the effects of various types of government spending on growth and poverty reduction. The country case studies avoid the problem of data comparability between countries, and a deeper understanding of the specific contexts within which expenditures occur facilitates empirical identification of country-specific factors. Countries may also have different priorities for their investments depending on their levels of economic development and their existing investment portfolios, among many other factors.

Many such case studies look only at the effects of public spending on poverty at the aggregate level. The aggregate effects are typically determined in two stages. First the relationship between spending and spending outcomes (e.g., spending in education leads to an improvement in the literacy rate or the average schooling of the population) is estimated, and then the effects of the spending outcomes on growth and poverty reduction are modeled. Combining these two steps will allow the calculation of the marginal growth and poverty reduction effects per unit of spending. While there have been many studies to quantify the effects of spending outcomes, the relationship between spending and spending outcomes depends crucially on specific factors generating these relationships. For example, weak relationships may reflect poor program selection, design, or implementation.

There has been a growing recognition of the importance of social security expenditures in the development process, particularly in protecting the welfare of some of the most disadvantaged and vulnerable groups in society. However, as practiced, the design and implementation of social security programs are often perceived as having numerous shortcomings that seriously undermine their effectiveness. These programs are often very badly targeted and implemented, with substantial leakage to non-poor households, incurring high administrative costs and involving corruption. All too often they fail to generate any long-term benefits. In addition, the overall effectiveness of social safety net systems is compromised by an unnecessarily large number of uncoordinated and duplicative program components. In this book we ask how these expenditures can be made more effective in achieving their objectives, including improved human capital outcomes, in both the short and the long run.

Although government expenditures are allocated to different sectors to achieve specific social or economic development objectives, their impact often goes beyond the targeted sector through their general equilibrium and economywide effects. While adopting an economywide approach is very data intensive and requires complicated modeling that limits its use more widely, it is important to understand how much bias will occur if general equilibrium effects are ignored.

The Organization of This Book

Based on the conceptual framework shown earlier, this book is organized into seven chapters.

To provide a background for the rest of the book, Chapter 2 analyzes the trends, compositions, and impact of government expenditures in developing countries over the past two decades. This is done by compiling data from various sources on government expenditures of different types between 1980 and 2002 and by conducting cross-country regressions. The data collected incorporate government spending by different sectors, including agriculture, education, health, infrastructure, social security and welfare, and defense, and cover 44 developing countries in Asia, Africa, and Latin America. Total government spending and allocation and their effects on GDP growth and agricultural GDP growth were estimated using the data set.

Chapter 3 reviews and synthesizes major issues, methodologies, and findings related to the impacts of government expenditures, conventionally classified as sectors or functions, such as agriculture, education, health, and infrastructure, on growth and poverty reduction. Specifically, emphasis is placed on the channels through which public investment can affect rural poverty. The studies analyze the differential impacts not only on economic growth, but also on poverty reduction and regional inequality. Because the achievement of growth and poverty reduction depends on country-specific conditions, the effects are separated into different geographic regions, even within the same country.

Chapter 4 examines human capital expenditures, such as those on nutrition, health, and education, and their impacts on the poor. The chapter begins with a synthesis of the various motivations provided in the literature to justify public sector involvement in each sector. Then, for each sector in turn, it examines the empirical evidence regarding the effectiveness of these expenditures in improving human capital outcomes, especially for poor households. The chapter reviews evidence using cross-country and cross-regional data, program evaluation data, and data used to evaluate the benefit-incidence analysis of expenditures. It then synthesizes the advantages and disadvantages of each empirical approach. The chapter concludes by identifying and summarizing implications for the policy research agenda.

Chapter 5 examines social security expenditures, which are defined to include expenditures aimed at protecting the welfare of the poorest and most vulnerable households in society. It evaluates programs commonly found in social safety net systems in developing countries from three perspectives, separately analyzing food subsidies,[16] public works and social fund programs, and targeted human capital subsidies. These programs typically account for the largest part of social security budgets, and many of the issues that arise in the context of these programs are relevant to all programs.

Together, Chapters 4 and 5 argue that improvements in program selection, design, and implementation could generate substantial improvements in the effectiveness of these expenditures. In particular, better targeting of these expenditures toward poor households through the appropriate choice of expenditure types and targeting methods (which help to avoid unnecessary "crowding out" of private sector expenditures) and improving the service delivery mechanisms for this population group are likely to generate significant improvements in the effectiveness of public expenditures. However, these are unlikely to be achieved without the prior development of government structures and institutions in addition to improved monitoring and evaluation techniques. Therefore, these institutional settings must also be understood, because they are crucial in determining the feasibility and effectiveness of policy interventions.

Chapter 6 draws from the findings presented in the previous five chapters to explore the impact of different government policies on long-run growth and poverty using the case of Sub-Saharan Africa (SSA). Here insights are obtained from a large body of research on the direct and indirect effects of different public spending policies on economic performance. Methodologically, the chapter analyzes growth in a "prototype" SSA country using a dynamic computable general equilibrium (CGE) model that is an extension of the static standard CGE model used extensively in the literature. This model is applied to a database that captures stylized, structural characteristics of the economies of SSA.

Finally, Chapter 7 brings together the major conclusions and policy implications of the previous chapters, focusing on major challenges and alternative strategies for public spending on education, health and safety nets, infrastructure, agriculture, and agricultural research and development. In particular, setting the right priorities for allocating public expenditures and improving the efficiency of the use of these expenditures by better targeting and reforming institutions are imperative for many developing countries to achieve the MDGs under their tight government budgets. The chapter also presents the lessons learned that can be applied in future research on public spending in developing countries. In addition, it provides guidelines for IFPRI and other relevant re-

---

16. These food subsidies include universal food subsidies, rationed food subsidies, and food stamps.

search institutions to use in setting their future research agendas related to the subject.

References

Alston, J., C. Chan Kang, M. Maria, P. Pardey, and J. Wyatt. 2000. A meta analysis of returns to agricultural R&D: Ex pede herculem? Environment and Production Technology Division Research Report 113. Washington, D.C.: International Food Policy Research Institute.

Aschauer, D. 1989. Is public expenditure productive? *Journal of Monetary Economics* 23: 177–220.

Atkinson, A. 1995. On targeting social security: Theory and western experience with family benefits. In *Public spending and the poor,* ed. D. Van de Walle and K. Nead. Baltimore, Md.: The Johns Hopkins University Press.

Atkinson, A., and J. Stiglitz. 1980. *Lectures in public economics.* New York: McGraw-Hill.

Banerjee, Abhijit V. 2001. Contracting constraints, credit markets and economic development. Cambridge, Mass.: MIT Press.

Banerjee, A., M. Kremer, P. Lanjouw, A. Banerjee, A. Kumer, and J. Lanjouw. 2000. The impact of supplementary teachers in non-formal education centers: A randomized evaluation. World Bank Development Research Group, New York.

Barro, J. R. 1990. Government spending in a simple model of endogenous growth. *Journal of Political Economy* 20 (2): 221–247.

Binswanger, Hans P., Shahidur R. Khandker, and Mark R. Rosenzweig. 1993: How infrastructure and financial institutions affect agricultural output and investment in India. *Journal of Development Economics* 41: 337–366.

Bourguignon, François. 1991. Optimal poverty reduction, adjustment, and growth. *World Bank Economic Review* (Oxford University Press) 5 (2): 315–338.

Canning, D., and E. Bennathan. 2000. The social rate of return on infrastructure investments. Policy Research Working Paper Series 2390. Washington, D.C.: World Bank.

Chen, S., and M. Ravallion. 2004. How have the world's poorest fared since the early 1980s? *World Bank Research Observer* 19 (1): 141–169.

Deacon, R. T. 1978. A demand model for the local public sector. *Review of Economics and Statistics* 60 (1): 169–173.

Dev, M., and L. Zhang. 2004. Anti-poverty strategies and programs: Lessons from China and India. Paper presented at the CAAS (Chinese Academy of Agricultural Sciences)–IFPRI (International Food Policy Research Institute) International conference of the Dragon and the Elephant, Beijing, November 10–11, 2003.

Drèze, J. 1991. Public action for social security foundations and strategy. In *Social security in developing countries,* ed. E. Ahmed, J. Drèze, and A. Sen. Oxford, England: Clarendon.

Drèze, J., and A. Sen. 1989. *Hunger and public action.* Oxford, England: Oxford University Press.

Dunne, J. P., and R. P. Smith. 1984. The allocative efficiency of government expenditure: Some comparative tests. *European Economic Review* 20: 381–394.

Easterly, W. 2001. *The elusive quest for growth: Economists' adventures and mis-adventures in the tropics.* London: MIT Press.

Goldstein, Ellen. 1993. The impact of rural infrastructure on rural poverty. Mimeo, World Bank, South Asia Region.

Haddad, L., H. Alderman, S. Appleton, and L. Song. 2003. Reducing child malnutrition: How far does income growth take us? *World Bank Economic Review* 17 (1): 107–131.

Haynes, K., and S. Grosskopf. 1984. The role of functional form in estimating the demand for local public goods. *Review of Economics and Statistics* 66: 63–179.

Hoddinott, J., and B. Baulch. 2000a. Economic mobility and poverty dynamics in developing countries. *Journal of Development Studies* 36 (1): 1–24.

Hoddinott, J., and B. Baulch, eds. 2002b. *Economic mobility and poverty dynamics in developing countries.* London: Frank Cass.

Hoff, K. 1994. The second theorem of the second best. *Journal of Public Economics* 54 (2): 223–242.

Hoff, K., and J. Stiglitz. 2001. Modern economic theory and development. In *Frontiers of development economics,* ed. G. Meier and J. Stiglitz. Oxford, England: Oxford University Press, 389–459.

Howe, J. D., and P. J. Richards. 1984. Rural roads and poverty alleviation: A study prepared for ILO within the framework of the World Employment Programme's Intermediate Technology Publications, London.

Jacoby, H. 2000. Access to markets and benefits of rural roads. *Economic Journal* 110 (465): 713–737.

Jimenez, Emmanuel. 1995. Human and physical infrastructure: Public investment and pricing policies in developing countries. In *Handbook of development economics,* vol. 3B, ed. J. Behrman and T. N. Srinivasan. North Holland: Elsevier Science.

Kessides, C. 1993. The contributions of infrastructure to economic development: A review of experience and policy implications. Discussion Paper 213, World Bank, Washington, D.C.

King, R. 1977. *Land reform.* London: C. Bell and Sons.

Lam, W. F. 1998. *Governing irrigation systems in Nepal—Institutions, infrastructure, and collective action.* Oakland, Calif.: ICS Press.

Lebo, J., and D. Schelling. 2001. Design and appraisal of rural transport infrastructure: Ensuring basic access for rural communities. Technical Paper 496. Washington, D.C.: World Bank.

Lipton, Michael, and Martin Ravallion. 1995. Poverty and policy. In *The handbook of development economics,* vol. 3, ed. J. Behrman and T. N. Srinivasan, 2251–2657. Amsterdam: Elsevier.

Little, I. 1982. *Economic development.* New York: Basic Books.

Lopez, Ramon, and Gregmar I. Galinato. 2007. Should governments stop subsidies to private goods? Evidence from rural Latin America. *Journal of Public Economics* 91 (5–6): 1071–1094.

Morduch, Jonathan. 1994. Poverty and vulnerability. *American Economic Review* 84 (2): 221–225.

North, D., and R. Thomas. 1973. *The rise of the western world: A new economic history.* Cambridge, England: Cambridge University Press.

North, D., and B. Weingast. 1989. Constitutions and commitment: The evolution of institutions governing public choice in seventeenth century England. *Journal of Economic History* 49: 803–832.

Piggott, John, and John Whalley. 1991. Public good provision rules and income distribution: Some general equilibrium calculations. *Empirical Economics* (Springer) 16 (1): 25–33.

Platteau, Jean-Philippe. 1991. Traditional systems of social security and hunger insurance. In *Social security in developing countries,* ed. E. Ahmad, J. Dreze, J. Hills, and A. Sen. Oxford: Clarendon Press, 112–170.

Powelson, J., and R. Stock. 1987. *The peasant betrayed: Agriculture and land reform in the third world.* Boston: Oelgeschlager, Gunn and Ham.

Pradhan, R. 2000. Water land and law: Changing rights to land and law in Nepal. Katmandu: Legal Research and Development Forum (FREEDEAL), Wageningen Agricultural University (WAU), and Erasmus University Rotterdam (EUR).

Psacharapoulos, G. 1994. Returns to investment in education: A global update. *World Development* 22 (9): 1325–1343.

Ravallion, M. 2002. *Targeted transfers in poor countries: Revisiting the trade-offs and policy options.* Paper presented at the International Food Policy Research Institute / World Bank Vulnerability Workshop at the Third Asia Development Forum, Bangkok.

Rodrik, D. 1999. Where did all the growth go? External shocks, social conflict, and growth collapses. *Journal of Economic Growth* 4 (4): 385–412.

———. 2000. *Development strategies for the next century.* Paper presented at the Institute for Developing Economies conference, Chiba, Japan, January 26–27.

Sahn, D., and D. Stifel. 2000. Poverty comparisons across time and over countries in Africa. *World development* 28 (12): 2123–2155.

Schultz, T. 1988. Economic investment and returns. In *Handbook of development economics,* Vol. 1, ed. H. Chenery and T. Srinivasan. Handbooks in Economics 9. Amsterdam: North-Holland.

Sen, A. 1985. Rights and capabilities. In *Morality and objectivity,* ed. T. Honderich. London: Routledge.

———. 1987. Equality of what? In *Tanner Lectures on Human Values,* Vol. 1, ed. S. McMurrin. Cambridge, England: Cambridge University Press.

———. 1992. *Inequality reexamined.* Oxford, England: Oxford University Press.

Stern, N. 1989. The economics of development: A survey. *Economic Journal* 397 (99): 597–685.

Stiglitz, J. 1988. *The economics of the public sector,* 2nd ed. New York: Norton.

———. 2000. More instruments and broader goals: Moving towards a post-Washington consensus. World Institute for Development Economic Research (WIDER) Annual Lecture 2, Snellmaninkatu, Finland.

Streeten, P. 1984. Basic needs: Some unsettled questions. *World Development* 12 (9): 73–79.

Tanzi, V., and H. Zee. 1997. Fiscal policy and long-run growth. *IMF Staff Papers* 44 (2): 179–209.

Torero, M., and J. von Braun. 2006. *Information and communication technologies for the poor.* Baltimore, Md.: The Johns Hopkins University Press.

Tridimas, G. 2001. The economics and politics of the structure of public expenditure. *Public Choice* 106 (3–4): 299–316.

Van de Walle, D. 1996. Assessing the welfare impacts of public spending. Policy Research Working Paper Series 1670. Washington, D.C.: World Bank.

———. 1998. Assessing the welfare impacts of public spending. *World Development* 26 (3): 365–379.

———. 2003. Are returns to investment lower for the poor? Human and physical capital interactions in rural Vietnam. *Review of Development Economics* (Blackwell Publishing) 7 (4): 636–653.

Van de Walle, D., and K. Nead. 1995. *Public spending and the poor: Theory and evidence.* Baltimore, Md.: The Johns Hopkins University Press.

Walters, E., and M. Auriol. 2005. The marginal cost of public funds in Africa. Mimeo, World Bank, Washington, D.C.

World Bank. 1990–2006. *World development indicators.* Washington, D.C.

———. 1990. *World development report: Poverty.* New York: Oxford University Press.

———. 1993. *World development report 1993.* New York: Oxford University Press.

———. 1997. *World development report 1997: The state in a changing world.* New York: Oxford University Press.

2 Public Spending in Developing Countries: Trends, Determination, and Impact

SHENGGEN FAN, BINGXIN YU, AND ANUJA SAURKAR

Government spending patterns in developing countries have changed dramatically over the past several decades. Thus it is important to monitor trends in the levels and composition of government expenditures and to assess the causes of change over time. It is even more important to analyze the relative contribution of various expenditures to production, growth, and poverty reduction, because this will provide important information for more efficient targeting of these limited and often declining financial resources in the future.

There have been numerous studies on the role of government spending in the long-term growth of national economies (Aschauer 1989; Barro 1990; Tanzi and Zee 1997). These studies found conflicting results regarding the effects of government spending on economic growth. Barro was among the first to formally endogenize government spending in a growth model and to analyze the relationship between size of government and rates of growth and saving. He concluded that an increase in resources devoted to nonproductive (but possibly utility-enhancing) government services is associated with a lower rate of per capita growth. Tanzi and Zee also found no relationship between government size and economic growth. On the other hand, Aschauer's empirical results indicate that nonmilitary public capital stock is substantially more important in determining productivity than is the flow of nonmilitary or military spending, that military capital bears little relation to productivity, and that the basic stock of infrastructure of streets, highways, airports, mass transit, sewers, and water systems has the greatest power to explain productivity. Many studies also attempted to link government spending to agricultural growth and poverty reduction (Elias 1985; Fan and Pardey 1998; Fan, Hazell, and Thorat 2000; Fan, Zhang, and Zhang 2004; and Lopez 2005). Most of these studies found that government spending contributed to agricultural production growth and poverty reduction, but different types of spending may have differential effects on growth and poverty reduction.

The purpose of this study is to review and analyze the trends in and causes of change in government expenditures and their composition in the developing

The authors thank Annie White and Neetha Rao for their able research assistance.

world and to develop an analytical framework for determining the differential impacts of various government expenditures on economic growth. This chapter links to the overall conceptual framework for the book by assessing the effects of different types of government spending on growth (and therefore their trickle-down effects on poverty reduction) using cross-country data sets and regressions. The chapter also provides important background for other chapters of the book by highlighting major trends in and the composition of government expenditures over time. We first review trends in and the composition of government expenditures across developing regions of Africa, Asia, and Latin America. We then model determinants of the composition of government expenditures. Next we model the effects of government expenditures on gross domestic product (GDP) growth by estimating a GDP function and the impact of various forms of public capital on agricultural GDP growth. We conclude with the study's major findings.

Government Spending: Trends, Size, and Composition

Trends in Government Spending

Total expenditures are broken down into the various sectors found in the International Monetary Fund's (IMF's) *Government Financial Statistics* (GFS) *Yearbook*. This study concentrates on six sectors, namely agriculture, defense, education, health, social security, and transportation and communication. Appendix Table 2A.1 provides definitions of these sectors.

Prices were first deflated from current local currency expenditures to a set of base year (2000) prices using each country's implicit GDP deflator. We then used 2000 exchange rates measured in 2000 purchasing power parity as reported by the *World Development Indicators* (World Bank 2006) to convert local currency expenditures measured in terms of 2000 prices into a value aggregate expressed in terms of 2000 international dollars.

We included 44 developing countries from three regions in our analysis, partly reflecting the availability of data and partly because these countries are important in their own right while representing broader rural development throughout all developing countries. The 17 countries included for Africa were Botswana, Burkina Faso, Cameroon, Côte d'Ivoire, Egypt, Ethiopia, Ghana, Kenya, Malawi, Mali, Morocco, Nigeria, Togo, Tunisia, Uganda, Zambia, and Zimbabwe. We included 11 countries from Asia: Bangladesh, China, India, Indonesia, Korea, Malaysia, Myanmar, Nepal, the Philippines, Sri Lanka, and Thailand. For Latin America we included 16 countries: Argentina, Belize, Bolivia, Brazil, Chile, Colombia, Costa Rica, the Dominican Republic, Ecuador, El Salvador, Guatemala, Mexico, Panama, Paraguay, Uruguay, and Venezuela. In 2002 these countries accounted for more than 80 percent of both total GDP and agricultural GDP in developing countries.

The data for the Asian countries include both central and subnational expenditures in the GFS. Many of the African countries have minimal local government expenditures or lack subnational government entities. In addition, expenditures by the local governments are central government transfers that are reflected in the central government's budget. However some Latin America countries have made significant decentralization efforts in recent decades. These efforts have been captured in the data for the large countries, such as Argentina, Bolivia, Chile, Colombia, Mexico, and Paraguay. But for smaller countries in the region, some of the local government expenditures may have not been captured by the IMF's data set. Budgetary support for social sectors provided to local nongovernmental organizations is not captured by the data.

Finally, we geometrically extrapolated data for countries whose values were missing to ensure the continuity of data (see Appendix Table 2A.2 for a summary of these extrapolations by country).

The Size of Government Spending

Over the past two decades, total government expenditures in the 44 developing countries considered in this study experienced overall growth. During the 1980s, expenditures increased from $993 billion in 1980 to $1,595 billion in 1990, with an annual growth rate of 4.8 percent (Table 2.1). In the 1990s, governments increased their spending power by 5.6 percent per year. By 2000, total government expenditures increased to $2,748 billion. They further reached $3,347.6 billion in 2002. Therefore, we have seen accelerated growth in government expenditures in developing countries.

However, among developing countries, regional deviations from these averages were quite marked. Across all regions, government expenditures in Asia experienced the most rapid growth, while those in Africa and Latin America increased at a much slower pace. In fact, most of the increase in total government expenditures came from Asia, accounting for 67 percent of total expenditures in 2002, up from 50 percent in 1980. This was due to the fact that most Asian countries experienced rapid growth in per capita GDP. With the exception of Sri Lanka and Myanmar, all countries in the region at least doubled their total expenditures for the period 1980–2002. The Republic of Korea and Bangladesh had the most rapid growth over 1980–2002, followed by India and Thailand.

For African countries, government expenditures grew at a rate of 3.8 percent over 1980–2002. Growth was much slower in the 1980s, at 2.92 percent per annum. In fact, there was a brief contraction after 1982, and it was not until 1986 that total government expenditures recovered to 1982 levels after many African countries implemented macroeconomic structural adjustments. However, during the 1990s African countries gained momentum in expanding their government expenditures, which grew at a rate of 4.8 percent per annum. Botswana had the most rapid growth, mainly due to the outstanding performance of its national economy: more than 10 percent growth per annum during 1980–2002.

TABLE 2.1 Government expenditures, 1980, 1990, 2000, and 2002

	2000 international dollars (billions)				Percentage of GDP			
	1980	1990	2000	2002	1980	1990	2000	2002
Africa	114.21	152.30	244.64	279.46	28.43	26.72	31.42	33.82
					24.11	*25.14*	*30.70*	*32.09*
Asia	500.13	870.81	1,786.98	2,228.66	19.30	17.09	17.99	20.20
					19.82	*19.32*	*18.12*	*19.07*
Latin America	379.23	571.55	716.97	839.45	18.22	23.13	20.94	24.73
					20.62	*19.68*	*22.38*	*25.48*
Total	993.57	1,594.65	2,748.59	3,347.57	19.58	19.60	19.44	21.95
					21.82	*21.79*	*24.63*	*26.47*

SOURCE: Calculated using data from International Monetary Fund, *Government Financial Statistics Yearbook,* various years.

NOTES: Values in italics are unweighted shares. The data for the Asian countries include both central and subnational expenditures in the GFS. Many of the African countries have minimal local government expenditures or lack subnational government entities. In addition, expenditures by the local governments are central government transfers that are reflected in the central government budget. However, some Latin America countries have made significant decentralization efforts in recent decades. The IMF data set may not have captured increased local government spending in these countries.

Latin American countries had the slowest growth in government spending between 1980 and 2002. The share of the total expenditures in the 16 countries was reduced from 38 percent in 1980 to 26 percent in 2000. The annual growth rate in the 1980s was 4 percent, and it was much less in the 1990s, 2.29 percent. Many countries in the region, including large ones like Argentina and Brazil, were faced with structural adjustment programs that led to lower spending in the social sectors and to overall lower government expenditures.

Measurement of total government expenditures as a percentage of GDP measures the amount a country spends relative to the size of its economy. For countries in this study, the percentage increased from 19 percent in 1980 to 22 percent in 2002.[1] On average, developing countries spend much less than developed countries. For example, total government outlays as a percentage of GDP in the Organisation for Economic Co-operation and Development (OECD) countries ranged from 27 percent in 1960 to 48 percent in 1996 (Gwartney, Holcombe, and Lawson 1998), compared to 13–35 percent in most developing countries. (For detailed information on each country, refer to Appendix Table 2A.3.)

For Asia, the percentage increased from 19 percent in 1980 to 20 percent in 2002. There is a strong correlation between the level of economic development and government spending power in this region, with the exception of Sri

1. Because the weighted averages commonly calculated at the regional and global levels may bias toward large countries, we also report unweighted averages at the regional and global levels.

Lanka. In 2002, Myanmar spent the least, only 8 percent of its GDP, while the rest of the Asian countries spent 14–25 percent of their GDP. India has been spending 17 percent of its GDP since it liberalized its economy in the 1990s, whereas China has accelerated its spending since 2000. Thailand has also accelerated its spending to a quarter of its GDP.

Surprisingly, among the three regions, Africa spent the most as a percentage of its GDP. Government spending in Africa as a percentage of GDP was roughly 27–34 percent over the past two decades, almost 10 percentage points higher than in Asia and Latin America. Among all countries in the region, Botswana, Nigeria, Malawi, Ethiopia, Tunisia, and Zimbabwe were among the largest spenders, often spending 35–67 percent of their GDP. Uganda and Côte d'Ivoire spent only a fraction as much, about 3–16 percent, the least among African countries in our study.

Latin America experienced even more of an erratic spending pattern. Their spending as a percentage of GDP increased at a rate of 2–3 percent per year until 1986, then declined thereafter at a rate of 1–2 percent per year from 1987 to 1991. After 1992, the percentage began another upward trend. For the region, the percentage averaged 25 percent in 2002, slightly higher than in Asian countries. Uruguay spent over 30 percent, while Guatemala spent roughly 14 percent of their respective GDPs.

The Composition of Government Spending

Equally important is the composition of government expenditures, which reflects government spending priorities. The composition of total expenditures across regions reveals many differences (Table 2.2).[2]

The top three sectors receiving expenditures in Africa in 2002 were education, defense, and health. Although the percentage of expenditures in education was the largest (14 percent), that percentage was smaller than that in Asia and comparable to that in Latin America. Defense accounted for 8 percent of total government expenditures in the region, similar to the percentage in Asia. African countries spent 8 percent of their total government expenditures on health. A discouraging trend was that African countries and Latin America spent very little on transportation and telecommunication. Africa's share in total government expenditures gradually declined from 6.4 percent in 1980 to 3.8 percent in 2002. The decline was much sharper in the case of Latin America, from 6.6 percent to 2 percent from 1980 to 2002.

Education spending represented the largest percentage of all government expenditures in Asia, accounting for 16 percent in 2002. It is not surprising that

2. Comparisons are made across six sectors, namely agriculture, education, health, defense, social security, and transportation and communication. Other sectors, such as mining, manufacturing and construction, fuel and energy, and general administration, are not included in our analysis and are collectively termed "other" expenditures.

TABLE 2.2 Composition of total expenditures, 1980, 1990, 2000, and 2002 (percent)

	Africa				Asia				Latin America			
	1980	1990	2000	2002	1980	1990	2000	2002	1980	1990	2000	2002
Agriculture[a]	6.42	5.15	4.05	4.52	14.80	12.23	9.11	8.60	8.04	2.02	2.53	2.53
	9.76	*5.29*	*3.95*	*4.85*	*14.44*	*9.31*	*8.33*	*6.70*	*9.34*	*4.40*	*3.15*	*2.74*
Education	12.33	14.60	14.72	13.98	13.66	17.31	16.18	15.23	10.04	7.74	14.10	14.06
	15.18	*16.15*	*16.00*	*17.01*	*13.70*	*15.50*	*16.86*	*16.29*	*16.58*	*14.09*	*17.78*	*18.29*
Health	3.75	4.58	8.38	8.26	5.25	4.25	4.61	4.37	5.86	6.10	6.93	7.61
	5.17	*6.08*	*10.10*	*10.93*	*5.92*	*4.64*	*6.12*	*5.68*	*8.69*	*9.07*	*15.39*	*15.65*
Transportation and communication	6.49	3.98	3.49	3.76	11.68	5.16	4.85	5.27	6.66	2.52	2.23	2.00
	9.40	*7.37*	*5.96*	*7.37*	*14.06*	*7.28*	*8.57*	*8.47*	*8.90*	*6.83*	*6.39*	*7.35*
Social security	5.69	6.72	6.05	7.17	1.87	2.40	3.77	4.27	24.00	22.24	39.18	38.38
	3.80	*4.60*	*6.25*	*10.21*	*3.48*	*4.29*	*6.19*	*7.26*	*13.65*	*16.80*	*22.56*	*21.05*
Defense	14.87	13.63	8.67	7.50	17.48	12.71	9.78	9.04	5.93	4.53	4.72	4.52
	18.09	*15.03*	*7.69*	*6.54*	*15.97*	*12.67*	*11.31*	*10.63*	*9.33*	*9.74*	*6.11*	*7.67*
Other[b]	50.46	51.33	54.63	54.81	35.27	45.94	51.69	53.22	39.47	54.85	30.32	30.90
	38.59	*45.48*	*50.05*	*43.09*	*32.43*	*46.30*	*42.62*	*44.97*	*33.52*	*39.07*	*28.63*	*8.39*
Total	100.00	100.00	100.00	100.00	100.00	100.00	100.00	100.00	100.00	100.00	100.00	100.00

SOURCE: Calculated using data from International Monetary Fund, *Government Financial Statistics Yearbook*, various years.

NOTES: Values in italics are unweighted shares.

[a]Includes agriculture, forestry, fishing, and hunting.

[b]Includes fuel and energy, mining, manufacturing, construction, and general administration.

Asia has the highest-quality human capital among the regions. Defense and agriculture spending ranked second and third, accounting for 9 percent each, of total government expenditures in 2002, reduced from 18 percent and 15 percent, respectively, in 1980.

Governments in Asia slightly reduced their spending on health as a share of total government spending from 1980 to 2002. This indicates that as the Asian economy continued to recover from the 1997 Asian financial crisis, governments in the region may have been spending less on health, though spending in that sector is much needed to protect disadvantaged groups. Although defense spending declined from 18 percent in 1980 to 9 percent in 2002, the percentage was still high compared to that in Latin America, which spent 4.5 percent on defense, and was substantially higher than the percentage of the region's spending on infrastructure, social security, and health.

In Latin America, social security spending ranked at the top of all government expenditure items, indicating that a higher rate of income inequality among population groups in the region may call for government intervention. In addition, Latin America spent 10–14 percent of its total government expenditures on education between 1980 and 2002. Agricultural expenditures accounted for a small fraction of total government expenditures (2.5 percent), mainly due to the small share of agriculture in national GDP.

Other expenditures (which include government spending on fuel and energy, mining, manufacturing and construction, and general administration) accounted for roughly 50 percent of total government spending in Africa over 1980–2002. For Asia, the share of this type of expenditures increased from 35 percent in 1980 to 53 percent in 2002. For Latin America, it also accounted for more than 31 percent of total government spending in 2002. Most of these expenditures were for either government subsidies or expenses relating to general administration. The large and increasing share of these expenditures may have competed with the shares of spending on more productive items such as agriculture, education, and infrastructure.

Agricultural Spending

Agriculture is the largest sector in many developing countries in terms of their shares in GDP and employment. More important, the majority of the world's poor live in rural areas and depend on agriculture for their livelihood. Sustainable agricultural development is therefore imperative in the quest for development. Therefore, agricultural expenditures represent one of the most important government instruments for promoting economic growth and alleviating poverty in rural areas of developing countries. Agricultural expenditures increased at an annual growth rate of 3.2 percent between 1980 and 2002 (Table 2.3). During the same period of time, rural population grew at approximately 1 percent per year and agricultural GDP by 4.2 percent. Therefore, we saw a slight

TABLE 2.3 Agriculture expenditures, 1980, 1990, 2000, and 2002

Region	Billions of 2000 international dollars				Percentage of agricultural GDP			
	1980	1990	2000	2002	1980	1990	2000	2002
Africa	7.33	7.85	9.90	12.62	7.40	5.44	5.71	6.72
					2.29	*1.37*	*1.20*	*1.47*
Asia	74.00	106.54	162.84	191.76	9.44	8.51	9.54	10.57
					2.96	*1.71*	*1.35*	*1.23*
Latin America	30.48	11.52	18.16	21.23	19.51	6.79	11.10	11.57
					1.66	*0.78*	*0.64*	*0.60*
Total	111.80	125.91	190.89	225.61	10.76	8.04	9.34	10.32
					2.23	*1.24*	*1.03*	*1.09*

SOURCE: Calculated using data from International Monetary Fund, *Government Financial Statistics Yearbook,* various years.

NOTE: Values in italics are unweighted shares.

increase in agricultural expenditures per capita of rural population and a decrease of agricultural expenditures per unit of agricultural GDP.

In Africa, government expenditures on agriculture increased gradually at an annual rate of 2.5 percent. Agricultural expenditures in Asia more than doubled in the past two decades, with an annual growth rate of 4.4 percent, the highest rate of growth among the three regions. Latin America was the only region that reduced its spending in agriculture, with an annual reduction of 1.6 percent. Six out of the 16 Latin American countries included in this study reduced their government expenditures in agriculture.

Agricultural expenditures as a percentage of agricultural GDP measure government spending on agriculture relative to the size of the sector. Agricultural spending as a percentage of agricultural GDP is extremely low in developing countries compared to developed countries. The former usually averages less than 10 percent, while the latter is more than 20 percent. In Africa, agricultural expenditures as a percentage of agricultural GDP remained at relatively similar levels (5.4–7.4 percent) throughout the study period. About half of African countries decreased their agricultural expenditures relative to their agricultural GDP. Asia's performance was much better than that of Africa; its percentage remained constant at 8.5–10.5 percent. For Latin America, agricultural spending as a percentage of agricultural GDP decreased from 19.5 percent in 1980 to 11.5 percent in 2002.

Among all types of agricultural expenditures, those on agricultural research and development are the most crucial to growth in agricultural and food production. Beintema and Stads (2004) show that agricultural research and development (R&D) expenditures as a percentage of agricultural GDP have been flat in the past three decades. For example, in 2000 the share of agricultural R&D expenditures in agricultural GDP in Africa and Asia was between 0.5 and 0.9 percent, and Latin America's share was 0.98 percent. These rates are relatively low compared to 2–3 percent in developed countries.

The Determination of Government Expenditures

In this section we attempt to gain insights by modeling government spending patterns. The determination of total government spending and its patterns is complex and may include many factors, such as fiscal conditions and political, cultural, and economic factors.

In the nineteenth century, economists generally advocated a state with minimal economic functions, or the so-called laissez-faire state. This was a response to failures in the eighteenth century due to heavy government distortions (Tanzi and Schuknecht 2001). After World War I, the perception about the role of government changed again due to the influence of John Maynard Keynes, who argued that the government still had many things to do that were not being done. In response to the Great Depression, the United States introduced major public expenditure programs to generate public goods and create employment. This period continued until the 1980s. For the OECD countries, percentages of total government expenditures in total GDP increased sharply, from 13.1 percent in 1913 to 23.8 percent in 1937, 28 percent in 1960, and 41.9 percent in 1980. During the 1980s and 1990s, skepticism about the large size of the government grew increasingly over time due to government failures to use public spending to achieve higher rates of growth and better income distribution outcomes. But for many OECD countries, the size of government continued to grow, but at a much slower pace (for example, government spending as a percentage of GDP grew from 43.1 percent in 1980 to 44.8 percent in 1990 and 45.6 percent in 1996).

More complicated is the determination of the composition of government spending. Rent-seeking behavior, economic and political structures, and economic development levels, among other factors, are all important in this process. The government can act as a social planner when allocating public spending. The social planner determines the optimal allocation by maximizing a weighted social welfare function. Under this approach, the government maximizes a utility function—defined in terms of a set of public services consumed by individuals or the electorate—subject to a budget constraint equal to the sum of public service expenditures (Deacon 1978).

Rent-seeking behavior has been an increasingly important subject under study in determining the allocation of government spending. Specifically, the distribution of potential individual beneficiaries of rents, the number of groups competing, the rule used to distribute private good transfers within groups, and the individual valuation of the local public good shape public spending patterns (Nitzan 1994). Public choice economics provides a theoretical basis for studying the role of political processes with regard to the level and composition of public expenditures. Sass (1991), for example, constructed a model of municipal government choice based on the constitutional choice model of Buchanan and Tullock (1962) to analyze the impact of differing government structures on two categories of public spending: educational and noneducational expenditures.[3] The results suggest that voter preferences appear to determine not only the level of municipal expenditures but the structure of local governments as well.

Ideological differences between groups and the parties that represent these groups matter, suggesting that lower-income groups favor a large and active state, while upper-income groups aim at minimizing the role of the state. Cusack (1997) analyzed the role of ideologically based partisan preferences in influencing public spending levels in a regression analysis using data from 15 OECD countries over the period 1950–89. To account for the impact of partisan politics, the author constructed two indexes with similar structures to represent the ideological preferences of government and the electorate on a left–right scale. These indexes represented the ideological preferences of the government party, which shapes the preferences for more or less spending. The results support the partisan politics model in that the left was found to increase the size of the public sector while the right reduced it.

While political factors influence the level and structure of public expenditures, economic and demographic factors are also important to consider. For example, Rodrik (1998) relates the degree of openness of the economy to the level of government spending. Demographic variables also influence the level and composition of public spending, because an aging population demands greater spending on health, housing, and social security (Feldstein 1996). Similarly, a rise in the proportion of young people affects the demand for education spending (Marlow and Shiers 1999). Structural differences, such as the degree of urbanization or population density, also affect government spending (Dao 1995). Dao found that population density has a positive influence on per capita expenditures on housing, social security and welfare, and education in developed economies. On the other hand, urbanization helps explain variations in per capita expenditures on social security and welfare among developing countries.

It is not our objective in this chapter to model the political and cultural factors. Our major purpose is to analyze how the structural adjustment programs have affected spending patterns. However, in order to avoid bias due to the

---

3. Buchanan and Tullock's (1962) constitutional choice model shows that individuals select the collective choice mechanism, which minimizes the costs associated with group decisionmaking. The optimal form of government involves a trade-off between external and internal or decision-making costs.

omission of these variables, we use country dummies to control for these effects, assuming that these factors have not changed over time.

Total Government Spending

When we control for political, social, and cultural factors, how much a government can spend depends on its revenues and its ability to borrow from international and domestic sources. For many small developing countries, international aid also has become a significant source of government expenditures. In Uganda, Tanzania, and Ghana, total foreign aid accounts for 15–30 percent of total GDP (World Bank 2006). The relative importance of these factors changes over time. In particular, when a government introduces budget cuts under the aegis of macroeconomic reforms and adjustments, spending patterns are likely to be affected. We use the following specification to model changes in government expenditures:

$$GEPGDP_t = f(RGDP_t, AID_t, SA_t, X_t), \tag{1}$$

where $GEPGDP_t$ is government expenditures as a percentage of GDP and $RGDP_t$ is government revenues as a percentage of GDP. AID_t is total aid received by the country, measured as a percentage of GDP. The variable SA_t is a dummy variable that is equal to one when macroeconomic adjustments are implemented and equal to zero otherwise.[4] Apart from revenue and structural adjustment variables, X_t captures the effects of other factors on government spending. Because it is difficult to quantify them, we use both year and country dummies to proxy these factors. Because revenue, aid, and structural adjustment programs can also be functions of government revenue, there may be a reverse causality. The ordinary least squares estimation technique will lead to a biased estimation. To avoid the potential endogeneity problem of the independent variables, the generalized method of moments (GMM) instrumental variable approach is used. Two years' lagged independent variables in difference are used as instruments. Another estimation issue that may cause spurious regressions is the possible existence of unit roots or the nonstationarity of variables included in the analysis. However, when the number of cross-sectional units (N) is much larger than the number of time periods (T), the nonstationarity problem commonly seen in time-series data can be attenuated (Holtz-Eakin, Newey, and H. Rosen, 1988). Just to ensure that there is no unit root problem in our panel data set, we used the Dickey-Fuller approach to conduct various tests. When we conducted tests country by country, we found that for government revenues, expenditures, foreign aid, and agricultural expenditures, the hypothesis of unit root is rejected

---

4. The initiation years of structural programs by country were reported by the IMF (Barro and Lee 2005). The initiation year is defined as the first year that the IMF implemented its structural adjustment program loans.

for most of the countries. For GDP and agricultural GDP, however, the hypothesis is rejected for only one-third of the countries. However, when we pool all countries together, all variables do not show the existence of unit root when country dummies are added or both country and year dummies are added. When dummies are not added, only GDP and agricultural GDP show an existence of unit root. Therefore, to avoid the problem of unit root, at least country dummies must be added. More details on the estimation procedures used in a panel data set are found in Appendix 2A.

Regression results are presented in Table 2.4. We have four different specifications. Regression 1 includes only revenue and structural adjustment program variables. In regression 2 we added GDP per capita ($GDPP_t$) and urbanization ($URBANP_t$) variables. These two variables illustrate how economic development levels and demographic shifts affect government spending. Regressions 3 and 4 are results from variable coefficient models in which all parameters in the regressions vary by region. This is because determination of government expenditures may differ by region even after controlling for all variables in the equations.

The results in regression 1 indicate that government expenditures are largely determined by revenues and structural adjustments. The latter were found to reduce government expenditures (the coefficient of the structural adjustment variables is negative and statistically significant). Regression 2 shows that after controlling for GDP per capita and for urbanization, the structural adjustment program variable is still statistically significant and negative. When we break our analysis into regions, we find that for all regions, structural adjustments reduced government spending. All these coefficients are statistically significant except for those of Africa when per capita GDP and urbanization are not controlled for and for those of Asia when these two variables are controlled for. This finding is by and large inconsistent with the objective of the structural programs of cutting down government spending.[5]

The Composition of Government Spending

Some studies have analyzed the impact of the composition of government spending on economic growth (Devarajan, Swaroop, and Zou 1996), but few have modeled the determination of such composition. Understanding why certain countries spend more on one sector than on others will help developing countries reallocate their government resources to the most productive sectors by focusing on major forces behind existing patterns. The composition of government spending is modeled in the following specification:

$$S_{i,t} = g(GEPGDP_t, GDPP_t, SAP_t, Z_{i,t}), \tag{2}$$

---

5. Barro and Lee (2003) found no significant effects of SAPs on government consumption.

TABLE 2.4 Determinants of total government expenditures

	Regression 1	Regression 2	Regression 3	Regression 4
RGDP	0.322	0.339		
	(5.26)*	(5.87)*		
Africa			0.271	0.307
			(3.27)*	(3.86)*
Asia			0.065	0.314
			(5.28)*	(4.62)*
Latin America			0.123	0.441
			(4.13)*	(3.83)*
GDPP		−0.010		
		(−0.20)		
Africa				0.302
				(3.04)*
Asia				−0.432
				(−4.46)*
Latin America				−0.194
				(−3.72)*
AID	0.015	0.119		
	(2.34)*	(1.64)*		
Africa			0.034	0.005
			(1.74)*	(0.58)
Asia			−0.002	−0.800
			(−0.37)	(−9.01)*
Latin America			0.007	−0.000
			(0.77)	(−0.001)
URBANP		0.403		
		(3.94)*		
Africa				0.176
				(1.44)
Asia				1.448
				(5.27)*
Latin America				0.795
				(3.42)*
SA_t	−0.089	−0.133		
	(−4.01)*	(−5.39)*		
Africa			−0.620	−0.090
			(−1.54)	(−1.96)*
Asia			−0.069	−0.307
			(−2.41)*	(−1.23)
Latin America			0.163	−0.155
			(−3.86)*	(−3.73)*
R^2	0.739	0.743	0.745	0.870
Number of observations	836	836	836	836

NOTES: The dependent variable is the percentage of government expenditures in total GDP. The figures in parentheses are *t*-values. * indicates significance at the 10 percent level. All regressions included country dummies to capture country-fixed effects. The total number of observations was 836 (for the years of 1984–2002 and 44 countries). Three years of observations were lost due to two years' lag of differencing. GMM instrumental variables are used with lagged independent variables in difference as instruments. Arellano–Bond dynamic panel data estimation was also employed. The results are, by and large, consistent with the results presented in the table.

where $S_{i,t}$ is the share of the ith sector in total government expenditures, $GEPGD_t$ is government expenditures as a percentage of GDP, $GDPP_t$ is per capita GDP, SAP_t is structural adjustment program, and $Z_{i,t}$ comprises other factors that may affect government spending in the sector. Again, we use year and country dummies to proxy for Z and to control for other factors excluded from the equation. Much as in equation 1, we also use a GMM instrumental estimator for estimating the share equations.[6] The regression results are presented in Table 2.5.

For all regressions, we disaggregated our analysis into regions. As total government expenditures increased, the share of agricultural expenditures (S_1) declined in all regions, although the coefficient is statistically significant only for Latin America. The share of the agriculture sector in total GDP ($GDPS_1$) is not statistically correlated with shares of government expenditures in agriculture in Asia and Latin America. In Africa, as the share of the agricultural sector increased, the share of the government spending on agriculture also increased. The most important finding is that structural adjustments reduced government expenditure shares in the agricultural sector in all regions. Since agricultural spending is the most pro-poor type of spending and contributes to overall economic growth, a cut in agricultural spending may adversely affect the poor and overall economic growth.

The results for S_2 (the education sector) indicate that as a country becomes richer, the share of its educational expenditures becomes larger, as evidenced by the positive and statistically significant coefficients of the per capita GDP variable in the education share equation. Structural adjustments increased the spending share on education in Africa, but reduced this share in Latin America. They had no statistically significant impact on educational spending in Asia.

Much as in the case of education, as countries become richer, they tend to spend more on health. The coefficients of per capita GDP are all positive and statistically significant. The structural adjustment programs increased spending on health in Africa and Latin America, but reduced the share of such spending in Asia.

The results from S_4 show that the share of social security in total government expenditures in Africa has generally had no relationship with the African countries' economic development levels (per capita GDP). By contrast, as Asian and Latin American countries' economies expand, governments tend to spend more on social security. The structural adjustment programs increased social

---

6. The Tobit model was also run using the lagged *GEPGDP* and *GDPP* as instruments for the structural adjustment program variable. The results are similar. In particular, all signs and significance levels of the coefficients of the structural adjustment programs changed very little. We also checked the shares of government expenditures in each sector, and they do not show lumpiness of observations close to either zero or one.

TABLE 2.5 Determinants of sector share in total government expenditures

	S_1	S_2	S_3	S_4	S_5	S_6
GEPGDP						
Africa	−0.100	−0.048	0.008	−0.002	−0.059	−0.024
	(−1.60)	(−6.21)*	(0.97)	(−0.12)	(−4.60)*	(−1.99)*
Asia	−0.014	−0.064	−0.030	0.015	−0.089	−0.009
	(−0.98)	(−7.37)*	(−4.13)*	(1.97)*	(−7.86)*	(−0.66)
Latin America	−0.016	−0.014	0.093	−0.034	−0.177	−0.021
	(−1.87)*	(−1.06)	(4.45)*	(−1.82)*	(−2.84)*	(−2.38)*
GDPP						
Africa	0.030	0.086	0.064	−0.029	0.476	−0.007
	(2.28)*	(6.35)*	(4.36)*	(−0.84)	(2.13)*	(−0.37)
Asia	−0.029	0.023	0.023	0.044	−0.076	0.015
	(−1.49)	(3.62)*	(4.29)*	(7.79)*	(−8.95)*	(1.36)
Latin America	−0.034	0.066	0.062	0.053	0.094	−0.006
	(−2.31)*	(3.33)*	(1.95)*	(1.85)*	(3.69)*	(−0.45)
SA$_t$						
Africa	−0.029	0.136	0.021	0.013	−0.322	−0.033
	(−5.42)*	(2.05)*	(2.98)*	(0.81)	(−2.93)*	(−3.13)*
Asia	−0.023	−0.005	−0.023	−0.002	−0.007	−0.041
	(−2.43)*	(−0.88)	(−4.49)*	(−0.38)	(−0.90)	(−3.97)*
Latin America	−0.026	−0.021	0.031	0.041	−0.070	−0.017
	(−4.37)*	(−2.34)*	(2.15)*	(3.20)*	(−1.67)*	(−2.80)*
GDPS1						
Africa	0.023					
	(2.54)*					
Asia	0.011					
	(0.54)					
Latin America	−0.005					
	(−0.57)					
R^2	0.778	0.728	0.846	0.526	0.536	0.223
Number of observations	836	836	836	836	836	836

NOTES: S_1, agriculture; S_2, education; S_3, health; S_4, social security; S_5, transportation and communication; S_6, defense. The figures in parentheses are *t*-values. * indicates significance at the 10 percent level. All regressions include country dummies to capture country-fixed effects. GMM estimators are used with two years' lagged differenced independent variables as instruments. Observations for 19 years (1984–2002) for 44 countries are used.

security spending in Latin America, but had no statistically significant impact in Asia or Africa.

Structural adjustments had an adverse impact on government spending on infrastructure across all regions, although they are statistically insignificant in Asia (regression S_5 in Table 2.5). This implies that governments may have reduced their infrastructure investments during macroeconomic structural adjustment programs, particularly in Africa and Latin America.

The relationship between government spending on defense and economic development levels is not statistically significant. As government revenues increase, developing countries tend to reduce their shares of spending on defense. Structural adjustment programs have reduced the shares of government spending on defense in all regions.

The Impact of Government Spending on Growth

Many studies have analyzed how government expenditures contribute to economic growth (Barro 1990; Kelly 1997). However, they have focused on the impact of total government expenditures and overall GDP growth. Very few studies have attempted to link different types of government spending to growth, and even fewer have attempted to analyze the impact of government spending at the sector level. In this section we first model the impact of different types of government spending on overall GDP growth, then analyze the effect of agricultural spending on agricultural GDP.

Spending and Overall GDP Growth

We estimate a production function with national GDP as the dependent variable and labor, capital investment, and various government expenditures as independent variables as follows:

$$GDP_t = h(LABOR_t, K_t, KGE_{i,t}, SA_t, W_t), \qquad (3)$$

where GDP_t is GDP in year t, $LABOR_t$ and K_t are labor and private capital inputs in year t, and KGE_{it} is capital stock constructed from current and past government spending in the ith sector, with $KAGEXP_t$ representing government stock in the agricultural sector, $KEDEXP_t$ that in the education sector, $KHEXP_t$ that in the health sector, $KTCEXP_t$ that in the transportation and telecommunication sector, $KSSEXP_t$ that in the social security sector, and $KDEXP_t$ that in the defense sector.[7] Usually this stock cannot be observed directly, so it serves more as a part of the conceptual apparatus than as an empirical tool. To con-

---

7. When the structural adjustment program variables are included, the coefficients are not statistically significant. This implies that the structural adjustment programs reduce GDP growth indirectly, mainly through reduced government spending in the productive sectors.

struct a capital stock series from data on capital formation, we used the following procedure:

$$K_t = S_t + (1 - \delta)K_{t-1},$$ (4)

where K_t is the capital stock in year t, I_t is gross capital formation in year t, and δ is the depreciation rate. Because the depreciation rate varies by country, we simply assumed a 10 percent depreciation rate for all the countries. To obtain initial values for the capital stock, we used a procedure similar to that of Kohli (1982):

$$K_{1980} = \frac{I_{1980}}{(\delta + r)}.$$ (5)

Equation 5 implies that the initial capital stock in 1980 (K_{1980}) was capital investment in 1980 (I_{1980}) divided by the sum of the real interest rate (r) and the depreciation rate.

Other factors not included in the equations are captured through the year and country dummies of W_t.

Because the government expenditure variables on the right-hand side of the equation can also be a function of GDP, there might be reverse causality. In addition, there might be unit root in many of the variables included in the analysis. There have been many empirical studies to address these problems by using different econometric techniques, for example, a differencing approach and an instrumental variables approach. Arrellano and Bond (1991) used a dynamic GMM technique (difference equations with lagged levels as instruments) to avoid the unit root problem as well as to address the dynamic nature of the relationship between dependent and independent variables. But this technique may lead to efficiency loss during the estimation. The lagged levels are also weak instruments of difference variables. Blundell and Bond (1998a), therefore, proposed to use an extended system estimator that uses lagged differences as instruments for equations in levels, in addition to lagged levels as instruments for equations in first difference. The system GMM estimator is shown to have dramatic efficiency gains over the basic first difference GMM both by simulations and by empirical estimation (Blundell and Bond 1998b). Zhang and Fan (2004) applied a system GMM method to empirically test the causal relationship between productivity growth and infrastructure development using the India district-level data over 1970–94.

For the purpose of this study, we report results from the Arrellano and Bond first-difference GMM and system GMM estimators. For the system GMM estimator, we stack first-difference equations with two years' lagged levels of dependent and independent variables as instruments and level equations with two years' lagged-differenced dependent and independent variables.

The results are shown in Table 2.6. The first two columns report results from the whole sample of the countries. The Sargan test rejects the hypothesis that the model is overidentified, all at the 5 percent significance level. The tests

TABLE 2.6 Estimated GDP function

	Pooled		Africa		Asia		Latin America	
	Difference	System	Difference	System	Difference	System	Difference	System
GDP_{t-1}	0.782 (55.09)**	0.759 (50.59)**	0.686 (26.42)**	0.731 (23.44)**	0.784 (40.22)**	0.784 (35.82)**	0.833 (36.58)**	0.830 (31.59)**
$LABOR_t$	−0.036 (0.96)	−0.070 (1.66)+	0.139 (1.38)	0.104 (1.01)	−0.076 (1.35)	−0.076 (1.20)	0.005 (0.11)	−0.006 (0.11)
K_t	0.097 (16.05)**	0.104 (15.84)**	0.094 (8.95)**	0.108 (9.29)**	0.122 (12.40)**	0.122 (11.04)**	0.085 (10.65)**	0.085 (9.16)**
$KAGEXP_t$	0.014 (2.48)**	0.020 (3.08)**	0.031 (2.44)*	0.056 (2.42)*	0.023 (1.78)*	0.023 (1.59)	0.001 (0.09)	0.001 (0.10)
$KEDEXP_t$	0.014 (1.35)	0.013 (1.07)	0.061 (2.52)*	0.101 (2.48)*	−0.023 (0.98)	−0.023 (0.88)	0.010 (1.00)	0.009 (0.73)
$KHEXP_t$	−0.043 (6.13)**	−0.048 (6.12)**	−0.072 (3.45)**	−0.028 (3.74)**	−0.012 (0.87)	−0.012 (0.78)	−0.008 (1.21)	−0.009 (1.14)
$KDEXP_t$	0.001 (0.19)	−0.003 (0.40)	−0.013 (0.96)	−0.038 (1.36)	−0.009 (0.82)	−0.009 (0.73)	0.005 (0.52)	0.006 (0.57)
$KSSEXP_t$	−0.008 (1.84)*	−0.009 (1.76)*	−0.010 (1.42)	−0.008 (0.90)	−0.040 (3.95)**	−0.040 (3.51)**	−0.000 (0.07)	−0.001 (0.10)
$KTCEXP_t$	0.002 (0.41)	0.003 (0.45)	0.013 (1.41)	0.033 (1.55)	−0.011 (1.74)+	−0.011 (1.55)	0.014 (1.61)	0.016 (1.53)
Sargan test χ^2	1,175.2**	958.8**	463.6**	391.0**	292.5**	232.0**	480.4**	355.0**
AR(1)	−8.21**	−6.94**	−5.65**	−4.93**	−4.10**	−3.66**	−5.05**	−4.32**
AR(2)	−5.09**	−4.30**	−3.82**	−3.35**	−1.21	−1.08	−2.57**	−2.19**
Number of observations	934	978	374	391	221	232	339	355

NOTE: ** and * indicate significance at the 5 and 10 percent level, respectively; AR indicates autoregressive.

also show that for the Arrellano and Bond first-difference GMM estimator, we accept at the 5 percent significance level the null hypothesis that there are second-order autocorrelations for Africa and Asia pooled. For Latin America, the second-order autocorrelation is not significant at the 10 percent level. But for all system GMM estimators except that for Asia, the second-order auto-correlations are not statistically significant. For Asia, it is significant at the 10 per-cent level. The results indicate that when all countries are pooled together, the elasticities of agricultural spending are 0.014 and 0.020, respectively, and they are statistically significant. The coefficients of educational spending are posi-tive, and their magnitudes are similar to those of agricultural spending. But their statistical significance is less than 10 percent. The coefficients of the health and social security spending variables are negative and statistically significant, which implies that this type of spending is an opportunity cost for other productive in-vestments in growth. The defense and the transportation and telecommunica-tion spending variables are not statistically significant.

The pooled analysis may cover large regional variations in the effects of various types of spending on growth. In Table 2.6 we also report both Arrellano and Bond first-difference GMM and system GMM results for Africa, Asia, and Latin America. Indeed, they show large regional differences. In Africa, it is spending in agriculture and education that has contributed to growth at the sta-tistically significant level, while the coefficient of investment in infrastructure is positive but only marginally statistically significant when the system GMM is used. In Asia, only the coefficient of agricultural spending seems to be sta-tistically significant and positive. In Latin America, the coefficients of agricul-tural spending are significant and positive and those of infrastructure are mar-ginally statistically significant. Although those of education and defense spending are also positive, they are not statistically significant.

Agricultural Spending and Growth in Agriculture

Because agricultural growth has been one of the most effective means of poverty reduction through the so-called trickle-down process, we estimate the determinants of agricultural growth in developing countries. We pay special attention to how government spending can promote growth in the agricultural sector. We include in the agricultural production function an explanatory vari-able that measures government expenditures on agriculture to identify output-enhancing effects of public expenditures. The production function to be esti-mated is specified as

$$AGOUT_t = h(AGLAND_t, LABOR_t, FERT_t, TRACT_t, ANIMALS_t,$$
$$ROADS_t, LITE_t, KAGEXP_t, U_t), \qquad (6)$$

where $AGOUT_t$ is agricultural output, the dependent variable; the independent variables are labor ($LABOR_t$), land ($AGLAND_t$), fertilizer ($FERT_t$), number of tractors ($TRACT_t$), number of draft animals ($ANIMALS_t$), and public input variables such as road density ($ROADS_t$), literacy rate ($LITE_t$), and an agricultural expenditure capital variable ($KAGEXP_t$). Traditionally, an irrigation variable is often also included. But irrigation is a result of government spending, and inclusion of this variable may double-count the effects of government spending. The variable U_t is used to capture the other factors not included in the equation and is proxied by year and country dummies.

We further disaggregate government expenditures into research ($KAGREXP_t$) and nonresearch expenditure capitals ($NKAGREXP_t$) to capture the separate effects of these two types of expenditures. These capital variables are converted from government expenditures using procedures similar to those described in equations 4 and 5.

Output is measured as the agricultural output index reported by the Food and Agriculture Organization (FAO), where agriculture is broadly defined as including crop, livestock, forestry, and fishery production. All these variables were incorporated into the estimating equation as indexes and in logarithm forms to minimize the bias that may arise from using different scales or units of input and output for each country.

Two different specifications were estimated, and the results are presented in Table 2.7. The first specification includes conventional inputs such as labor, land, fertilizer, machinery, and draft animals; physical public inputs such as road density and literacy rate; and a stock variable of total government expenditures on agriculture. The second specification disaggregates total agricultural expenditures into agricultural and nonagricultural research expenditures (total agricultural expenditures net of agricultural research expenditures). Due to the limited number of observations (24 countries), we were unable to conduct this analysis at the regional level. The statistical tests also show that the second-order autocorrelations are not significant for all specifications.

The estimation procedure used was similar to that of the GDP function. Similar to the results in Table 2.6, total agricultural expenditures had a significant effect on agricultural GDP, as shown in the first regression of Table 2.7. The coefficients for fertilizer and draft animal inputs are also statistically significant.

Disaggregating total agricultural expenditures into research and nonresearch expenditures reveals an interesting finding: the coefficient for agricultural research is statistically significant and positive, while that for nonresearch spending variable is not statistically significant. This is prima facie evidence that productivity-enhancing expenditures such as agricultural research investments have much larger output-promoting effects than other forms of public spending (including subsidies).

Major Findings

In this study we compiled government expenditures by type across 44 developing countries for the years from 1980 to 2002. We then analyzed the trends,

TABLE 2.7 Estimated agricultural production function

	Differences		System
	R_1	R_2	R_3
$AGOUT_{t-1}$	0.222	0.411	0.638
	3.48**	4.38**	18.91**
$KAGEXP_t$	0.085		0.041
	2.15**		1.83*
$KAGREXP_t$		0.038	
		1.76*	
$KNAGREXP_t$		−0.070	
		−2.6**	
$AGLAND_t$	0.085	−0.386	−0.027
	0.34	−0.93	−0.67
$LABOR_t$	−0.089	−0.615	−0.016
	−0.52	−1.76*	−0.18
$FERT_t$	0.029	0.023	0.027
	1.59*	0.57	1.91**
$TRACTS_t$	0.038	0.032	0.021
	0.84	0.44	1.16
$ANIMALS_t$	0.282	0.399	0.087
	2.85**	2.47**	1.69*
$ROADS_t$	−0.087	−0.092	0.002
	−1.30	−0.54	0.08
$LITE_t$	0.0218	0.362	0.083
	0.09	0.86	1.03
Sargan test χ^2	246.55**	142.85**	554.05**
AR(1)	−11.01**	−3.02**	11.08**
AR(2)	1.55	−1.08	1.56
Number of observations	476	174	476

NOTES: R_1, R_2, and R_3 are estimates from three regressions. AR indicates autoregressive. The dependent variable is the agricultural production index. The figures in parentheses are *t*-values. ** and * indicate significance at the 5 and 10 percent level, respectively. All regressions included country dummies to capture country-fixed effects. Due to a lack of data on research spending, only 24 countries are included in regression R_2. Due to a time lag and shorter time series of R&D spending, 12 years of observations of each country are included.

determination, and impact of various forms of government spending. The following are the major findings of this study.

The total government expenditures for the 44 countries included in the study increased over time. Macroeconomic adjustment programs did indeed reduce the total amount of government spending. However, they had different consequences for different sectors. For almost all regions, the programs reduced the shares of spending on agriculture and on infrastructure. Because many studies have shown that investments in these two productive sectors have large returns to GDP growth and poverty reduction, the structural adjustment programs adversely affect these final development indicators by cutting down spending in these two sectors.

The performance of government spending with regard to economic growth is mixed. In Africa and Asia, government spending on agriculture and education were particularly strong in promoting economic growth. In Latin America, spending on agriculture and infrastructure had positive growth-promoting effects.

Agricultural spending contributed strongly to agricultural growth. Disaggregating total agricultural expenditures into research and nonresearch spending reveals that research spending had a larger productivity-enhancing impact than nonresearch spending.

Several lessons can be drawn from this study. First, various types of government spending have differential impacts on economic growth, implying that there is a greater potential to improve the efficiency of government spending by reallocation among sectors. Second, governments should reduce their spending in unproductive sectors such as defense and curtail excessive subsidies in fertilizer, irrigation, power, and pesticides. Third, all regions should increase their spending on agriculture, particularly on production-enhancing investments such as agricultural R&D. This type of spending not only yields high returns to agricultural production, but also has a large impact on poverty reduction because most of the poor still reside in rural areas and their main source of livelihood is agriculture.

Appendix 2A: Supplementary Tables

See tables on pages 42–50.

TABLE 2A.1 Definitions of government revenue and of government and sectoral expenditures

Type of expenditure	What it includes
Government revenue	Current revenue (tax and nontax revenue), capital revenue, and grants.
Government expenditures	Expenditures on central government (government departments, offices, establishments, and other bodies that are agencies or instruments); state, provincial, or regional government; local government; and supranational authorities.
Defense	Expenditures on the administration of military defense affairs and services; operation of land, sea, air, and space defense forces; operation of engineering, transport, communication, intelligence, personnel, and other noncombat defense forces; operation or support of reserve and auxiliary forces of the defense establishment.
	Includes offices of military attachés stationed abroad and field hospitals. Excludes military aid missions, base hospitals, and military schools.
	Expenditures on the administration of civil defense affairs and services; formulation of contingency plans; organization of exercises involving civilian institutions and populations; operation or support of civil defense forces; administration of military aid and operation of military aid missions accredited to foreign governments or attached to international military organizations or alliances; military aid in the form of grants (in cash or in kind), loans (regardless of the interest charged), or loans of equipment; contributions to international peacekeeping forces, including the assignment of manpower.
	Expenditures on the administration and operation of government agencies engaged in applied research and experimental development related to defense; grants, loans, or subsidies to support applied research and experimental development related to defense undertaken by nongovernment bodies such as research institutes and universities.
Health	Expenditures on the administration, operation, or support of activities such as formulation, administration, coordination, and monitoring of overall health policies, plans, programs, and budgets; preparation and enforcement of legislation and standards for the

TABLE 2A.1 *Continued*

Type of expenditure	What it includes
	provision of health services, including the licensing of medical establishments and medical and paramedical personnel; and production and dissemination of general information, technical documentation, and statistics on health.
Education	Government outlays for education include expenditures on services provided to individual pupils and students and expenditures on services provided on a collective basis. Collective educational services are concerned with matters such as the formulation and adminis-tration of government policy; setting and enforcement of standards; regulation, licensing, and supervision of educational establishments; and applied research into and experimental development of education affairs and services. The breakdown for education is based on the levels established in the 1997 International Standard Classification of Education (ISCED–97) of the United Nations Educational, Scientific, and Cultural Organization (UNESCO).
Social security and welfare	Expenditures for transfer payments, including payments in kind (to compensate for reduction or loss of income or inadequate earning capacity); administration, management, or operation of social security affairs involving chiefly provision of benefits for loss due to sickness, childbirth, or temporary disability resulting from industrial and other accidents, including maternity benefits; administration, management, or operation of retirement, pensions, or disability plans for government employees, both civil and military, and their survivors; administration, operation, and support of old age, disability, or survivor's benefits; unemployment compensation benefits; family and child allowances; welfare affairs and services (for children's and old age residential institutions, handicapped persons, and other residential institutions).
Agriculture, forestry, fishing, and hunting	Agriculture: Expenditures on the administration of agricultural affairs and services; conservation, reclamation, or expansion of arable land; agrarian reform and land settlement; supervision and regulation of the agricultural industry; construction or operation of flood control, irrigation, and drainage systems, including grants, loans, or subsidies for such works;

(Continued)

TABLE 2A.1 *Continued*

Type of expenditure	What it includes
	operation or support of programs or schemes to stabilize or improve farm prices and farm incomes; operation or support of extension services or veterinary services to farmers, pest control services, crop inspection services, and crop grading services; production and dissemination of general information, technical documentation, and statistics on agricultural affairs and services; compensation, grants, loans, or subsidies to farmers in connection with agricultural activities, including payments to restrict or encourage output of a particular crop or to allow land to remain uncultivated.
	Forestry: Expenditures on the administration of forestry affairs and services; conservation, extension, and rationalized exploitation of forest reserves; supervision and regulation of forest operations and issuance of tree-felling licenses; operation or support of reforestation work, pest and disease control, forest firefighting and fire prevention services, and extension services to forest operators; production and dissemination of general information, technical documentation, and statistics on forestry affairs and services; grants, loans, or subsidies to support commercial forest activities.
	Fishing and hunting: Expenditures on both commercial fishing and hunting and on fishing and hunting for sport (outside natural parks and reserves). Include the administration of fishing and hunting affairs and services; protection, propagation, and rationalized exploitation of fish and wildlife stocks; supervision and regulation of freshwater fishing, coastal fishing, ocean fishing, fish farming, wildlife hunting, and issuance of fishing and hunting licenses; operation or support of fish hatcheries, extension services, stocking or culling activities, etc.; production and dissemination of general information, technical documentation, and statistics on fishing and hunting affairs and services; grants, loans, or subsidies to support commercial fishing and hunting activities, including the construction or operation of fish hatcheries.

TABLE 2A.2 Extrapolation of expenditure data

Countries	Sectors for which expenditure data are available	Years extrapolated[a]
Africa		
Botswana	Agriculture, education, health, defense	2002, 2001–2, 2002, 2002
	Transportation and communication, social security	1999–2002, 2001–2
	Total expenditures	1997–2002
Burkina Faso	Agriculture, health	1994–99, 2000–2001
	Transportation and communication, social security	1999–2002, 1999–2002
	Total expenditures	1994–2001
Cameroon	Agriculture, education, health	2002–2, 2002, 2001–2
	Transportation and communication, social security, defense	2001–2, 2001–2, 2002
	Total expenditures	2000–2002
Côte d'Ivoire	Agriculture	1986–2002
	Education	2002
	Health	2000–2002
	Transportation and communication, social security	1999–2001, 2001–2
	Defense	1999–2002
	Total expenditures	1981–83 and 1991–93
Egypt	Social security	2002
	Total expenditures	1998–2001
Ethiopia	Agriculture, transportation and communication, social security	2001, 2001, 2002
	Total expenditures	1993–96 and 2000–2001
Ghana	Agriculture, education, social security, defense	2001, 2001, 2002, 2002
	Total expenditures	1994–2001
Kenya	Transportation and communication, total expenditures	1999–2001, 1999–2001

(Continued)

TABLE 2A.2 *Continued*

Countries	Sectors for which expenditure data are available	Years extrapolated[a]
Malawi	Agriculture, education, health, social security	2002, 2002, 2002, 2002
	Transportation and communication, defense, total expenditures	2002, 2002, 1991–2001
Mali	Agriculture, transportation and communication, total expenditures	1989–2002, 1999–2002, 1989–2001
	Defense, social security	1989–90, 2002
Morocco	Agriculture, health, defense	2002, 2002, 2002
	Total expenditures, transportation and communication, social security	1996 and 2000–2001, 1988–90, 2002
Nigeria	Agriculture, education, health, transportation and communication, defense	2002, 2002, 2002, 2002, 2002
	Total expenditures	1980–83 and 1988–2001
Togo	Agriculture, education, health, transportation and communication	1999–2002, 1999–2000, 2002, 1999–2002
	Social security, defense	2002, 1999–2002
	Total expenditures	1998–2001
Tunisia	Agriculture, education, health, transportation and communication	2001–2, 2001–2, 2002, 2000–2002
Uganda	Transportation and communication	1987–90
Zambia	Agriculture, education, defense, health	2002–2, 2000–2002, 2002, 2002
	Transportation and communication, social security	2000–2002, 2002
	Total expenditures	1989–2001
Zimbabwe	Agriculture, education, transportation and communication, health	2002, 2002, 2000–2002, 2000–2002
	Social security, defense	2002, 2002
	Total expenditures	1998–2001
Asia		
Bangladesh	Health	1986–88 and 1997–2000
	Total expenditures	1990–98 and 2000–2001
	Transportation and communication, social security	1998–2001, 2002

China	Health, transportation and communication, social security	1998, 2001, 2002
India	Health, social security	2000–2001, 1998–2002
	Transportation and communication	2000–2001
Indonesia	Social security	1980–93
Korea, Republic of	Agriculture, education, health, transportation and communication	1998–2002, 2002, 2002, 1998–2002
	Defense, social security, total expenditures	2002, 2002, 1998–2001
Malaysia	Agriculture, education, health, defense	1999–2002, 2002, 2001–2, 2002
	Transportation and communication, social security, total expenditures	1999–2002, 2002, 1998–2002
Myanmar	Social security	2002
Nepal	Data for all sectors and years available	
Philippines	Data for all sectors and years available	
Sri Lanka	Data for all sectors and years available	
Thailand	Data for all sectors and years available	
Latin America		
Argentina	Education	1986–88
	Health	1980–88
	Social security	2002
Belize	Agriculture, education, health, transportation and communication	1998–2002, 2002, 2002, 1998–2002
	Social security, defense	2002, 1999–2001
	Total expenditures	1986–2001
Bolivia	Agriculture, transportation and communication	1985–86, 1985–86
	Total expenditures	1980–85
Brazil	Agriculture, education, health, transportation and communication,	1995–96, 1995–96, 1995–96,
	social security, total expenditures	1995–96, 1995–96, 1995–96,
		1999–2002
Chile	Agriculture	1989–2001
	Transportation and communication, social security	1999–2002, 2002

(*Continued*)

TABLE 2A.2 *Continued*

Countries	Sectors for which expenditure data are available	Years extrapolated[a]
Colombia	Agriculture, health	1985–89 and 2000–2001, 1985–89 and 2000–2001
	Transportation and communication, social security, total expenditures	2000–2001, 2000–2001, 2000–2001
	Defense, social security	1985–88, 1985–88
Costa Rica	Defense	1999–2002
Dominican Republic	Agriculture, education, health, total expenditures	2001, 2001
Ecuador	Data for all sectors and years available	
El Salvador	Education, health	2001, 2001
Guatemala	Agriculture, transportation and communication, social security	1999–2001, 1999–2001, 1999–2001
	Total expenditures	1984–2001
Mexico	Agriculture, education, health	2001–2, 2001–2, 2001–2
	Transportation and communication, defense, total expenditures	2002, 2002, 2001–2
Panama	Agriculture, education, health, transportation and communication, defense	2002, 2002
	Total expenditures	2002
Paraguay	Agriculture, education, health	1999–2002, 2002, 2002
	Transportation and communication, social security, defense	2002, 2002, 2000–2002
Uruguay	Agriculture, education, health, transportation and communication	2002, 2002, 2002, 2002
	Defense	2000–2002
Venezuela	Education	1995–98

[a]The year or range of years for which data are not available for each sector at left.

TABLE 2A.3 Government expenditures, 1980, 1990, 2000, and 2002

Region/country	Billions of 2000 international dollars				Percentage of GDP			
	1980	1990	2000	2002	1980	1990	2000	2002
Africa	114.21	152.30	244.64	279.46	28.43	26.72	31.42	33.82
Botswana	0.86	2.54	5.39	6.30	31.76	33.58	42.17	46.91
Burkina Faso	0.59	1.01	2.35	2.39	10.81	13.27	20.74	19.62
Cameroon	2.79	5.21	5.69	6.39	15.74	21.17	20.16	21.33
Côte d'Ivoire	5.81	4.82	4.52	3.91	31.68	24.48	17.94	15.73
Egypt	44.30	41.73	57.95	66.26	50.28	27.81	25.53	25.99
Ethiopia	4.06	12.17	20.28	21.90	n.a.	37.99	47.00	45.50
Ghana	2.21	3.33	10.53	10.90	10.89	13.25	27.51	26.15
Kenya	5.12	8.25	7.43	8.38	25.26	27.46	24.87	23.62
Malawi	1.23	1.13	2.15	2.43	34.59	25.45	35.25	40.62
Mali	1.07	1.86	2.71	2.83	19.44	32.01	31.40	27.85
Morocco	18.35	23.36	32.68	33.13	33.09	28.82	32.36	29.92
Nigeria	9.80	20.86	47.46	72.41	12.80	24.49	42.87	67.01
Togo	1.65	0.99	1.77	2.04	30.80	16.70	26.03	28.40
Tunisia	8.26	12.86	18.90	21.33	31.56	34.60	32.02	33.89
Uganda	0.21	1.85	6.14	9.78	6.17	11.70	20.41	28.68
Zambia	2.33	1.97	1.87	2.15	37.05	27.26	24.31	25.71
Zimbabwe	5.55	8.36	16.83	6.94	27.92	27.32	51.40	38.54
Asia	500.13	870.81	1,786.98	2,228.66	19.30	17.09	17.99	20.20
Bangladesh	6.18	25.52	27.37	24.35	7.13	20.45	13.24	11.11
China	226.12	335.92	872.12	1,179.44	27.20	16.62	17.76	21.05
India	102.39	233.14	408.35	446.69	12.54	16.26	16.69	16.64
Indonesia	50.10	77.08	133.56	146.17	22.14	18.36	23.12	24.59
Korea, Republic of	31.02	65.76	144.64	191.46	17.37	16.22	21.00	25.90
Malaysia	16.55	30.94	41.98	46.16	27.98	29.26	20.02	21.07

(Continued)

TABLE 2A.3 *Continued*

Region/country	Billions of 2000 international dollars				Percentage of GDP			
	1980	1990	2000	2002	1980	1990	2000	2002
Myanmar	7.58	8.70	9.39	9.95	15.85	16.03	8.67	7.67
Nepal	1.64	3.12	4.75	5.41	14.30	17.22	16.02	17.42
Philippines	25.43	44.10	58.46	64.21	13.36	19.60	19.25	19.60
Sri Lanka	11.23	11.61	17.42	14.18	41.36	28.37	25.61	20.32
Thailand	21.90	34.92	68.94	100.64	18.80	14.08	17.97	24.38
Latin America	379.23	571.55	716.97	839.45	18.22	23.13	20.94	24.73
Argentina	57.17	30.56	76.55	117.33	18.23	10.57	16.97	30.53
Belize	0.12	0.23	0.33	0.32	22.87	28.40	24.08	23.00
Bolivia	2.17	2.26	4.74	8.88	15.91	16.38	23.73	43.26
Brazil	157.79	335.24	324.56	329.96	20.19	34.87	25.90	25.50
Chile	14.50	15.27	30.38	32.90	28.01	20.38	21.89	23.45
Colombia	19.21	23.66	55.80	71.54	13.37	11.58	21.32	26.67
Costa Rica	4.03	5.23	7.56	9.48	25.04	25.61	22.27	26.85
Dominican Republic	3.92	3.48	8.48	9.89	16.92	11.66	16.02	17.27
Ecuador	4.05	5.29	8.54	8.96	14.02	14.97	20.20	19.50
El Salvador	0.95	1.76	4.96	0.76	17.14	10.90	17.01	2.51
Guatemala	3.94	3.01	5.46	5.75	14.32	10.04	12.17	12.25
Mexico	82.18	111.90	140.27	192.07	15.75	17.88	15.95	22.07
Panama	2.91	2.59	4.31	4.85	30.53	23.70	23.49	26.35
Paraguay	1.54	1.93	4.83	4.71	9.85	9.40	19.38	19.15
Uruguay	4.80	5.12	9.30	8.21	21.84	23.35	31.47	32.20
Venezuela	19.95	24.02	30.90	33.86	18.74	20.73	21.66	25.67
Total	993.57	1,594.65	2,748.59	3,347.57	19.58	19.60	19.44	21.95

SOURCE: Calculated using data from International Monetary Fund, *Government Financial Statistics Yearbook*, various years.

NOTE: n.a., not available.

Appendix 2B: Data Sources and Econometric Estimation

The main source of expenditure data used in the chapter was the IMF's *Government Financial Statistics Yearbook,* various years. Their measures have been discussed in the text.

Total GDP, agricultural GDP, total population, agricultural population, employment, and private investments by sector, road density, and literacy rate were taken from the World Bank database (World Bank 2006). Agricultural land, agricultural labor, number of tractors, and number of draft animals were taken from the FAO database (FAO 2006). All data on agricultural research and development expenditures were taken from Pardey, Roseboom, and Beintema (1997).

Because the panel data set was used and there may be a strong reverse causality between government spending and GDP growth, special attention is needed to avoid or minimize the bias by using certain econometric estimation techniques. To avoid these econometric problems' arising from endogeneity in a panel data set, scholars have used different approaches. First, if the endogeneity comes from regional targeting (for example, the government targets its investment to high-potential areas or to poor areas), regional dummies are often used to minimize the potential bias (Hsaio 1986). Another commonly used approach is differencing. However, differencing would destroy the long-term relationship in the data and leave just indications of short-term impact (Hsiao 1986; Munnel 1992). Thus the differencing may not be justified. Instrumental variables have also been used, but it is difficult to find instruments that are correlated with independent variables to be instrumented but are not correlated with dependent variables. Arellano and Bond (1991) proposed a GMM estimator for a dynamic estimation for a panel data set. To illustrate, assume that N cross-sectional units are observed over T periods. Let i index the cross-sectional unit (country) and t the time periods. Further assume the existence of an individual effect η_i for the ith cross-sectional unit. The model to be estimated is specified as

$$y_{it} = \alpha_0 + \sum_{e=1}^{m} \alpha_e y_{i,t-e} + \sum_{k=1}^{n} \beta_k x_{i,t-k} + \eta_i + u_{it},$$

where y is dependent variable; x is a set of independent variables, $i = 1, \ldots, N$; $t = m + 2, \ldots, T$; α's and β's are parameters; and the lag lengths m and n are sufficient to ensure that u_{it} is a stochastic error. Although it is not essential that m equal n, we follow typical practice by assuming that they are identical.

But in this dynamic panel model, including an individual effect together with a lagged dependent variable generates biased estimates for a standard LSDV (least squares dummy variable) estimator, especially when N is much larger than T (Hsiao 1986). A common way to deal with this problem is to take the first difference and exploit a different number of instruments in each time period using either an instrument variable estimator or a GMM estimator as an estimation method (Holtz-Eakin, Newey, and Rosen 1988; Arellano and Bond 1991):

$$\Delta y_{it} = \sum_{e=1}^{m} a_e \Delta y_{it-e} + \sum_{e=1}^{m} \beta_e \Delta x_{it-e} + \Delta u_{it}.$$

Expressed in matrix, the general model is a single equation,

$$Y_i = W_i \delta + \phi_i \eta_i + u_i,$$

where δ is a parameter vector including the α's and β's, W_i is a data matrix containing the time series of the lagged y's and x's, and ϕ_i is a vector of ones. Assuming that we found a set of suitable instrumental variables Z_i, and that H_i is the covariance matrix of the transformed errors, the linear GMM estimators of δ could be computed as

$$\hat{\delta} = [(\sum_i W_i^{*\prime} Z_i) A_N (\sum_i Z_i' W_i^*)]^{-1} (\sum_i W_i^{*\prime} Z_i) A_N (\sum_i Z_i' Y_i^*),$$

where $A_N = \frac{1}{N}(\sum_i Z_i' H_i Z_i)^{-1}$ and W_i^* and Y_i^* denote some transformation of W_i and Y_i (levels, first difference, combinations of first differences and levels).

For the first-difference equation, suitably lagged endogenous variables can be used as instruments, and Z_i may consist of submatrixes with the block diagonal form (exploiting all or part of the moment restrictions available). A judicious choice of the Z_i matrix should strike a compromise between prior knowledge (from economic theory and previous empirical work) and the characteristics of the sample. For example, if u_{it} are not serially correlated with each other, for time $t = m + 2$ $(y_{i1}, y_{i2}, \ldots, y_{im})$ are uncorrelated with $y_{i,m+2}$ and therefore can be used as valid instruments at time $m + 2$. Similarly, the instruments for time period T are $(y_{i1}, y_{i2}, \ldots, y_{i(T-2)})$. In the case of first-order difference with one lag, $Y_i^* = (\Delta y_{i3}, \ldots, \Delta y_{iT})$, $W_i^* = (\Delta y_{i2}, \ldots, \Delta y_{i,T-1})$,

$$Z_i = Z_i^D = \begin{bmatrix} y_{i1} & 0 & 0 & \ldots & 0 & 0 & \ldots & 0 \\ 0 & y_{i1} & y_{i2} & \ldots & 0 & 0 & \ldots & 0 \\ 0 & 0 & 0 & \ldots & 0 & 0 & \ldots & 0 \\ 0 & 0 & 0 & \ldots & y_{i1} & y_{i2} & \cdots & y_{i,T-2} \end{bmatrix},$$

$$\text{and } H_i = H_i^D = \begin{bmatrix} 2 & -1 & . & . & 0 \\ -1 & 2 & . & . & 0 \\ . & . & . & . & . \\ . & . & . & 2 & -1 \\ 0 & 0 & . & -1 & 2 \end{bmatrix}.$$

In models with explanatory variables, a predetermined regressor x_i correlated with the individual effect could be added to the instrumental variable matrix, and the corresponding Z_i matrix would be given by

$$
Z_i = \begin{bmatrix}
y_{i1} & x_{i2} & x_{i2} & 0 & 0 & 0 & 0 & 0 & \cdots & 0 & \cdots & 0 & 0 & \cdots & 0 \\
0 & 0 & 0 & y_{i1} & y_{i2} & x_{i1} & x_{i2} & x_{i3} & \cdots & 0 & \cdots & 0 & 0 & \cdots & 0 \\
\cdot & \cdot & \cdot & \cdot & \cdot & \cdot & \cdot & \cdot & \cdots & \cdot & \cdots & \cdot & \cdot & \cdots & \cdot \\
\cdot & \cdot & \cdot & \cdot & \cdot & \cdot & \cdot & \cdot & \cdots & \cdot & \cdots & \cdot & \cdot & \cdots & \cdot \\
\cdot & \cdot & \cdot & \cdot & \cdot & \cdot & \cdot & \cdot & \cdots & \cdot & \cdots & \cdot & \cdot & \cdots & \cdot \\
0 & 0 & 0 & 0 & 0 & 0 & 0 & 0 & \cdots & y_{i1} & \cdots & y_{i,T-2} & x_{i1} & \cdots & x_{i,T1}
\end{bmatrix}.
$$

But this technique may lead to efficiency loss during the estimation. Blundell and Bond (1998a), therefore, proposed to use an extended system estimator that used lagged differences as instruments for equation in levels, in addition to lagged levels as instruments for equations in first difference. In other words, we "stack" both difference and level equations together for estimation. This implies a set of moment conditions relating to the equations in first differences and a set of moment conditions relating to the equations in levels. When combined together, we are able to obtain a dramatic efficiency gain over the basic first-difference GMM estimator. If the simple autoregressive AR(1) model is mean-stationary, the first differences Δy_{it} will be uncorrelated with individual effects, and thus $\Delta y_{i,t-1}$ can be used as instruments in the level equations. Zhang and Fan (2004) applied a system GMM method to empirically test the causal relationship between productivity growth and infrastructure development using the India district-level data from 1970 to 1994.

In this case, we define $Y_i^* = (\Delta y_{i3}, \ldots, \Delta y_{iT}, y_{i3}, \ldots, y_{iT})'$, $W_i^* = (\Delta y_{i2}, \ldots, \Delta y_{i,T-1}, y_{i2}, \ldots, y_{i,T-1})'$,

$$
Z_i = \begin{bmatrix}
Z_i^D & 0 & \cdots & 0 \\
0 & \Delta y_{i2} & \cdots & 0 \\
0 & \Delta y_{i2} & \cdots & 0 \\
\cdot & \cdot & \cdots & \cdot \\
0 & 0 & \cdots & \Delta y_{i,T-1}
\end{bmatrix},
$$

and the covariance matrix $H_i = \begin{bmatrix} H_i^D & 0 \\ 0 & I_i \end{bmatrix}$, where Z_i^D is the matrix of instruments for the equations in first differences, as described earlier, and I_i an identity matrix with dimension equal to the number of level equations. Again Z_i would include instruments of suitably lagged explanatory variables if they were uncorrelated with individual effects and the error terms. Using these instruments and following the estimation strategy outlined by Blundell and Bond (1998a,b), the coefficients for the lagged dependent variables and predetermined variables can be estimated.

References

Arellano, M., and S. Bond. 1991. Some tests of specification for panel data: Monte Carlo evidence and an application to employment equations. *Review of Economic Studies* 58: 277–297.

Aschauer, D. 1989. Is public expenditure productive? *Journal of Monetary Economics* 23: 177–220.

Barro, J. R. 1990. Government spending in a simple model of endogenous growth. *Journal of Political Economy* 20 (2): 221–247.

Barro, R. J., and J. W. Lee. 2005. IMF programs: Who is chosen and what are the effects? *Journal of Monetary Economics* 52 (7): 1245–1269.

Beintema, N., and G. Stads. 2004. Sub-Saharan African agricultural research: Recent investment trends. *Outlook on Agriculture* 33 (4): 239–246.

Blundell, Richard, and Stephen Bond. 1998a. Initial conditions and moment restrictions in dynamic panel data models. *Journal of Econometrics* 87: 115–143.

———. 1998b. GMM estimation with persistent panel data: An application to production functions. Working Paper W99/4. Institute for Fiscal Studies, London.

Buchanan, J., and G. Tullock. 1962. *The calculus of consent: A logical foundation of constitutional democracy.* Ann Arbor: University of Michigan Press.

Cusack, T. R. 1997. Partisan politics and public finance: Changes in public spending in the industrialized democracies, 1955–1989. *Public Choice* 91: 375–395.

Dao, M. Q. 1995. Determinants of government expenditures: New evidence from disaggregative data. *Oxford Bulletin of Economics and Statistics* 57: 67–76.

Deacon, R. T. 1978. A demand model for the local public sector. *Review of Economics and Statistics* 60 (1): 169–173.

Devarajan S., V. Swaroop, and H. Zou. 1996. The composition of public expenditure and economic growth. *Journal of Monetary Economics* 37 (2–3): 313–344.

Elias, V. 1985. *Government expenditures on agriculture and agricultural growth in Latin America.* Research Report 50. Washington, D.C.: International Food Policy Research Institute.

Fan, S., and P. Pardey. 1998. Government spending on Asian agriculture: Trends and production consequence. In *Agricultural public finance policy in Asia.* Tokyo: Asian Productivity Organization.

Fan, S., P. Hazell, and S. Thorat. 2000. Government spending, agricultural growth and poverty in rural India. *American Journal of Agricultural Economics* 82 (4): 1038–1051.

Fan, S., L. Zhang, and X. Zhang. 2004. Investment, reforms and poverty in rural China. *Economic Development and Cultural Change* 52 (2): 395–422.

Feldstein, M. 1996. How big should government be? NBER Working Paper 5868. Cambridge, Mass.: National Bureau for Economic Research.

Food and Agriculture Organization (FAO). 2006. FAOStat database, June. Rome.

Gwartney, J., R. Holcombe, and R. Lawson. 1998. The scope of government and the wealth of nations. *Cato Journal* 18 (2): 163–190.

Holtz-Eakin, D., W. Newey, and H. Rosen. 1988. Estimating vector autoregressions with panel data. *Econometrica* 56: 1371–1395.

Hsaio, C. 1986. *Analysis of panel data.* Cambridge, England: Cambridge University Press.

International Monetary Fund. 1973–2005. *Government financial statistics yearbook.* Washington D.C.

Kelly, T. 1997. Public expenditures and growth. *Journal of Development Studies* 34 (1): 60–84.

Kohli, Ulrich. 1982. A gross national product function and the derived demand for imports and supply of exports. *Canadian Journal of Economics* 18: 369–386.

Lopez, R. 2005. Under-investing in public goods: Evidence, causes and consequences for agricultural development equity and the environment. *Agricultural Economics* 32 (51): 211–224.

Marlow, M. L., and A. F. Shiers. 1999. Do law enforcement expenditures crowd-out public education expenditures? *Applied Economics* 31 (2): 255–266.

Munnel, A. 1992. Infrastructure investment and economic growth. *Journal of Economic Perspective* 6 (4): 0189–198.

Nitzan, S. 1994. Transfers or public good provision? A political allocation perspective. *Economics Letters* 45: 451–457.

Pardey, P. G., J. Roseboom, and N. M. Beintema. 1997. Investments in African agricultural research. *World Development* 25 (3): 409–423.

Rodrick, D. 1998. Why do more open economies have bigger governments? *Journal of Political Economy* 106 (5): 997–1032.

Sass, T. R. 1991. The choice of municipal government structure and public expenditures. *Public Choice* 71: 71–87.

Tanzi, V., and L. Schuknecht. 2001. Public spending in the 20th century: A global perspective. *Public Choice* 108 (1–2): 197–200.

Tanzi, V., and H. Zee. 1997. Fiscal policy and long-run growth. *IMF Staff Papers* 44 (2): 179–209.

World Bank. 2006. *2006 world development indicators.* Washington, D.C.

Zhang, X., and S. Fan. 2004. How productive is infrastructure? New approach and evidence from rural India. *American Journal of Agricultural Economics* 86 (2): 492–501.

3   Public Investment, Growth, and Rural Poverty

SHENGGEN FAN AND NEETHA RAO

The objective of this chapter is to improve our understanding of the relationship between government spending and poverty reduction through long-term growth by reviewing and synthesizing major issues, methodologies, and findings of major studies by the International Food Policy Research Institute (IFPRI). As shown in Figure 3.1, public spending affects poverty reduction through different channels. Understanding these different channels will enable policymakers to design more effective policies. Much of the evidence reviewed in the chapter was drawn from case studies undertaken by IFPRI over the last several years. These case studies have analyzed the impact of differential investments not only on economic growth, but also on poverty reduction and regional inequality. Moreover, they have distinguished the effects by different geographic regions.

The spending considered in this chapter is public investment at the different levels of government that leads to long-term growth from which the poor will benefit. This type of spending is very different from the targeted welfare or social safety net spending considered in Chapter 5. Welfare or safety net spending reduces poverty mainly through changes in income distribution, at least in the short run. As will be illustrated in Chapter 5, this type of spending has also been increasingly used for long-term growth and thus poverty reduction through enhanced human capital.

We will first review a framework for the assessment of public investment for poverty reduction. We pay particular attention to how public investment affects rural poverty through different channels. We then use select case studies to illustrate how different types of public investment can have differential impacts. Finally, we summarize lessons learned from this synthesis, note knowledge gaps that remain, and offer policy recommendations for a public investment strategy to achieve the twin goals of economic growth and poverty reduction.

How Public Investment Affects Rural Poverty

This section aims to assess the current state of knowledge on public investment linkages for poverty reduction. As we mentioned earlier, public investment affects

FIGURE 3.1 Government spending and rural poverty

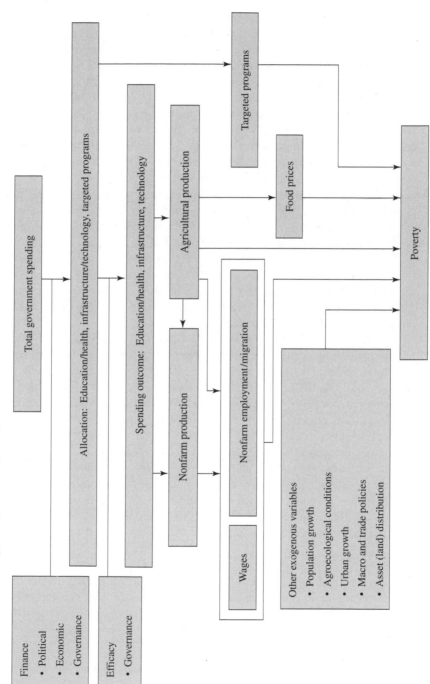

rural poverty through many channels (see Figure 3.1). For example, public investment in agricultural research, rural education, and infrastructure increases farmers' income directly by increasing agricultural productivity, which in turn reduces rural poverty. Indirect impacts come from the higher agricultural wages and improved nonfarm employment opportunities induced by growth in agricultural productivity. Agricultural output from rural investment often yields lower food prices, again helping the poor indirectly because they are often net buyers of foodgrains. The redistribution of land caused by higher rates of agricultural growth also impacts rural poverty. In addition to indirectly affecting wages, nonfarm employment and migration directly promote rural wages, nonfarm employment, and migration through increased productivity and public investments in rural education, health, and infrastructure, thereby reducing rural poverty. For example, improved infrastructure access will help farmers set up small rural nonfarm businesses such as food processing and marketing enterprises, electronic repairs shops, transportation and trade businesses, and restaurant services. As seen in a recent study by Torero and von Braun (2005), the effects of information and communication technologies on the poor can come through many different channels, such as promoting the development of small and medium-sized enterprises, improved health and education services, and finally higher per capita consumption.

Investments in rural sectors not only contribute to growth, employment, and wages in rural areas, but also help the development of the national economy by providing labor, human and physical capital, less expensive food, and markets for urban industrial and service development. Growth in the national economy reduces poverty in both rural and urban sectors. Understanding these different effects provides useful policy insights to improve the effectiveness of national poverty reduction strategies. In particular, it provides information on how public investment can be used to strengthen weak links between poverty reduction channels to increase the efficiency of targeting public resources for poverty reduction. More efficient targeting has become increasingly crucial as many developing countries have committed to achieving poverty reduction goals using the framework provided by the Millennium Development Goals with limited public resources.

Agricultural Growth

The relationship between general economic growth and poverty reduction is well established after more than three decades of debate. This chapter will not repeat these arguments.[1] Instead it will focus on evidence of the poverty reduc-

---

1. For debates on this issue, refer to the *World Development Report* for 2000/2001 (World Bank 2001), and Dollar and Kraay (2001). One type of study is particularly relevant: that estimating elasticity of poverty reduction with respect to economic growth. For example, Ravallion obtained a growth elasticity of poverty of –2.0 to –2.5 using a cross-country regression, and Warr

tion impacts of *agricultural growth* for the following reasons: (1) a majority of the world's poor live in rural areas, and a large share of their income comes from agriculture; (2) growth in agriculture contributes to poverty reduction indirectly through increased rural wages and both farm and nonfarm employment; and (3) agricultural growth may also contribute to poverty reduction in urban areas by lowering food prices for urban residents and helping national economic growth.

The most remarkable evidence on the poverty reduction effects of agricultural growth is probably that from the green revolution in South Asia from the late 1960s to the 1980s. Before the green revolution was well under way in the late 1960s, the incidence of rural poverty in India fluctuated widely, between 50 and 60 percent. But after the green revolution began in the mid-1960s, due to the widespread use of high-yielding varieties developed jointly by national and international agricultural research centers, the yield of wheat and rice doubled, tripled, or even quadrupled in farms in just two decades. The incidence of rural poverty declined, from 64 percent in 1966 to 34 percent in 1989.

However, it was not until the late 1970s that Ahluwalia (1978a) formally constructed a formula for the relationship between agricultural growth and poverty reduction. The correlation between agricultural growth and rural poverty became much stronger and more statistically significant after the green revolution. After Ahluwalia's seminal study, a greater consensus began to emerge in the literature on the poverty-reducing impacts of agricultural growth. In particular, rapid agricultural growth and poverty reduction in India during the 1980s triggered numerous other studies in the 1990s. Using state-level data from India, Datt and Ravallion (1998a) found that there was a strong negative relationship between farm yield and rural poverty. The short-run elasticity of various measures of poverty relative to farm yield ranged from –0.18 to –0.41, and the range of long-run elasticity, from –0.88 to –1.93, was substantially larger for the same measures. Fan, Hazell, and Thorat (2000) obtained a poverty reduction elasticity of agricultural productivity growth of –0.250 after considering all direct and indirect impacts of growth on poverty reduction and after controlling for all other investments.[2]

There is strong evidence of a growth effect on poverty in rural China, where there has been tremendous poverty reduction over the last two decades. The number of poor declined from 260 million in 1978 to 26 million in 2004 (China, Ministry of Agriculture 2005). The most rapid reduction occurred during the initial phase of rural reforms, from 1978 to 1984, and was highly correlated with agricultural growth due to institutional and policy changes in agricultural

(2001) estimated this elasticity for several Asian countries: India (–0.92); Taiwan, China (–3.82); Thailand (–2.04); Indonesia (–1.38); Malaysia (–2.06); and the Philippines (–0.73).

2. Among the total impacts of agricultural productivity growth, the direct impact from higher farm income accounted for 70 percent, higher wages for 8.6 percent, better nonfarm employment for 14 percent, and lower food prices for 16 percent (Fan, Hazell, and Thorat 2000).

production. However, between 1984 and 1989 rural poverty began to rise, and that rise is attributed to stagnation of agricultural growth during this period. The Chinese evidence convincingly shows that whenever agricultural growth is strong, there is rapid poverty reduction, and whenever agricultural growth is lacking, poverty reduction is slow. Fan, Zhang, and Zhang (2004) estimated the poverty elasticity of agricultural growth as –1.50.[3] This elasticity is much greater than that of India, measured by Datt and Ravallion (1998a).[4] This is largely due to the fact that land is equally distributed in China, so even the very poor have access to land, while in India many of the poor are landless laborers. This strongly suggests that more equal distribution of production assets will lead to more poverty reduction given the same rate of growth.

The importance of agricultural growth for poverty reduction has also been demonstrated for the countries of Latin America. This evidence is particularly significant for two reasons. First, because many of the Latin American countries belong to the middle-income rather than the low-income category, one would expect a somewhat diminished role for agricultural growth. Second, unlike in Asia and Africa, poverty in Latin America is not predominantly a rural phenomenon. The debt and adjustment crisis of the 1980s created a whole new class of urban poor, although even before advent of the crisis, almost half of the poor population lived in urban areas.

For the reasons just cited, one might suspect that agricultural growth does not play a crucial role in reducing poverty in Latin America, but some recent analyses suggest otherwise. De Janvry and Sadoulet (1993) analyzed the linkage between growth, inequality, and poverty in a number of Latin American countries for the period 1970–90. Their analysis distinguished between rural and urban poverty and looked separately at periods of growth and recession to allow for the possibility that the effect of per capita income change on poverty might have differed in the two time periods. Some of their findings are particularly relevant in the present context.

First, changes in agricultural value added are significantly related to rural poverty in periods of both growth and recession; growth reduces poverty, and

---

3. Among the total impacts of agricultural growth, the direct impact of growth from higher farm income accounted for 81 percent, rural nonfarm wages for 4 percent, and rural nonfarm employment for 15 percent. The price effect induced by agricultural growth was insignificant.

4. It is obvious that growth-poverty elasticities not only are specific to each context, but will change for a different poverty line and a different initial mean income or a different initial degree of poverty. We should also be careful in interpreting the higher elasticity of poverty reduction with respect to agricultural growth. If resources are shifted to the agriculture sector (a lower-productivity sector), this may slow down overall growth, and therefore result in less poverty reduction in other sectors. But this is largely an empirical question. Recent IFPRI studies have shown that the poverty reduction elasticities of agricultural growth are larger than those from urban growth when the economywide model is used and both redistribution and aggregate growth effects are considered (Diao et al. 2006). This is because agricultural growth also trickles down to other sectors through growth linkages and also because a large share of the poor are engaged in agriculture.

recession increases it. By contrast, urban poverty is sensitive to recession but not to the growth of urban income. In other words, while agricultural growth has been effective in reducing overall poverty in Latin America, urban income growth has played no part in this process. Second, bias toward agriculture, as indicated by a positive deviation from the growth trend of agricultural income, had an independent effect on poverty in addition to the effect of the growth trend, especially in spells of recession. When the overall economy was faltering, differential agricultural growth provided a source of vertical mobility.

Irz, Thirtle, and Wiggins (2001) were the first to link poverty reduction with agricultural growth using a cross-country regression that included many developing countries in the sample. They found that poverty reduction is correlated more with labor productivity than with land productivity, –0.83 for labor productivity and –0.37 for land productivity. The higher labor productivity elasticity of poverty reduction implies that the ability of agriculture to generate employment, bolster rural economy linkages, and reduce food prices is crucial for the maximum impact of productivity on poverty reduction.

Another set of studies analyzed the impact of regional growth patterns on rural poverty reduction. A study done by Fan and Hazell (2000) on rural India showed that it is now the rain-fed areas, including many less favored areas, rather than the irrigated areas (as during the green revolution) that offer the most productive growth for an additional unit of investment. Furthermore, investments in rain-fed areas have a much larger impact on poverty alleviation, making them a "win-win" development strategy. Fan, Zhang, and Zhang (2002) found that in rural China, all types of public investments, most importantly rural education and agricultural research and development (R&D), reduced regional inequality in the least developed (western) region, but additional investments worsened it in the developed (coastal and central) regions.

In summary, agricultural growth facilitates poverty reduction. Poverty reduction elasticity is often greater than that of overall or urban growth. However, the patterns of growth and its distributional impacts also matter. Better distribution of production assets and more growth in the less developed areas and in the small farm sector will foster more poverty reduction given the same rate of agricultural growth. On the other hand, poverty reduction promoted by agricultural growth may also have opportunity costs. For example, investing in agriculture may offset some growth in the urban sector and therefore urban poverty reduction. It is therefore also very important to analyze the poverty reduction effects of nonagricultural growth or urban growth. Growth in agriculture and that in nonagricultural sectors are often interlinked through product markets, labor and migration, and capital movement. This calls for a general-equilibrium analysis of the effects of various government interventions as well as trade-offs and synergies in different sectors. Chapter 7 will make an initial attempt in this regard.

Rural Wages

In the majority of developing countries, the bulk of the poor are either landless or live on small farms with inadequate land to meet their food needs. Therefore, they depend heavily on the only available capital of production—labor. The poor gain from economic growth by increasing their productivity if they own land and/or by participating in the labor market. For example, with the advent of the green revolution in India, the poor took advantage of the extra labor demand and of higher wages. Another factor of production, namely land, is also crucial in giving small-scale and landless farmers access to rural wages. Thiesenhusen and Melmed-Sanjack (1990) found that land distribution from large-scale farmers to small-scale farmers sharply increased family labor used per hectare and, to a lesser extent, labor hired per hectare.

Empirical evidence from India shows that agricultural wages can be affected by other factors in addition to agricultural growth, labor, and land. During the green revolution period of the 1970s and 1980s, the incidence of rural poverty in India declined in many states that experienced higher rates of agricultural growth. But it also declined in many states that did not benefit so much from higher agricultural growth, particularly in the 1980s (Sen 1997). A significant feature of this later period, however, was that the agricultural wage rate, which had been stagnant until the mid-1970s, subsequently increased sharply in most parts of India and appears to have been a major factor in (or a significant explanation for) the decline in rural poverty (Ravallion and Datt 1995; Tendulkar and Jain 1995; Mukherjee 1996; Sen 1997). Nonfarm employment opportunities, migration to cities, and government programs to generate wage employment all contributed to higher agricultural wages during this period (Mukherjee 1996; Sen 1997).

In many developing countries, such as India, the labor market is competitive and rural nonagricultural wages and agricultural wages are highly correlated. Both these types of wages have strong links to rural poverty. Public investment in infrastructure, health, and education promotes increases in these wages by supporting agricultural productivity and nonfarm employment activities. While the poverty effect of agricultural wages on rural poverty reduction is well noted, the effect of rural nonagricultural wages is often ignored. Ignoring this effect is likely to lead to underestimation of the impact of government spending on poverty because wage increases induced by improved infrastructure and human capital can be potentially large, albeit direct. Fan, Zhang, and Zhang (2004) obtained results showing a poverty reduction elasticity of rural nonfarm wages of –0.37.

Nonfarm Employment

Traditional rural households in developing countries are viewed mainly as agricultural producers and sources of agricultural wage laborers. However, there is increasing empirical evidence that rural households are often diversified in their activities, with nonagricultural sources of income often contributing significantly to household incomes. For the poor, different forms of nonfarm employment are a source of supplementary income and are ways to diversify and spread risk across a number of livelihood strategies. For the nonpoor, nonfarm activities are an avenue to the generation of more income and assets in addition to other factors of production, such as land, capital, and technology.

Indeed recent evidence suggests that nonfarm activities are generally associated with lower absolute poverty rates. Newman and Canagarajah (2000) concluded that poverty reduction in Ghana between 1988 and 1992 can be attributed mainly to improvements in both average levels of income and the pattern of its distribution in the informal and nonfarm sectors in cities and rural areas outside the capital city, Accra. Datt and Ravallion (1998b) illustrated the important role of growth in nonfarm output, in addition to growth in agricultural output in poverty reduction across Indian states. The impact of the nonfarm economy on inequality is less clear-cut, however. A recent study of Ecuador explored these questions directly (Elbers and Lanjouw 2001). A key finding was that, irrespective of an association with income inequality, employment shares in both high-productivity and low-productivity nonfarm activities are associated with sharply lower absolute poverty rates. Thus, while inequality and poverty are clearly related, they are not equivalent. The authors suggest that the high-productivity subsector acts as an engine of growth by lifting the poor out of poverty either directly or by generating higher wage rates, while the low-productivity subsector acts as a safety net that helps prevent more households from falling below the poverty line.

Various studies also show that the poor, particularly those who are landless, receive a higher percentage of their income from nonfarm occupations, suggesting an equalizing influence (Bagachwa and Stewart 1992; Adams Jr. 1999). Although high-return nonfarm activities such as shopkeeping, tailoring, and carpentry exist in rural areas, the poor are not typically involved in such occupations. They participate in activities that require little investment and few skills, and they are likely to face entry barriers to high-return options. Similarly, Fabrizio et al. (2000) have pointed out that among farming households in Thailand, the larger the farm size, the lower the share of income earned from nonfarm sources.

There is evidence that women's nonfarm activities help reduce poverty. A study done in two economically and culturally different countries—Ghana and Uganda—showed that in both countries rural poverty rates were lowest and fell most rapidly for female heads of household engaged in nonfarm activities (Canagarajah, Newmann, and Bhattamishra 2001). Participation in nonfarm activities increased more rapidly for women, particularly married women and female heads of household, than for men. Women were more likely than men to combine agriculture and nonfarm activities. In Ghana it was nonfarm activities that provided the highest average incomes. More important, women earned the highest income shares. Elsewhere in Africa, there is evidence of the crucial role of women in the success of the nonfarm economy. For example, female non-farm participation rates in West Africa are very high—60 percent in western Nigeria and 41 percent in Benin (Haggblade, Hazell, and Brown 1989).

The returns to education are one of the main factors determining productivity, access to employment, and income in the nonfarm sector. For example, people with secondary or higher levels of education in the Brazilian northeast and southeast have better prospects in the nonfarm sector (Ferreira and Lanjouw 2001). This effect is magnified when broken down into low- and high-return nonfarm activities. This breakdown also yields a more striking result: gender differentiation in nonfarm activity. Women tend to work in the low-pay activities, while the opposite is true for men. De Janvry and Sadoulet (2001) also showed that Mexicans who have 3 to 9 years of schooling were more able to participate in nonfarm activities. Gains were highest for those who had a secondary or higher level of education. However, education played no role in access to agricultural labor. Yúnez-Naude and Taylor (2001) have further argued that preparatory and technical education yielded high returns and increased labor productivity in Mexico. They contend that it would serve Mexico to focus on these types of education to increase the establishment of manufacturing enterprises in the rural nonfarm economy.

Migration

Public investment can have a large impact on migration both from rural to rural areas and from rural to urban areas. For example, the green revolution in South Asia was initially concentrated in irrigated regions and only later spread to more favorable rain-fed areas. Technological change, therefore, can contribute to widening disparities between regions. Worse, if technology leads to lower production costs per unit of output in the adopting regions, producer prices may fall, leaving nonadopting regions with lower prices and stagnant yields, so their incomes actually decline. Interregional migration serves to buffer these gaps and provides an efficient way of spreading the benefits to poorer regions with limited agricultural growth potential.

In such instances, migrants leave their villages to settle permanently in other rural parts of the country or travel from their villages to other villages (where there is a need for surplus labor or where there is windfall productivity) and return to their villages, as was the case during the green revolution. Many people, both landless and landowning, migrated to Punjab and Haryana in India from neighboring states such as Uttar Pradesh and Bihar because of the increased productivity of high-yielding crop varieties and the subsequent increase in labor demand. Such migration sees the return of migrants to their own villages and is termed seasonal migration. It is estimated that the green revolution led to the seasonal migration of more than a million agricultural workers each year from the eastern states to Punjab and Haryana (Westley 1986). Moreover, in a study of the impact of the green revolution in a sample of Asian villages, David and Otsuka (1994) found that seasonal migration played an important role in spreading the benefits between technology-adopting and nonadopting regions.

Lack of economic and/or employment opportunities leads to rural-to-urban migration, with scores of people looking for better opportunities in cities. In China, due to lax rural-to-urban migration restrictions, many farmers migrated to urban centers to work in service and construction sectors. It is estimated that there were more than 150 million rural migrants working in various urban sectors in 2004, but this number was negligible even 20 years ago (China, Ministry of Agriculture 2005). Never before in China's history had there been such a large-scale relocation of the population, reducing by a large number the poor in rural areas and contributing to a large share of rapid economic growth in the past two decades. The migration from rural to urban areas and from agricultural to nonagricultural sectors in rural China accounted for 14 percent of the total poverty reduction and even a larger share of income growth in rural China from 1978 to 1997 (Fan, Zhang, and Zhang 2004). Among all factors, education was the key factor in the ability of the poor to migrate to urban sectors (Yang 1997; Zhao 1999).

Land Distribution

Improvement in the asset base of the poor is viewed as one of the ways to lift them out of poverty, which in a poor agrarian economy means improving access to land. The relationship between agricultural growth and land distribution has been debated over the past several decades. The consensus is that better land distribution through land reforms not only is good for better income distribution and consequently poverty reduction, but also helps agricultural growth, which in turn alleviates poverty. However, the effect of agricultural growth on land distribution has been less clear-cut. In fact, one of the earliest controversies on the green revolution was whether a higher rate of agricultural growth worsened land distribution.

Critics argue that large farm owners who had better access to irrigation water, fertilizers, seeds, and credit were the main adopters of new technologies, and smallholders were either unaffected or made worse off because the green revolution resulted in lower product prices, higher input prices, and owners' efforts to increase rents or force tenants off the land. However, a recent study does not support this argument. Fan, Hazell, and Thorat (1999) used state-level data from India for several decades and found that both relationships—between poverty and land distribution and between agricultural growth and land distribution—have been very weak. However, the fact that agricultural growth did not contribute to worsening land distribution does not mean that rural poverty is not correlated with land ownership. In fact, today many rural poor are either landless laborers or smallholders. Therefore, future growth must be ensured to benefit these landless or marginal landholding peasants. Alternatively, other policies have to be introduced to move them out of poverty.

Food Prices

Public investment in rural areas can lead to an increase in aggregate agricultural output, and this will in turn reduce food prices. This has proved to be one of the most important ways in which both rural and urban poor people will be affected by public investment (Scobie and Posada 1978; Rosegrant and Hazell 2000; Fan, Zhang, and Zhang 2002; Fan, Fang, and Zhang 2003). The impact of reduced food prices is particularly important for the urban poor because they often spend more than half of their income on food. These price reductions may not be very large in an open economy with low transport costs. Indeed many countries now fall into this category than did previously due to recent market liberalization policies. However, many poor countries still face high transport costs because of poor infrastructure, remoteness from world markets, or inefficient marketing institutions, and may still face considerably higher endogenous domestic prices even after market liberalization. For example, domestic prices still fall sharply when domestic food production increases suddenly in many Asian countries, such as China and India, and in landlocked African countries. Furthermore, the prices of many traditional food crops also continue to be endogenously determined within these countries because they are not traded in world markets.

The impact of reduced food prices on rural poverty is less clear-cut, however. This largely depends on whether the rural poor are net sellers or buyers of food. In the case of China, a majority of the rural poor are net sellers of food. Fan, Zhang, and Zhang (2004) found a strong relationship between lower food prices and higher rates of rural poverty in rural China. In this case, lower food prices from public investment may offset certain benefits of poverty reduction, although the net impact of public investment on rural poverty reduction is enormous. Ignoring the price effects would lead to overestimation of the poverty reduction effects.[5] On the other hand, many of India's rural poor are net buyers of food because of land constraints. As a result, they benefit from lower food prices induced by public investment.

The nutrition–food prices nexus is significant for the welfare of the poor. This is especially important during periods of structural adjustment. Therefore, it is very informative to observe consumption and poverty patterns as a result of changes in food prices. Research has also shown that there are considerable effects of food prices on child survival (Benefo and Schultz 1994; Lavy, Strauss, and DeVreyer 1995). Therefore, any reduction in food prices from public in-

---

5. How much net sellers will gain from increased productivity depends on the relative magnitude of demand or supply elasticities.

vestment may also help the nutritional and health status of the poor, particularly that of children and women.

Empowerment

Public investment can also affect rural poor through empowerment. For example, decentralization of public provisions and participation of the poor in managing public services can increase the impact and efficiency of public spending. The *World Development Report* (World Bank 2001) incorporates the concept of empowerment, opportunity, and security in a three-pronged approach to poverty reduction. This broader definition of poverty requires a broader set of actions to fight it and in doing so increases the challenge of measuring poverty. The term *empowerment* has many definitions aimed either at capturing one aspect of empowerment (such as group-based microfinance lending to empower low-income women) or at capturing a comprehensive and complex definition (such as the definition used by the World Bank in its latest report on poverty reduction). As a consequence, there is a conspicuous absence of empirical evidence of the impact of government spending on participation and empowerment activities.

Actions to improve the functioning of state and social institutions can lead to increased economic and social mobility such that the poor can lift themselves out of poverty. Involving the poor in decisions that affect them goes a long way in promoting empowerment by giving them access to information and by holding governments accountable for their actions. Participation in community development and agricultural R&D and extension is seen not only as a practical and feasible way of making use of indigenous knowledge in farming practices and nonfarm activities, but also as a viable form of empowerment (Kerr and Kolavalli 1999).

Similarly, decentralization can give more autonomy to state and local governments to provide constituent-specific public services. Division of responsibility between central, state, and local governments can mean efficient delivery of services because it helps to minimize corrupt bureaucratic practices. An important step in empowering the poor is to reform legal and political systems to make them more effective in allowing people to exercise their rights. For example, China began to promote direct elections of local village leaders beginning in the early 1990s. In a recent study Zhang et al. (2004) concluded that elected officials tend to tax constituents less and provide them with more public services than do appointed cadres.

A Theoretical Framework and Methodology to Link Public Investment to Poverty

In this section we review the conceptual framework and model used in linking public investment to poverty reduction. The framework reviewed has been used by many IFPRI case studies, although it may have to be adjusted to the national context, data availability, and issues analyzed. We then discuss some of the econometric problems in estimating the empirical model and possible solutions to these problems.

A Conceptual Framework and Model

A significant feature of the literature on public investment and rural poverty is that most of the previous studies have considered only one type of government spending or investment. It is difficult to compare the relative returns to these types of spending or investment in terms of both growth and poverty reduction. Most of these empirical studies used a single-equation approach (Ahluwalia 1978b; Saith 1981; Gaiha 1989; Ravallion and Datt 1995; Datt and Ravallion 1997). There are at least four disadvantages to this approach. First, many poverty determinants, such as income, production or productivity growth, prices, wages, and nonfarm employment, are generated from the same economic process as rural poverty. In other words, these variables are also endogenous variables, and ignoring this characteristic leads to biased estimates of poverty effects (Van de Walle 1985; Bell and Rich 1994). Second, certain economic variables affect poverty through multiple channels. For example, improved rural infrastructure will reduce rural poverty not only through improved agricultural productivity, but also through improved wages and nonfarm employment. It is very difficult to capture these different effects in a single-equation approach. Third, including only one type of public investment when estimating poverty reduction will lead to an upward bias in the estimation of the impact of that particular investment. Finally, it is difficult to rank the effects of different types of investment on both growth and poverty reduction.

For the past several years, IFPRI has developed a simultaneous-equations model to estimate the various effects of government expenditure on production, inequality, and poverty through different channels (Fan, Hazell, and Thorat 1999; Fan, Zhang, and Zhang 2002; Fan, Zhang, and Rao 2004). Table 3.1 describes the variables that are typically used in these case studies.[6] The main equations used in the simultaneous-equations model are as follows:

- *Poverty equation*

$$P = f(Y, WAGE, NAGEMPLY, APP, POP_{-1}).$$ (1)

- *Agricultural production function*

$$Y = f(LABOR, LAND, FERT, MACH, RDE, RDE_{-1}, \ldots RDE_{-i}, \\ IR, SCHY, ROADS, RTR, ELECT, ANRAIN).$$ (2)

---

6. The equations specified and variables defined are generic. The actual specifications and data used in case studies may vary.

- *Rural nonfarm wage equation*

$$WAGE = f(ROADS, RTR, SCHY, ELECT, Y, POP, UGDP_{-1}). \qquad (3)$$

- *Rural nonfarm employment equation*

$$NAGEMPLY = f(ROADS, RTR, SCHY, ELECT, Y, UGDP_{-1}). \qquad (4)$$

- *Technology, infrastructure, and education equations*

$$IR = f(IRE, IRE_{-1}, \ldots, IRE_{-j}). \qquad (5)$$

$$ROADS = f(ROADE, ROADE_{-1}, \ldots, ROADE_{-k}). \qquad (6)$$

$$SCHY = f(EDE, EDE_{-1}, \ldots, EDE_{-m}). \qquad (7)$$

$$RTR = f(RTRE, RTRE_{-1}, \ldots, RTRE_{-1}). \qquad (8)$$

$$ELECT = f(PWRE, PWRE_{-1}, \ldots, PWRE_{-n}). \qquad (9)$$

- *Terms-of-trade equation*

$$APP = f(Y, WFP). \qquad (10)$$

In this model rural poverty defined as poverty incidence is modeled as a function of growth in agricultural production, changes in rural wages, growth in rural nonfarm employment, and changes in agricultural prices (equation 1).[7] Growth in agricultural production is included as a variable in the poverty equation because agricultural income still accounts for a substantial share of total income among rural households. This percentage is particularly high for poor households. Nonfarm employment income is the second most important source of income after agricultural production. It accounts for 30–40 percent of rural household income in many developing countries. In the case of China, in many advanced regions the share of income from nonfarm employment accounts for more than 60 percent of total household income (Fan, Zhang, and Zhang 2002). The wage and number of nonfarm laborers are good proxies for nonfarm income. Moreover, we can distinguish the differential impacts of changes in wages and number of workers in the nonfarm sector on rural poverty reduction. These differential impacts may have important policy implications for further poverty reduction. If improvement in rural wages reduces rural poverty more than increased rural nonfarm employment does, government resources should be targeted to improve rural wages, or vice versa.

The terms-of-trade variable measures the impact on rural poverty of changes in agricultural prices relative to nonagricultural prices. Price policy can have a large effect on the rural poor. We hypothesize that in the short run the poor may suffer from higher agricultural prices if they are net buyers of food-

---

7. A subscript denotes years of lag. The lagged values of population and urban GDP growth are used to avoid the endogeneity problem of these two variables.

TABLE 3.1 Definitions of variables in the simultaneous-equations model

Variable	Definition
P	Rural poverty incidence
Y	Agricultural production
WAGE	Wage rate of nonagricultural labor in rural areas
NAGEMPLY	Percentage of nonagricultural employment in total rural employment
APP	Terms of trade, measured as agricultural prices divided by a relevant nonagricultural GNP deflator
POP	Rural population
LABOR	Total number engaged in agricultural labor
LAND	Total agricultural land
FERT	Fertilizer use
MACH	Machinery input
UGDP	Urban GDP per capita
RDE	Government spending on agricultural R&D
IR	Percentage of total cropped area that is irrigated
SCHY	Average years of schooling of rural population
ROADS	Road density in rural areas
RTR	Rural telephone
ELECT	Electricity consumption
ANRAIN	Annual rainfall
IRE	Government spending on irrigation
ROADE	Government spending on roads
EDE	Government spending on education
RTRE	Government spending on rural telecommunication
PWRE	Government spending on rural power supply
WFP	World food price

grains. But they may gain from higher prices if they are net sellers of agricultural products. In the long run, however, increased agricultural prices may induce government and farmers to invest more in agricultural production, shifting the supply curve outward. Population growth also affects rural poverty because fast growth in population may increase rural poverty if there is insufficient growth in rural employment. This is particularly important for countries like China and India, in which resources are limited and the population base is large.

Agricultural production is modeled as a function of conventional inputs such as labor, land, fertilizer, machinery, and public investment variables such as the use of high-yielding varieties, public irrigation, roads, electrification, and education (equation 2).

Rural wages and nonfarm employment are modeled as functions of growth in agricultural production as well as public investment variables (equations 3 and 4). These equations are reduced forms of the equations for labor supply and demand, where equilibrium wages clear the labor market. The derived labor and wages are a function of labor productivity. Labor productivity, in turn, is a function of the capital-labor ratio and of production shifters such as infrastructure and improvements in education. Therefore, the final labor and wage equations are functions of capital-labor ratios and production shifters. But due to data unavailability, we did not include the capital-labor ratio variable in most IFPRI case studies. This may not cause a serious problem because this variable does not vary across regions and regional dummies introduced in the case studies should reduce the potential bias from omitting this variable. The supply shifters included are improved infrastructure, education, agricultural growth, and urban growth. Numerous studies have shown the important linkage between agricultural and nonagricultural growth. Ignoring the effect of public investment on rural poverty through this linkage could lead to underestimation of the poverty reduction effects of government investment in agriculture.[8]

Government investments in R&D, roads, education, and irrigation can have long lead times to affect agricultural production, as well as long-term effects once they kick in. One of the thornier problems to resolve when including government investment variables in a production or productivity function concerns the choice of an appropriate lag structure. Most past studies used stock variables, which are usually weighted averages of current and past government expenditures on certain investments, such as R&D. But which weights and how many years' lag should be used in the aggregation are currently under hot debate. Because the shape and length of these investments are largely unknown, a free-form lag structure can be used in the analysis; that is, we include current and past government expenditures on certain investment items, such as R&D, irrigation, roads, and education, in the respective productivity, technology, infrastructure, and education equations (equations 5–9). Then, statistical tools can be used to test and determine the appropriate length of lag for each type of expenditure.[9] We will further discuss this issue in the next section, on estimation techniques.

Equation 10 determines the agricultural terms of trade. Growth in agricultural productivity increases the supply of agricultural products and thus reduces agricultural prices. These changed prices will, in turn, affect poverty reduction. If poor households are net sellers of agricultural products, reduced prices will offset poverty reduction effects. If they are net buyers, they will benefit from reduced prices.

In addition to its ability to track the relevant linkages between public investments and rural poverty, a systems approach enables other endogenous vari-

---

8. Here we measure the long-term effects of infrastructure improvement on wages and nonfarm employment. The short-run effects of the construction of infrastructure have not been considered here.

9. For details about the methodology, refer to Fan, Hazell, and Thorat (2000) and Fan, Zhang, and Zhang (2004).

ables to be properly specified. Once the model is estimated, the total effects of public investment variables on growth and poverty reduction can also be calculated by totally differentiating the equations system with respect to each public investment variable.

The marginal impact of public spending can be derived from these three equations as follows, taking agricultural research and rural education as examples.

The impact of government investment in agricultural R&D in year $t - i$ on poverty in year t can be derived as

$$dP/dRDE_{-i} = (\partial Y/\partial Y)\,(\partial Y/\partial RDE_{-i})$$
$$+ (\partial P/\partial NAGEMPLY)\,(\partial NAGEMPLY/\partial Y)\,(\partial Y/\partial RDE_{-i})$$
$$+ (\partial P/\partial WAGE)\,(\partial WAGE/\partial Y)\,(\partial Y/\partial RDE_{-i})$$
$$+ (\partial P/\partial APP)\,(\partial APP/\partial Y)\,(\partial Y/\partial RDE_{-i}). \tag{11}$$

Equation 11 measures the marginal effect on poverty reduction of the research stock variable. The first term on the right-hand side of the equation is the direct poverty impact of growth in agriculture due to increased agricultural research, while the remaining terms measure the effects of agricultural research through improved nonfarm employment and rural wages due to research-induced production growth in agriculture.[10] By summing the marginal returns over the lag years, the total effect of research investment over the lag period is obtained:

$$dP/dEDE_{-i} = (\partial P/\partial Y)\,(\partial Y/\partial SCHY)\,(\partial SCHY/\partial EDE_{-i})$$
$$+ (\partial P/\partial NAGEMPLY)\,(\partial NAGEMPLY/\partial Y)\,(\partial Y/\partial SCHY)\,(\partial SCHY/\partial EDE_{-i})$$
$$+ (\partial P/\partial WAGE)\,(\partial WAGE/\partial Y)\,(\partial Y/\partial SCHY)\,(\partial SCHY/\partial EDE_{-i})$$
$$+ (\partial P/\partial APP)\,(\partial APP/\partial Y)\,(\partial Y/\partial SCHY)\,(\partial SCHY/\partial EDE_{-i})$$
$$+ (\partial P/\partial NAGEMPLY)\,(\partial NAGEMPLY/\partial SCHY)\,(\partial SCHY/\partial EDE_{-i})$$
$$+ (\partial P/\partial WAGE)\,(\partial WAGE/\partial SCHY)\,(\partial SCHY/\partial EDE_{-i}). \tag{12}$$

Equation 12 measures the marginal poverty reduction effects of government spending in education. Much as in equation 11, the first four terms on the right-hand side are the poverty reduction effects of education spending, directly through growth in agricultural production and indirectly through improved nonfarm employment opportunities, increased rural wages, and changes in agricultural prices. The last two terms capture the impact on poverty reduction of directly improving nonfarm employment and rural wages due to education spending.

---

10. The terms are separated by + marks. Definition of all variables is the same as in equations 1–10.

Estimation Techniques

There are several challenges in estimating the overall effects of different types of government spending on growth and poverty reduction. In this section we point out how the IFPRI studies have dealt with these challenges.

ENDOGENEITY, REVERSE CAUSALITY, AND ESTIMATION OF SYSTEM EQUA-TIONS.   Government investment itself may be an endogenous variable. Binswanger, Khandker, and Rosenzweig (1989) argue that government may allocate its investment based on agroclimatic conditions; that is, high-potential areas may receive more resources from government. If this is true, a simple ordinary least squares technique may result in biased estimates. In this case, the return to public investment in terms of growth may be overstated. On the other hand, if the government targeted its resources to poor areas for poverty reduction purposes, the poverty reduction impact may be understated if the endogeneity problem is not properly dealt with. These biases may vary by region and by type of investment.

Similarly, the existence of reverse causality between government investment and development outcome may also result in biased estimates if it is not taken into consideration. Reverse causality occurs because income growth may increase the demand for infrastructure or other forms of public capital.[11] However, more infrastructure or other forms of public capital may also induce increases in income.

Besley and Case (1994) argued that endogeneity could also be a result of political and economic factors, which vary over time as well as space. In this case, the fixed-effects approach used by many economists does not resolve the endogeneity problem because it fails to control for the omitted time-varying differences across space, which help to determine policies and outcomes (Van de Walle 1998).

One of the most common approaches to avoid the potential biases in the estimates due to endogeneity and reverse causality is the instrumental approach. Broadly speaking, an instrumental variable is a variable that is uncorrelated with the error term but correlated with the explanatory variables in the model. But in reality it is hard to find such as instrument (or instruments). Davidson and MacKinnon (1993) demonstrate that the validity of the choice of instruments may be tested in this context via an auxiliary regression.

When panel data are available, the two-way fixed-effects model can eliminate most of biases due to time- or regional-invariant fixed effects. For example, if government always targets its resources to a particular region (e.g., either a high-potential or a poor region), the regional fixed-effects model should be able to eliminate the endogeneity bias.

---

11. For more information on reverse causality see World Bank (1994), Canning and Bennathan (2000), and Zhang and Fan (2004).

The general methods of moment (GMM) approach has recently been introduced to reduce the potential endogeneity of many independent variables when panel data are available. In general, a model in levels captures the long-term relationship, while the model in differences captures short-term effects. However, models in level cannot avoid the inherent endogeneity problem of independent variables such as government spending variables. Zhang and Fan (2004) used a dynamic GMM approach to estimate the effects of infrastructure on agricultural productivity using the Indian district level. They estimated the model in level, but used differences of lagged independent variables as instruments in order to maintain the long-run relationship between infrastructure investment and productivity growth and to control for the endogeneity of the infrastructure variable. They found that the effect of infrastructure using this approach is between those of the level and difference estimations, but more toward the level estimation. They also showed that if two-way fixed effects are used, the bias in the level estimation due to the endogeneity problem is very small.

The instrumental variables approach and other econometric techniques within a single-equation approach can reduce the bias due to endogeneity. But it is still difficult to model the multiple effects of public investment on poverty reduction. In this case, the system equation estimation technique is preferred. The rapid development of computational tools has made the system estimation much easier in recent years. The full information maximum likelihood estimation was chosen for the cases of China and India given the simultaneous nature of the system of equations (autonomous equations, with variables jointly determined by the system). In the case of not only a system of equations, but a simultaneous-equations model with variables jointly determined by the system, the single-equation estimation approach fails to use the information arising from the joint determination of key variables, potentially resulting in a very high efficiency loss.

TIME LAG OF INVESTMENT.   Most past studies used stock variables, which are usually weighted averages of current and past government expenditures on certain investments, such as R&D. But which weights and how many years' lag should be used in the aggregation are currently issues of some contention in the literature.[12] We propose that when there is a lack of long time series data on government investment (by types and regions), the stock approach can be used as a crude proxy. Some of our sensitivity analysis from China and India shows that the ranking of different types of public investment in terms of their growth

---

12. Alston et al. (2000) argue that the research lag may be much longer than previously thought, or even infinite. But many developing countries have national agricultural research systems that are much younger than those in developed countries (often 30 to 50 years old), and they use more applied types of research. Therefore, it is certain that research lags in developing countries are much shorter than those in developed countries.

and poverty reduction effects changes very little, but the magnitudes of the effects may change.

However, when long time series data on investment are available, we can use the following procedures to determine the lag structure or the dynamic relationship between government investment and the final development outcome. A first step is to use statistical tools to test and determine the appropriate length of lag for each investment expenditure. For example, we include annual agricultural research expenditures for a certain number of past years in the agricultural production function. How many years should be included depends on statistical test values. Various procedures have been suggested for determining the appropriate lag length. The adjusted R^2 and Akaike's information criteria (AIC) are often used by many economists (Greene 1993). The optimal length is determined when the adjusted R^2 reaches its maximum or AIC reach the minimum.

However, we cannot directly use the coefficients of the past annual government expenditures in calculating the effects on growth in agricultural production because these variables are often highly correlated, making the estimated coefficients statistically insignificant. To avoid this problem, the most popular approach is to use what are called polynomial distributed lags, or PDLs. In a polynomial distributed lag, the coefficients are all required to lie on a polynomial of some degree d. PDLs with degree 2 are often used. In this case, we need to estimate only three instead of $i + 1$ parameters for the lag distribution. For more detailed information on this subject refer to Davidson and MacKinnon (1993).

CONTROLLING FOR OTHER FACTORS. Many other factors may affect the development outcome in addition to public investment. These variables may include changes in international trade and prices, domestic macroeconomic conditions, urban development, and regional agroecological conditions. For example, institutional changes and policy reforms have made large contributions to rapid growth in agricultural and nonagricultural production and to poverty reduction in China's rural areas since 1979. In India, market and trade liberalization introduced in the early 1990s has also had profound effects on economic growth as well as on poverty reduction. If these variables are not controlled, the estimated results on the poverty reduction impact of public investment will be biased, and in many cases returns to public investment will be overestimated. A common practice is to use year and regional dummies to control for year- and region-specific fixed effects.

Country Case Studies

For the last several years, IFPRI has conducted numerous case studies to quantify the effects of various types of government spending on poverty reduction through long-term growth. The common framework described in the previous section was used, although the number of equations and specifications have varied across these cases due to limited data availability and the specific contexts of these countries. Most of these case studies have been peer reviewed and published in various international journals. These publications have been cited and used by many national and international institutions in their policy debates related to the setting of their spending priorities. These institutions include the World Bank, the Asian Development Bank, and the government agencies and policy advisors in China, India, Uganda, and Vietnam. In this section we synthesize only the major findings from these case studies. For more detailed information readers can refer to the relevant publications, which we will provide in the footnotes when we describe these cases. We have also included the data sources and definitions of various variables used, estimation techniques, and estimated results in Appendix 3A.

India

Poverty in rural India has declined substantially in recent decades.[13] This steady decline in poverty has been strongly associated with agricultural growth, particularly the green revolution, and with rural nonfarm activities, which represent a response to massive public investments in agriculture and rural infrastructure. Fan, Hazell, and Thorat (2000) used the system of econometric equations discussed in the previous section to identify the relative roles of different forms of government spending in agricultural growth and rural poverty reduction using state-level data from 1970 to 1993. The model was structured to enable identification of the various channels through which different types of government expenditures affect the poor. The study also distinguished between direct and indirect effects. The direct effects arise in the form of benefits the poor receive from employment programs directly targeted to the rural poor. The indirect effects arise when government investments in rural infrastructure, agricultural research, health, and the education of rural people stimulate agricultural and nonagricultural growth, leading to greater employment, more income-earning opportunities, and less expensive food for the poor.

The results from the model show that additional government expenditures on roads have the largest impact on poverty reduction as well as a significant impact on productivity growth (Table 3.2). For every 1 million rupees spent on rural roads, 124 poor are lifted above the poverty line, the largest amount of poverty reduction among all types of investment. One rupee invested in rural roads generates more than 5 rupees in returns in agricultural production, the second-largest production growth effect, following only agricultural R&D. Therefore, government investment in roads is a dominant "win-win" strategy. Additional government spending on agricultural research and extension has the largest impact on agricultural productivity growth, with a cost-benefit ratio of 13, and it also leads to large benefits for the rural poor, second only to rural road investment. It is another dominant win-win strategy. Additional government

---

13. The India case study was drawn from Fan, Hazell, and Thorat (1999, 2000).

TABLE 3.2 Returns to agricultural research in India, state-level analysis, 1993

	Returns in rupees per rupee spending	No. of poor reduced per million rupees' spending
R&D	13.45	84.5
Irrigation	1.36	9.7
Roads	5.31	123.8
Education	1.39	41.0
Power	0.26	3.8
Soil and water conservation	0.96	22.6
Health	0.84	25.5
Antipoverty programs	1.09	17.8

SOURCE: Calculated by the authors from Fan, Hazell, and Thorat (2000).

spending on education has the third-largest impact on rural poverty reduction, largely as a result of the increases in nonfarm employment and rural wages that it induces.

Additional irrigation investment has an impact similar to that of education investment on growth in agricultural productivity but only a small impact on rural poverty reduction, even after trickle-down benefits have been allowed for. Additional government spending on rural and community development, including integrated rural development programs, contributes to the reduction in rural poverty, but its impact is smaller than that of expenditures on roads, agricultural R&D, and education. Additional government expenditures on soil and water conservation and health have no impact on productivity growth, and their poverty effects through employment generation and increased wages are also small.

In another study, Fan and Hazell (2000) attempted to estimate the returns of various public investments in different regions of India using district-level data. The districts were classified into three categories: irrigated, high-potential rain-fed, and low-potential rain-fed. Districts were defined as irrigated if more than 25 percent of the cropped area was irrigated. Rain-fed districts were subdivided into high- and low-potential areas according to their agroecological characteristics. Using district-level data for 1970–95, an econometric model was developed to estimate the impact of different types of public investment on agricultural production and rural poverty. The model was then used to calculate the impact on growth and poverty of another unit of each type of investment by land type.

For every type of investment, the greatest marginal impact on agricultural production and poverty alleviation was seen in one of the two rain-fed areas, while the impact in irrigated areas ranked second or last. Moreover, many types of investment in low-potential rain-fed areas yielded some of the highest production returns, and all except those in education had some of the most favorable impacts on poverty. These results strongly support the hypothesis that investments in less favored areas are becoming win-win opportunities and that more investment should now be channeled to less favored areas.

China

China achieved immense success in reducing its rural poverty during the past two decades, despite the slow-down in global poverty reduction.[14] Contributing to this success were a series of policy and institutional reforms, promotion of equal access to social services and production assets, and public investments in rural areas. Yet as China's economy continues to grow, it is becoming harder to reduce poverty and inequality further. How the government can better design its policies, particularly its public investment policy, to promote growth while reducing poverty and regional inequality is debated in both academic and policy circles.

Using provincial-level data for 1970–2000, Fan, Zhang, and Zhang (2004) developed a simultaneous-equations model to estimate the effects of different types of government expenditure. The results show that government's production-enhancing investments, such as those in agricultural R&D, irrigation, rural education, and infrastructure (including roads, electricity, and telecommunications), contributed not only to agricultural production growth, but also to reduction of rural poverty and regional inequality (Table 3.3).

However, variations in the magnitude of the effects were large among different types of spending and across regions. Based on actual investments in 2000 and the parameters estimated from the model, the authors calculated the marginal returns to various investments of growth in agricultural and nonfarm production and reduction of rural poverty and regional inequality. These returns were calculated for the nation as a whole and for three different economic zones. Because the estimated returns are recent, they can serve as a direct input into the current policy debate.

Government expenditures on education had the largest impact in reducing rural poverty and regional inequality and had a significant impact on production growth. Increased rural nonfarm employment accounted for much of this poverty- and inequality-reducing effect. Government spending on agricultural R&D substantially improved agricultural production. In fact, this type of expenditure had the largest impact on agricultural production growth, which is much needed to meet the increasing food demands of a richer and larger population. Benefits of agricultural production growth also trickled down to the rural poor. The poverty reduction effect per unit of additional agricultural R&D investment ranked second after that of investment in rural education.

Government spending on rural infrastructure (roads, electricity, and telecommunications) had a substantial impact on reducing poverty and inequality,

---

14. The China case study drew heavily from Fan, Zhang, and Zhang (2002, 2004).

TABLE 3.3 Returns to public investment in China, 2000

	Coastal	Central	Western	Average
Returns to total rural GDP	Yuan per yuan expenditure			
R&D	5.54	6.63	10.19	6.75
Irrigation	1.62	1.11	2.13	1.45
Roads	8.34	6.90	3.39	6.57
Education	11.98	8.72	4.76	8.96
Electricity	3.78	2.82	1.63	2.89
Telephone	4.09	4.60	3.81	4.22
Returns to agricultural GDP	Yuan per yuan expenditure			
R&D	5.54	6.63	10.19	6.75
Irrigation	1.62	1.11	2.13	1.45
Roads	1.62	1.74	1.73	1.69
Education	2.18	2.06	2.33	2.17
Electricity	0.81	0.78	0.88	0.82
Telephone	1.25	1.75	2.49	1.63
Returns to nonfarm GDP	Yuan per yuan expenditure			
Roads	6.71	5.16	1.66	4.88
Education	9.80	6.66	2.43	6.79
Electricity	2.96	2.04	0.75	2.07
Telephone	2.85	2.85	1.32	2.59
Returns to poverty reduction	No. of poor reduced per 10,000 yuan expenditure			
R&D	3.72	12.96	24.03	10.74
Irrigation	1.08	2.16	5.02	2.31
Roads	2.68	8.38	10.03	6.63
Education	5.03	13.90	18.93	11.88
Electricity	2.04	5.71	7.78	4.85
Telephone	1.99	8.10	13.94	6.17
Poverty loan	3.70	3.57	2.40	3.03

SOURCE: Fan, Zhang, and Zhang (2004).

owing mainly to improved opportunities for nonfarm employment and increased rural wages. Investments in irrigation had only a modest impact on agricultural production growth and even less impact on rural poverty and inequality, even after trickle-down benefits were allowed for. A striking finding was the minimal impact of specifically targeted government antipoverty loans. In fact, the poverty reduction impact of these loans was the least of all the types of government spending considered in the study.

Disaggregating the analysis into different regions reveals that for all types of government spending, returns to investments in poverty reduction were highest in the (less-developed) west region, while returns in agricultural production growth were the highest in the central (more developed) region for most types of spending. Furthermore, investments in the western region led to the greatest reductions in regional inequality for all types of government spending, while investments in either coastal or central regions worsened existing large regional inequalities.

However, the government public investment variable is highly aggregated. While the total length of roads or average years of schooling is a useful indicator of the road infrastructure availability or education level in a country, it is important to account for quality differences, because different types of roads or education (e.g., rural versus urban) can have very different economic returns and poverty impacts. Second, most studies have focused only on rural poverty, because urban poverty has only recently emerged as an important and growing problem. To address these limitations, Fan and Chan-Kang (2005) disaggregated road infrastructure into different classes of roads to account for quality. Their study also estimated the impact of road investments on overall economic growth, urban growth, and urban poverty reduction, in addition to agricultural growth and rural poverty. The most significant finding of their study was that low-quality (mostly rural) roads have cost-benefit ratios for national gross domestic product (GDP) that are about four times larger than the cost-benefit ratios of high-quality roads. Even in terms of urban GDP, the cost-benefit ratios for low-quality roads are much greater than those for high-quality roads. As far as agricultural GDP is concerned, high-quality roads do not have a statistically significant impact, while low-quality roads not only have benefits that are significant but generate 1.57 yuan of agricultural GDP for every yuan invested. Investment in low-quality roads also generates high returns in rural nonfarm GDP. Every yuan invested in low-quality roads yields more than 5 yuan of rural nonfarm GDP. In terms of poverty reduction, low-quality roads raise far more rural and urban poor above the poverty line per yuan invested than do high-quality roads.

Thailand

Thailand is a middle-income country.[15] The question is whether public investment is still important in reducing rural poverty in such a country. Fan, Jitsuchon, and Methakunnavut (2004) show that despite Thailand's middle-income status, public investments in agricultural R&D, irrigation, rural education, and infrastructure (including roads and electricity), still have positive marginal impacts on agricultural productivity growth and rural poverty reduction (Table 3.4).

Using regional data from 1977–99, these authors showed that additional government spending on agricultural research and development improves agri-

---

15. The results of the Thailand case study were drawn from Fan, Jitsuchon, and Methakunnavut (2004).

TABLE 3.4 Returns to government investment in rural Thailand, 1999

Investment	Northeast	North	Central	South	Thailand
	Cost-benefit ratio (bhat/bhat)				
Agricultural R&D	n.a.	n.a.	n.a.	n.a.	12.62
Irrigation	0.76	1.11	0.55	0.62	0.71
Roads	1.23	1.23	0.44	1.24	0.86
Education	1.26	2.92	2.89	2.51	2.12
Electricity	8.66	8.04	2.59	5.48	4.89
Phone	n.s.	n.s.	n.s.	n.s.	n.s.
	No. of poor reduced per million bhat				
Agricultural R&D	n.a.	n.a.	n.a.	n.a.	138.10
Irrigation	21.05	5.22	1.74	4.53	7.69
Roads	394.09	67.43	15.88	106.08	107.23
Education	34.74	13.71	9.08	18.53	22.75
Electricity	1,253.02	198.57	42.79	211.99	276.07
Phone	n.s.	n.s.	n.s.	n.s.	n.s.

SOURCE: Fan, Jitsuchon, and Methakunnavut (2004).

NOTES: n.a., not available; n.s., statistically insignificant.

cultural productivity the most and has the second-largest impact on rural poverty reduction. Investments in rural electrification reduce poverty the most and have the second-largest growth impact. These two types of investment dominate all others and are win-win strategies for growth and poverty reduction. Road expenditures have the third-largest impact on rural poverty reduction, but only a modest and statistically insignificant impact on agricultural productivity. Government spending on rural education has only the fourth-largest impact on poverty, but a significant economic impact through improved agricultural productivity. Irrigation investment has the smallest impact on both rural poverty reduction and productivity growth in agriculture. Additional investments in the northeastern region contribute more to reducing poverty than do investments in other regions. This is because most of the poor are now concentrated in the northeastern region and it has suffered from underinvestment in the past. The poverty-reducing impacts of infrastructure investments, such as those in electricity and roads, are particularly high in this region. The growth impacts of many investments are also greatest in the northeastern region than in other regions; hence there is no evident trade-off between investments for growth and investments for poverty reduction.

Because Thailand is a middle-income country, insight can be gained by comparing these results with those of similar studies undertaken in low-income countries such as China, India, and Uganda. Some of the results are similar; for example, high returns to public investments in agricultural research and some kinds of rural infrastructure are seen in most countries because of the inherent market failures associated with these types of public goods. But other results are different. For example, the returns to public investment in education in Thailand are quite low, partly because of increasing private investment but also because of the inappropriate composition of much public spending on education. Within infrastructure, results from low-income countries often show higher returns to road investments than to investments in telecommunications and electricity. But in the case of Thailand, it is investments in electricity that show the highest rate of return. Thailand has invested heavily in rural roads, and a dense road network has already been built, suggesting that additional investment may yield diminishing returns. Also, there has been significant investment by the private sector in rural telecommunication, leading to a much reduced role for the public sector. This situation differs from that in many low-income countries, especially Africa, where the private sector is still embryonic and the public sector must play a dominant investment role for the foreseeable future.

Uganda

The Asian case studies conducted by IFPRI have generated interesting debates on the priorities of government investment and have led several countries to rethink their current investment strategies for future investment. However, all of these studies were done on Asia and secondary-level data were used, and the literature on the impact of public investment in Sub-Saharan Africa is sparse. One study undertaken at IFPRI estimated the productivity and poverty reduction effects of public investments in rural Uganda.[16] Using district and household-level data for 1992, 1995, and 1999, Fan, Zhang, and Rao (2004) estimated the effects of different types of government expenditure on agricultural growth and rural poverty in Uganda following the simultaneous multiple equations model described in the previous section. The authors considered six sectors of government spending, namely agriculture, defense, education, health, social security, and transportation and communication.

For the country as a whole, the results estimated from the poverty equation showed that growth in labor productivity, and growth in nonfarm employment are all important factors in explaining rural poverty in Uganda. In contrast, rural wages did not significantly affect rural poverty. This may be because there is surplus rural labor, consistent with the so-called efficiency wage theory.

Turning to the marginal returns to different types of government expenditures on growth and reduction of rural poverty, the authors found that all types of public spending reduce poverty while increasing agricultural production in Uganda (Table 3.5). However, there were sizable differences in production and poverty reduction gains among different types of expenditure. For the country as a whole, government expenditures on agricultural extension and research

---

16. The results of the Uganda case study were drawn from Fan and Chan-Kang (2005).

TABLE 3.5 Returns to government investment in rural Uganda, 1999

Investment	Central	East	North	West	Uganda
Cost-benefit ratio					
Agricultural R&D	12.49	10.77	11.77	14.74	12.38
Education	2.05	3.51	2.10	3.80	2.72
Feeder roads	6.03	8.74	4.88	9.19	7.16
Murram roads	n.s.	n.s.	n.s.	n.s.	n.s.
Tarmac roads	n.s.	n.s.	n.s.	n.s.	n.s.
Health	1.37	0.92	0.37	0.96	0.90
Number of poor reduced per million shillings					
Agricultural R&D	21.75	66.31	175.52	48.91	58.39
Education	3.57	21.60	31.38	12.62	12.81
Feeder roads	10.51	53.85	72.82	30.49	33.77
Murram roads	4.08	11.88	14.80	9.77	9.70
Tarmac roads	2.59	13.12	62.92	9.39	9.73
Health	2.60	6.15	5.95	3.46	4.60

SOURCE: Fan and Chan-Kang (2005).

NOTE: n.s., statistically insignificant.

have the highest return in terms of labor productivity and poverty reduction, followed closely by investments in feeder roads. Education ranked third in terms of productivity and poverty reduction effects, whereas health had the smallest impact.

Large regional variations have also been observed in the marginal impact of public expenditures on poverty alleviation. Uganda is characterized by a variety of agroclimatic conditions and is commonly divided into four regions. The central region enjoys good rainfall and is the most developed region in terms of social and economic indicators. The poverty incidence in central Uganda is the lowest among all regions. Eastern Uganda is the second-most developed region in terms of social and economic indicators, but the level of rural poverty is high, averaging 38.4 percent in 1999. The western region has mountainous areas where the altitude permits cultivation of temperate-zone fruits, vegetables, and some traditional food crops. The rural poverty rate there averaged 29 percent in 1999. The northern region is the poorest of the four and is home to 67 percent of Uganda's rural population. Incidentally, this region has also been struggling with war between the government and rebels for a long time.

Regional disaggregation revels that, for all types of investment except in health, the returns in terms of increased agricultural productivity were the highest in the western region. For agricultural extension, the eastern region had the lowest returns, while the central and northern regions fell in between. For education and roads, the central and northern regions had the lowest returns, while the eastern region ranked in the middle. In terms of poverty reduction, the northern region, which is Uganda's poorest region, had the highest returns except in health, whereas for all types of investment, the poverty impact was the smallest in the central region.

What We Have Learned and What We Still Need to Know

A large body of literature shows that public investments in rural areas have contributed significantly to agricultural growth and rural poverty reduction. These investments have also contributed to urban poverty reduction through growth in the national economy and lower food prices. Without these investments, agricultural growth and national economic growth would have been much slower, and there would be many more rural poor and urban poor in numerous developing countries.[17] Despite these successes, there are still more than 800 million rural poor, and governments in developing countries routinely cut budgets in rural areas. Many African countries are particularly affected.

Because significant increases in public rural investment seem unlikely, countries will have to give greater emphasis to using their public investment resources more efficiently. This will require better targeting of investments to achieve growth and poverty alleviation goals, as well as improved efficiency within the agencies that provide public goods and services. Reliable information on the marginal effects of various types of government spending is crucial for governments to make sound investment decisions. Without such information, it is difficult for governments to hone in on future investment priorities to achieve national development goals. Despite vast differences in the economic systems, natural resource endowments, socioeconomic conditions, and sizes of the countries treated in the case studies summarized here (all performed by IFPRI), these studies offer some important lessons:

1. Returns to public investments vary drastically across different types of investment and regions, even within the same country. This implies that there is a great potential for more growth and poverty reduction even with the same amount of investment if these public resources can be allocated optimally. It also strongly suggests that it is important to include all (or most) types of public investment when assessing their impact on growth and poverty reduction. To date, very few studies have done so.
2. Various studies that included only one type of spending and, more important, a few case studies that included most of government investment, all

---

17. Of course, the size of the effects of rural investment on poverty reduction has to be context-specific. Empirical evidence has shown that in many African countries, these effects are still large, but in many emerging countries like Brazil, China, and Vietnam, the effects may have declined (Diao et al. 2006).

concluded that agricultural research, education, and rural infrastructure are the three types of public spending that are most effective in promoting agricultural growth and poverty reduction (Table 3.6).

3. Limited evidence from China and Uganda also indicates that it is often the low-quality or low-cost types of infrastructure that may yield the highest payoff per unit of investment in growth and poverty reduction. In the case of China, rural road investments contribute not only to rural growth and rural poverty reduction, but also to urban growth and urban poverty reduction.

4. The trade-off between agricultural growth and poverty reduction is generally small among different types of investments and between regions. Agricultural research, education, and infrastructure development have large impacts on growth as well as poverty reduction. Regional analyses conducted for China and India suggest that more investments in many less developed areas not only offer the largest amount of poverty reduction per unit of spending, but also lead to the highest economic returns.

TABLE 3.6 Public investment and poverty reduction in China, India, Thailand, and Uganda

Type of public investment	China, 2000	India, 1993	Thailand, 1999	Uganda, 1999
	Ranking of returns to agricultural production			
Agricultural R&D	1	1	1	1
Irrigation	5	4	5	
Education	2	3	3	3
Roads	3	2	4	2
Telecommunications	4			
Electricity	6	8	2	
Health		7		4
Soil and water conservation		6		
Antipoverty programs		5		
	Ranking of returns to poverty reduction			
Agricultural R&D	2	2	2	1
Irrigation	6	7	5	
Education	1	3	4	3
Roads	3	1	3	2
Telecommunications	5			
Electricity	4	8	1	
Health		6		4
Soil and water conservation		5		
Antipoverty programs	7	4		

SOURCES: Fan, Hazell, and Thorat (2000); Fan, Jitsuchon, and Methakunnavut (2004); Fan, Zhang, and Rao (2004); and Fan, Zhang, and Zhang (2004).

5. Government spending on antipoverty programs generally has a small impact on poverty reduction, mainly due to inefficiency in its targeting and misuse of the funds. Although many governments have realized the seriousness of the problem, more efforts are needed to better target the funds to the poor or otherwise to use the investments to improve rural education and infrastructure, which promote long-term growth and thereby offer a long-term solution to poverty.

6. Government spending in irrigation played an important role in promoting agricultural growth and poverty reduction in the past. But today this type of spending has smaller marginal returns in terms of both growth and poverty reduction for many Asian countries. Increased investment in irrigation should be replaced by increasing the efficiency of current public irrigation systems.

Despite a vast literature on public investment and rural poverty reduction, there is much to be done in the future. First, developing countries must pay greater attention to systematically compiling public investment data in rural areas. Various international agencies, such as the World Bank, the Food and Agriculture Organization, and the International Monetary Fund, have made efforts to help developing countries establish national statistical systems to collect, compile, and monitor development indicators related to agricultural production and inputs, income, employment, wages, and poverty. But these efforts have seldom included government investment in rural infrastructure, technology, education, and related areas. Without such information, it is difficult to assess the potential holistic impacts of government intervention on agricultural growth and poverty reduction.

Second, a general-equilibrium analysis is needed to show how government investment in rural areas affects not only the agricultural sector and rural areas, but also other sectors and cities. To date, most of the studies conducted have been single-sector, partial-equilibrium analyses, which do not have the ability to track general-equilibrium and societal effects. Ignoring these impacts severely underestimates the overall impact of public investment on poverty.

Third, how to finance needed public investment in rural areas deserves more attention. There are two major means of financing expenditures for public goods—general government financing (for example, taxes) and cost recovery (for example, user fees) for service provision. The financing of public expenditures has important implications for efficiency and equity.

Fourth, an analysis of the political and institutional context of public investments and of the conditions for efficient provision of public goods and services is also much needed to improve the efficiency of public investments. In particular, how governments can design mechanisms (policies, regulations, fiscal systems) to mobilize public resources to invest in rural areas deserves much more research attention in the future. How to reform public institutions by improving incentives, accountability, human capital, and management is also an important issue for further research.

Finally, most research on public investment has been conducted on Asia. An important question to answer is whether the results obtained for Asia are similar to those for Africa and Latin America, where the poverty incidence is also very high.

Appendix 3A: Data, Variables, and Estimated Results of the Country Case Studies

India: Data Sources and Definition of Variables

Panel data for 14 states from 1953 to 1993 were used for the India study. However, results were estimated only for the period from 1970 to 1993 due to the long lag effects of expenditures on productivity growth and poverty reduction. The years 1971, 1974–76, 1978–82, 1984–85, and 1991 were also deleted because of missing values. A total of 154 observations was used in the final estimation. Most of the variables used in the study were reported as an appendix in an IFPRI research report (Fan, Hazell, and Thorat 1999).

The head-count ratio, which measures poverty as a percentage of the rural population falling below the poverty line, was used. The data were constructed by Gaurav Datt and published by the World Bank (World Bank 1997).

The total factor productivity (TFP) index is defined as the aggregate output index minus the aggregated input index and was calculated by the authors. The road density variable is defined as length of road per unit of geographic area. The education variable is the literacy rate, defined as the percentage of the total population that is literate. Public irrigation is defined as the percentage of the cropped area under canal irrigation, and private irrigation is defined as the percentage of the cropped area under well and tubewell irrigation. The electrification variable is the percentage of villages that have access to electricity. The rural wage used is the male labor rate in real terms deflated by the consumer price index for rural labor. These variables were aggregated from district-level data that were obtained from the Planning Commission through the National Center for Agricultural Policy and Economics Research, New Delhi.

Nonagricultural employment is measured as the percentage of nonagricultural employment in total rural employment. Data on nonagricultural employment have been reported by the National Sample Survey Organisation (NSS) for every five years beginning in 1973 (see NSSO 1973). The data for other years were estimated by geometric interpolation.

The terms-of-trade variable is measured as the change in agricultural prices relative to nonagricultural prices. The landless variable is measured as the percentage of rural households classified as landless. Because the data have been made available only every five years beginning in 1953, the data for intermediate years were estimated by geometric interpolation.

Government expenditure data by state were obtained from *Finances of State Governments* (various years), published by the Reserve Bank of India. All the expenditures were deflated to 1960/61 prices using a national GDP deflator. They include expenditures from both the current account (for maintenance) and the capital (investment) account.

Agricultural R&D expenditures include government expenditures on agricultural research and extension, while government expenditures on irrigation include spending on irrigation and flood control. Government expenditures on roads, education, power, and health in rural areas are calculated using the percentage of the rural population in the total population and total government expenditures on these items.

GDP at the state level is measured in 1960/61 prices and is reported in the official state statistical abstracts.

India: Model Estimation

All variables were measured in annual growth rates (or differences in logarithm of all variables) and are defined in Table 3A.1. This is equivalent to the first difference in logarithm. It has the ability to control for time-invariant fixed effects. The full information maximum likelihood (FIML) technique was used for the estimations given the simultaneous nature of the system of equations (autonomous equations, with variables jointly determined by the system) (Table 3A.2). As we have discussed in the chapter, the single-equation estimation approach fails to use the information arising from the joint determination of key variables, potentially resulting in very high levels of efficiency loss.

China: Data Sources and Definitions of Variables

Provincial-level data from 1970 to 2000 were used in the estimation. Most of the data (Table 3A.3) are from officials publications of the Chinese government. The data were also available at the Web site of the International Food Policy Research Institute.

POVERTY.   The present study used provincial-level poverty data from official sources (the State Council Leading Group on Economic Development and Poverty Alleviation).

AGRICULTURAL AND NONAGRICULTURAL GDP.   Both nominal GDP and real GDP growth indexes for various sectors are available in *The Gross Domestic Product of China* (China, National Bureau of Statistics, 1997). Data sources and construction of national GDP estimates were also published in *Calculation and Methods of China's Annual GDP* (China, State Statistical Bureau, 1997).

LABOR.   Agricultural labor is measured in stock terms as the number of persons engaged in agricultural production at the end of each year. The data prior to

TABLE 3A.1 Definitions of variables, India

Exogenous variables	
POP_{-1}	One-year lag of rural population growth
WAPI	World agricultural price index (average export price for rice, wheat, and corn)
GDP_{-1}	One-year lag of gross domestic product
ATT	Lagged five years' moving average of the terms of trade variable
TFPn	Total factor productivity growth at the national level
RAIN	Annual rainfall .
Endogenous variables	
IRE	Government expenditures on irrigation, both from revenue and capital accounts
RDE	Government spending (both revenue and capital) on agricultural R&D
ROADE	Government investment in and spending on rural roads
EDE	Government spending on rural education
PWRE	Government revenue from and capital spending on rural power
GCSSL	Government capital stock accumulated in soil and water conservation investment. It is the weighted average of past government expenditures on soil and water conservation, that is, $GCSSL_t = \varphi_m w_m S$, where $SOILE_{t-m}$ is government expenditures on soil and water conservation at time $t - m$. The weights are 0.4, 0.3, 0.2, and 0.1, respectively, with three years' lag.
GCSHEL	Government spending on medical and public health and on family welfare, measured in stock terms using three years' lag much as in the case of expenditures on soil and water conservation
GERDEV	Government expenditures on rural and community development, measured in stock terms using three years' lag much as in the case of expenditures on soil and water conservation
P	Rural population falling below the poverty line
LITE	Literacy rate of the rural population
ROADS	Road density in rural areas
IR	Percentage of total cropped area that is irrigated (sum of both public and private irrigation)
PUIR	Percentage of total cropped area under public irrigation (canal irrigation)
PRIR	Percentage of total cropped area under private irrigation (wells, tube wells, and tanks)
PVELE	Percentage of rural villages that are electrified
WAGE	Wage rate for rural labor
NAEMPLY	Percentage of nonagricultural employment in total rural employment
TFP	Total factor productivity growth (Tornqvist–Theil index)
LANDN	Percentage of rural households that are landless
TT	Terms of trade, measured as agricultural prices divided by a relevant nonagricultural GNP deflator

TABLE 3A.2 Estimated results for an Indian case study

Eqn. no.				Estimated equations		
1	P	$=$	−0.034 (−1.32)	−0.171 TFP (−2.58)**	−0.185 $WAGE$ (−2.24)**	+0.263 TT (2.52)**
2	TFP	$=$	−0.026 (−0.78)	+0.255 $TRDE$ (1.82)**	+0.215 IR (1.83)**	+0.242 $ROADS$ (2.43)**
				+0.0015 $GCSSL$ (0.37)	−0.141 GDP_{-1} (−0.97)	+0.272 $RAIN$ (5.47)**
3	$WAGE$	$=$	−0.035 (−1.39)	+0.129 TFP (1.86)**	+0.231 $ROADS$ (2.28)**	+0.062 $PVELE$ (0.57)
				+0.273 GDP_{-1} (1.32)		
4	$NAEMPLY$	$=$	−0.029 (−2.72)**	−0.058 TFP (−0.67)	+0.190 $ROADS$ (2.45)**	−0.045 $PVELE$ (−0.94)
				+0.209 GDP_{-1} (2.60)**		
5	$PUIR$	$=$	−0.021 (−0.66)	+0.087 $TIRE$ (4.49)**	+0.067 $PVELE$ (1.05)	
6	$PRIR$	$=$	0.017 (2.23)**	+0.918 $PUIR$ (18.61)**	+0.012 $PVELE$ (0.87)	
7	$ROADS$	$=$	0.088 (4.59)**	+0.232 $TROADE$ (2.83)**		
8	$LITE$	$=$	0.087 (4.59)**	+0.067 $TEDE$ (6.52)**		
9	$PVELE$	$=$	0.107 (6.34)**	+0.072 $TPWRE$ (2.56)**		
10	$LANDN$	$=$	−0.011 (−0.89)	+0.026 TFP (0.72)	+0.511 POP_{-1} (1.82)**	−0.142 $NAEMPLY$ (−1.46)
11	TT	$=$	0.025 (2.22)**	−0.175 TFP (−3.03)**	−0.792 $TFPn$ (−5.54)**	+0.271 $WAPI$ (8.03)**
12	RDE	$=$	0.107 (2.20)**	+0.363 GDP_{-1} (0.82)	+0.550 ATT (2.39)**	
13	$ROADE$	$=$	0.224 (5.45)**	+0.482 GDP_{-1} (0.31)	+0.534 ATT (2.43)**	
14	IRE	$=$	0.478 (5.20)**	−0.431 GDP_{-1} (−0.53)	−0.254 ATT (−0.61)**	
15	EDE	$=$	0.123 (5.77)**	+0.336 GDP_{-1} (1.79)**	−0.075 ATT (−0.79)**	
16	$GCSSL$	$=$	−0.140 (−3.52)**	+0.773 GDP_{-1} (2.31)	+0.594 ATT (2.32)**	
17	$PWRE$	$=$	0.133 (1.02)	+1.490 GDP_{-1} (2.24)**	+1.11 ATT (1.78)**	
18	$GERDEV$	$=$	0.113 (2.49)**	+1.476 GDP_{-1} (3.56)**	+0.677 ATT (3.11)**	
19	$GCSHEL$	$=$	0.177 (5.77)**	−0.123 GDP_{-1} (−0.224)	+0.173 ATT (0.85)	

SOURCE: Fan, Hazell, and Thorat (2000).

NOTES: ** indicates that coefficients are statistically significant at the 5 percent level.

−0.594 *NAEMPLY* (−3.12)**	+0.024 *LANDN* (0.43)	+0.320 POP_{-1} (0.31)	+0.072 GDP_{-1} (0.82)	$R^2 = 0.113$
+0.062 *PVELE* (0.60)	+0.708 *LITE* (1.95)**	+0.012 *GCSHEL* (0.39)	+0.022 *GERDEV* (0.63)	
				$R^2 = 0.301$
+0.939 *LITE* (2.01)**	+0.026 *GCSHEL* (0.83)	−0.024 *GERDEV* (−0.88)	+0.013 *GCSSL* (0.74)	
				$R^2 = 0.093$
+0.710 *LITE* (3.27)**	+0.011 *GCSHEL* (0.24)	+0.030 *GERDEV* (2.23)**	−0.003 *GCSSL* (−0.37)	
				$R^2 = 0.311$
				$R^2 = 0.087$
				$R^2 = 0.697$
				$R^2 = 0.147$
				$R^2 = 0.277$
				$R^2 = 0.028$
				$R^2 = 0.059$
				$R^2 = 0.363$
				$R^2 = 0.028$
				$R^2 = 0.018$
				$R^2 = 0.020$
				$R^2 = 0.056$
				$R^2 = 0.151$
				$R^2 = 0.017$
				$R^2 = 0.292$
				$R^2 = 0.058$

TABLE 3A.3 Definitions of variables, China

Exogenous variables

LANDPC	Land area per worker
AKPC	Agricultural capital per worker
NAKPC	Capital per worker in the rural nonagricultural sector
URBANP	Percentage of urban population in total population
UGDPPC	Per capita GDP produced by the urban sector
IRE	Government spending on irrigation, from both revenue and capital accounts
RDE	Government spending (both revenue and capital) on agricultural R&D
ROADE	Government investment in and spending on rural roads
EDE	Government spending on rural education
RTRE	Government spending on rural telecommunications
PWRE	Government spending on rural power
PLOAN	Government expenditures for poverty alleviation per capita, measured as last three years' moving average

Endogenous variables

P	Percentage of rural population below the poverty line
SCHY	Average years of schooling of rural population 15 years and older
ROADS	Road density in rural areas
IR	Percentage of total cropped area that is irrigated
ELECT	Electricity consumption
RTR	Rural telephone
WAGE	Wage rate for nonagricultural labor in rural areas
NAGEMPLY	Percentage of nonagricultural employment in total rural employment
AGDPPC	Agricultural GDP per laborer
AGDPPCn	Agricultural productivity growth at the national level
NAGDPPC	Nonagricultural GDP per worker in rural areas
TT	Terms of trade, measured as agricultural prices divided by a relevant nonagricultural GNP deflator

1978 were available in *Historical Statistical Materials for Provinces, Autonomous Regions, and Municipalities* (China, State Statistical Bureau, various years). The data after 1977 were taken from *China Agricultural Yearbook* (China, Ministry of Agriculture, various years), *China Statistical Yearbook* (China, National Bureau of Statistics, various years), and *China Rural Statistical Yearbook* (China, Ministry of Agriculture, various years).

The labor input for the nonfarm sector is calculated simply by subtracting agricultural labor from total rural labor.

CAPITAL STOCK.   Capital stocks for the agricultural and nonagricultural sectors in rural areas are calculated from data on gross capital formation and annual fixed asset investment. For the three sectors classified, data on gross capital formation by province have been published since 1978 (China, State Statistical Bureau, 1997). Gross capital formation is defined as the value of fixed assets and inventory acquired minus the value of fixed assets and inventory disposed of. To construct a capital stock series from data on capital formation, we used the following procedure: we defined the capital stock in time t as the stock in time $t - 1$ plus investment minus depreciation,

$$K_t = I_t + (1 - \delta)K_{t-1},$$ (A1)

where K_t is the capital stock in year t, I_t is gross capital formation in year t, and δ is the depreciation rate. To obtain initial values for the capital stock, we used a procedure similar to that of Kohli (1982). That is, we assumed that prior to 1978 real investment grew at a steady rate (r), which we assumed to be the same as the rate of growth of real GDP from 1952 to 1977. Thus

$$K_{1978} = \frac{I_{1978}}{(\delta + r)}.$$ (A2)

This approach ensures that the 1978 value of the capital stock is independent of the 1978–95 data used in our analysis. Moreover, given the relatively small capital stock in 1978 and the high levels of investment, the estimates for later years are not sensitive to the 1978 benchmark value of the capital stock.

R&D EXPENDITURES. Public investment in agricultural R&D is accounted for in the total national science and technology budget. The sources of agricultural R&D investment are different government agencies. Research expenditures and personnel numbers include those from research institutions at national, provincial, and prefectural levels, as well as from agricultural universities (only the research part).

IRRIGATION EXPENDITURES. Provincial irrigation expenditures refer to total government fiscal expenditures on reservoirs, irrigation and drainage systems, and flood and lodging prevention, as well as maintenance of these systems. However, government reports of such data are available only for the years after 1980 in the *China Water Conservancy Yearbook* (China, Ministry of Water Conservancy, various years). Prior to 1979, the Ministry of Water Conservancy reported total expenditures (not by item) on reservoirs, irrigation and drainage systems, flood and lodging prevention, water supply, and hydropower in *Thirty years of water conservancy statistical materials* (China, Ministry of Water Conservancy, 1980). This spending item is much broader than irrigation, because it also includes urban water supply, flood control, and hydropower generation. To calculate the cost solely of irrigation prior to 1979, we used the percentage of irrigation spending in total expenditures on water conservancy in 1980.

EDUCATION EXPENDITURES. Provincial expenditures for primary- and middle-school education in rural areas since 1990 are reported in various issues of the *China Education Yearbook* and the *China Education Expenditure Yearbook* (China, Ministry of Education, various years). Expenditures prior to 1990 are extrapolated using the percentage of rural students in total students. Because the education expenditure per student is higher in urban areas than in rural areas, we used the cost difference in 1990 to downwardly adjust the total education expenditures in rural areas.

ROAD EXPENDITURES.   Road expenditures are reported in *China Fixed Asset Investment Statistical Materials* (China, State Statistical Bureau, various years) and various issues of the *China Transportation Yearbook* (China, Ministry of Transportation, various years). However, there is no breakdown of rural and urban road expenditures. We used the percentage of the length of rural roads in total length of roads to extrapolate the cost of rural roads by assuming that the unit cost of constructing rural roads is one-third that for urban roads (China, Ministry of Transportation, various years).

POWER EXPENDITURES.   Provincial power expenditures are available in *China Fixed Asset Investment Statistical Materials* (China, State Statistical Bureau, various years) and in various issues of the *China Power Yearbook* (China, Ministry of Electric Power, various years). We used the unit cost of electricity per kilowatt to calculate power expenditures for rural areas.

TELECOMMUNICATIONS EXPENDITURES.   Telecommunications expenditures by province are available in *China Fixed Asset Investment Statistical Materials* (China, State Statistical Bureau, various years) and various issues of the *China Transportation Yearbook* (China, Ministry of Transportation, various years). However, much as in the case of expenditures on roads and power, there is no breakdown between rural and urban expenditures. We used the number of telephones in rural and urban areas to extrapolate the cost of rural telecommunications.

RURAL EDUCATION.   We used the percentage of rural labor with different education levels to calculate the average years of schooling as our education variable, assuming 0 years for a person who is illiterate or semi-illiterate, 5 years for one with a primary-school education, 8 years for one with a junior high school education, 12 years for one with a high-school education, 13 years for one with a professional-school education, and 16 years for one with a college or higher level of education. Education levels for rural labor were published by various issues of *China Rural Statistical Yearbook* (China, Ministry of Agriculture, various years).

ROADS.   The road variable is measured as road density, or road length in kilometers per 1,000 square kilometers of geographic area. The total length of roads by province is reported in various issues of the *China Statistical Yearbook* (China, National Bureau of Statistics, various years) and the *China Transportation Yearbook* (China, Ministry of Transportation, various years), while the length of rural roads in the 1980s is reported in various issues of the *China Rural Statistical Yearbook* (China, Ministry of Agriculture, various years). In more recent years, the *China Rural Statistical Yearbook* stopped reporting rural roads. We therefore used the trend in the total length of roads (except highways) to extrapolate the length of rural roads for the years for which data are not available.

ELECTRICITY.   Total rural electricity consumption for both production and residential uses by province are available in various issues of the *China Rural Statistical Yearbook* and the *China Agricultural Yearbook* (China, Ministry of Agriculture, various years). In more recent years, the *China Rural Energy Yearbook* (China, Ministry of Agriculture, various years) began publishing the use of electricity separately for residential and production purposes by province. We used this newly available information to back-cast the different uses by province for earlier years.

RURAL TELEPHONY.   The number of rural telephones is used as a proxy for the development of rural telecommunications. The number of rural telephones by province is published in various issues of the *China Rural Statistical Yearbook* (China, Ministry of Agriculture, various years), the *China Statistical Yearbook* (China, National Bureau of Statistics, various years), and the *China Transportation Yearbook* (China, Ministry of Transportation, various years).

China: Model Estimation

We used double-log functional forms for all equations in the system (Table 3A.4). More flexible functional forms such as Translog or quadratic forms impose fewer restrictions on estimated parameters, but many coefficients are not statistically significant due to multicollinearity problems among various interaction variables. For the system equations, the FIML estimation technique was used. For all equations in the system, the two-way (provincial and year) fixed-effects model was used to control for time and provincial invariant effects.

Thailand: Data Sources and Definitions of Variables

Most of the data used in this study come from either various agencies of the Thai government or from the Thailand Development Research Institute (TDRI) (Table 3A.5).

POVERTY.   The poverty variable is measured as the percentage of the rural population living below the poverty line. This percentage is calculated from rural household surveys completed in various years. For more details on poverty measures refer to Jitsuchon (2001).

AGRICULTURAL LABOR PRODUCTIVITY.   Agricultural labor productivity is measured as gross agricultural production value per agricultural worker.

NONFARM EMPLOYMENT.   Rural nonfarm employment is measured as the percentage of the rural labor force engaged in nonfarm activities such as manufacturing, construction, trading, and services.

WAGES.   Agricultural wages are the average daily compensation for agricultural workers. Nonagricultural wages are the average daily compensation for rural nonagricultural workers.

URBANIZATION.   Urbanization is measured as the percentage of the urban population in the total population.

TABLE 3A.4 Estimates from the simultaneous-equations model, China

Eqn. no.			Estimated equations		
1	ln$P$	=	−1.219 ln$AGDPPC$ (−2.99)*	−0.371 ln$WAGE$ (−1.22)	−0.937 ln$NAGEMPLY$ (−3.82)*
2	ln$AGDPPC$	=	0.438 ln$LANDPC$ (9.36)*	+0.113 ln$AKPC$ (5.16)*	+0.079 lnRDE (2.47)*
			+0.079 lnRTR (4.40)*	+0.010 ln$ELECT$ (0.32)	
3	ln$NAGDPPC$	=	0.576 ln$NAKPC$ (17.83)*	+0.173 ln$ROADS$ (4.26)*	+0.581 ln$SCHY$ (3.71)*
4	ln$WAGE$	=	0.090 ln$ROADS$ (2.05)*	+0.112 ln$ELECT$ (1.70)	+0.035 lnRTR (2.21)*
5	ln$NAGEMPLY$	=	0.100 ln$ROADS$ (3.16)*	+0.036 lnRTR (1.90)*	+0.406 ln$SCHY$ (3.04)*
6	lnIR	=	0.247 lnIRE (3.374)*		
7	ln$ROADS$	=	0.120 ln$ROADE$ (1.752)*		
8	ln$SCHY$	=	0.409 lnEDE (1.768)*		
9	lnRTR	=	0.270 ln$RTRE$ (2.13)*		
10	ln$ELECT$	=	0.328 ln$PWRE$ (5.56)*		
11	lnTT	=	−0.142 ln$AGDPPC$ (−2.15)*	−0.041 ln$AGDPPCn$ (−1.87)*	

NOTES: Region and year dummies are not reported. * indicates that coefficients are statistically significant at the 10 percent level. The coefficients for the technology, education, and infrastructure variables are the sum of those for past government expenditures.

TERMS OF TRADE.   The terms of trade are measured as agricultural prices relative to nonagricultural prices (or an agricultural GDP deflator divided by a nonagricultural GDP deflator).

AGRICULTURAL RESEARCH.   In Thailand agricultural research is conducted at the national level. But national research affects production throughout the country through so-called spillover effects. Therefore, we included the agricultural research stock variable constructed from past expenditures in all regions. When we calculated returns to agricultural research investment, we added agricultural extension to determine the total investment in agricultural R&D.

INFRASTRUCTURE.   Most of the infrastructure and education variables used in the model are defined in physical terms (Table 3.4), and data for suitable measures are available at the national and regional levels. The greatest dif-

−1.15 ln*TT* (−1.62)	−0.051ln*PLOAN* (−0.81)	−0.389ln*URBANP* (−0.87)	$R^2 = 0.655$
+0.099 ln*ROAD* (3.43)*	+0.481 ln*IR* (12.51)*	+0.301 ln*SCHY* (2.62)*	$R^2 = 0.914$
+0.011 ln*ELECT* (0.21)	+0.079 ln*RTR* (1.78)*		$R^2 = 0.810$
+0.690 ln*SCHY* (2.40)*	+0.587 ln*AGDPPC*$_{-1}$ (8.79)*	−0.148ln*UGDPPC* (−1.49)	$R^2 = 0.541$
+0.112 ln*ELECT* (2.04)*	−0.063 ln*AGDPPC*$_{-1}$ (−1.36)	+0.112 ln*UGDPPC* (2.19)*	$R^2 = 0.995$
			$R^2 = 0.976$
			$R^2 = 0.959$
			$R^2 = 0.975$
			$R^2 = 0.976$
			$R^2 = 0.976$
			$R^2 = 0.932$

ficulties arose in collecting data on government expenditures by type of investment and region, which are needed to calculate the value of the existing stocks of these investments and their unit costs. Like many countries, Thailand compiles data on public spending by different types of investment at the national level, but there are much fewer data on how these expenditures are allocated to different regions and by rural and urban areas. Therefore, the authors had to use some techniques and assumptions to make these allocations.

IRRIGATION. Data on both irrigated areas and investment costs are available at the regional level.

RURAL EDUCATION. Data on years of schooling are available by region, but public expenditure data are available only at the national level. The government of Thailand reported that 44.2 percent of the total education budget is

TABLE 3A.5 Definitions of variables, Thailand

Exogenous variables	
RDS	Stocks of agricultural R&D
RSCHY	Years of schooling of the rural population
RPHONE	Number of rural telephone sets per agricultural worker
RROADS	Length of rural roads per agricultural worker
IRRIST	Irrigation stock generated from past government investment
RELECT	Consumption of rural electricity per agricultural worker
UGDPP	Urban (or nonagricultural) GDP per capita
WFP	World food price
T	Time trend
Endogenous variables	
P	Percentage of rural population that falls below the poverty line
AWAGE	Wage rate for agricultural labor
NAWAGE	Wage rate for rural nonagricultural labor in rural areas
NAGEMPLY	Percentage of nonagricultural employment in total rural employment
URBANP	Percentage of urban population in total population
LP	Labor productivity of agricultural labor
TT	Terms of trade, measured as agricultural prices divided by a relevant nonagricultural GNP deflator

used for primary education. We used this percentage to calculate the budget for primary education. We then used the regional share of rural students in total students to calculate the expenditures for rural primary education by region, assuming that the per student expenditure in rural areas is one-fifth that in urban areas.[18]

RURAL ELECTRICITY.   Data on rural consumption of electricity in kilowatt units are available by region, but data on total public spending are available only at the national level. We used the electricity consumption data to apportion the total expenditures to different rural regions.

ROADS.   Road length and public expenditure data on roads are available by region from the government budget office. We used the share of the length of rural roads in the total length of roads to calculate the expenditures for rural roads, assuming that the cost per unit of rural roads is one-fifth that of urban roads.[19]

RURAL TELEPHONES.   Most of the investments in telephones are made by the private sector, and we do not have data on those. Consequently we did not try to estimate a capital value or cost for telephones, but simply used the physical data to control for telephones in the model.

---

18. Personal communication with TDRI staff.
19. This differential cost for different types of roads can be found and supported by the World Bank Road Information System, which provides unit costs for World Bank–funded road projects in different countries.

Thailand: Model Estimation

We used double-log functional forms for all equations in the system. Regional dummies were added to the equations for poverty, productivity, employment, migration, and terms of trade to capture the fixed effects of regional differences in agroclimatic and socioeconomic factors. The time trend variable was also added to these equations, except for the poverty equation, to control for any macroeconomic polices that have the same impact on every region. The estimation covers the period from 1977 to 2000.

All endogenous variables on the right-hand side of equations 1–7 were lagged for one year (Table 3A.6). This has two advantages. First, it allows for weak exogeneity of the endogenous variables. Second, because every equation has its own predetermined variables, the model is identified, which means it is possible to obtain an estimate of each parameter.

There are two approaches to estimating the results of an equation system: the single-equation approach and the multiple-equations system approach. Single-equation techniques such as instrumental variable estimators, two-stage least squares, and limited information maximum likelihood are easy to use and require only limited information. However, the single-equation techniques often neglect information contained in the other equations of the system. For this reason, we used the FIML estimation technique. Among all estimators, FIML is the most efficient. The only disadvantage is its estimation complexity, but with the rapid development of different forms of econometric software, this task has become increasingly easy and more accessible.

During our estimation we found that agricultural wages, rural nonfarm wages, urbanization, and rural nonfarm employment are highly correlated. When we included all these variables in the poverty equation, some of them became statistically insignificant. However, when we included them separately in the equation, all of them were statistically significant at the 1 percent level. It was obvious that we could not include all these variables in the equation. We used the principal-component technique to determine which variable should be included, following Mundlak (1981). Through this technique we kept the non-agricultural employment and urbanization variables in our final estimation for the poverty equation. In this case, when we interpreted the estimated results, the nonagricultural employment was a proxy for all rural wages and non-agricultural employment variables. Because all infrastructure and education variables affect poverty through nonagricultural employment, we did not need to report the results of wage equations.

Uganda: Data Sources and Definition of Variables

The unit of analysis for the Uganda case is a combination of national, regional, and district levels. Most of the data were collected from various agencies of the Ugandan government and/or aggregated from the Uganda National Household

Table 3A.6 Estimates from equations, Thailand

Eqn. no.					Estimated equations			
1	P	=	−0.417 LP (−1.68)*	−0.955 NAGEMPLY (−4.23)*	−0.117 URBANP (−0.12)	−2.42 TT (−3.99)*		$R^2 = 0.862$
			−0.797 RD1 (−2.05)*	−0.490 RD2 (−3.30)*	+0.134 RD3 (0.15)			
2	LP	=	0.099 IRRI (1.03)	+8.63 RSCHY (4.81)*	+0.464 RDS (2.21)*	+0.140 RROADS (0.50)	+0.175 RELECT (1.68)*	$R^2 = 0.921$
			+0.272 RPHONE (2.52)*	−0.265 T (−5.24)*	+0.239 RD1 (0.73)	+1.068 RD2 (3.83)*	−0.684 RD3 (−3.48)	
5	NAGEMPLY	=	−0.120 LP (−1.09)	−1.527 RSCHY (−0.81)	+0.820 RROADS (3.75)*	+0.388 RELECT (4.18)*	−0.068 RPHONE (−0.64)	$R^2 = 0.956$
			+2.97 UGDPP (5.03)*	+0.030 T (0.69)	+0.609 RD1 (2.23)*	+0.338 RD2 (1.30)	+0.925 RD3 (2.70)*	
7	TT	=	−0.068 LP (−1.29)	+0.438 WFP (5.54)*	+0.022 T (5.92)*	−0.001 RD1 (−0.02)	−0.083 RD2 (−3.31)*	$R^2 = 0.420$
			−0.083 RD3 (−3.31)*					

SOURCE: Fan, Jitsuchon, and Methakunnavut (2004).

NOTES: RD1 is the dummy variable for the northeast region, RD2 for the north region, and RD3 for the central region. The south region is the base region. * indicates that coefficients are statistically significant at the 10 percent level. Estimates of equations 3 and 6 are not reported because they are not used in calculation of the productivity and poverty effects of government spending.

Survey, crop surveys, and community surveys conducted by the Uganda Bureau of Statistics (UBOS). Crop production and land-use variables were generated from crop surveys, while most of infrastructure variables, such as access to markets, roads, schools, health services, and post offices were from community surveys. Data on poverty, income, employment, and wages by district were aggregated from different national household surveys. Most of the government spending variables at the national level were obtained from the Ministry of Planning and Finance, while spending data at the district level came from the Ministry of Local Governments and the Ministry of Planning and Finance.

POVERTY.   With respect to poverty estimation, we closely followed Appleton's method (2001) to estimate the values of consumption per adult equivalent. Based on regionally specific poverty lines described in Appleton (2001), we then calculated poverty rates at the district level.[20] The traditional approach uses a single national poverty line derived from a common "food basket." Uganda has a large amount of regional variation in diets, with six major staple foods eaten. For example, *matooke* is mainly consumed in the central and western regions, and not in the northern region. Therefore, a single national food basket approach may not be appropriate. Based on this concern, Appleton calculated region-specific poverty lines following the standard approach of Ravallion and Bidani (1994). By comparing the poverty incidence based on national and regional poverty lines, he showed that the region-specific poverty line is more appropriate for estimating regional patterns of poverty in Uganda.

OUTPUT VALUES.   Because the questionnaire used in the crop survey provides more than 30 units for each crop and many crops are produced only for self-consumption, it is difficult to aggregate output values across households and crops. For those crops with reported market sales in a household, we used the market price to derive the total output value. In cases where price information was not available for a particular crop, we used the median price for the same quantity among all the households within a district to derive the value for this particular output. If for the same quantity no price was available at the district level, we used the national median price as a proxy to calculate the output value of the crop produced by the household. The questionnaire includes the following crops: *matooke,* maize, finger millet, sorghum, rice, beans, field peas, cowpeas, pigeon peas, groundnuts, *sim-sim,* cotton, Irish potatoes, sweet potatoes, cassava, coffee, tea, tobacco, trees, flowers, oranges, passionfruit, pineapples, mangoes, papaw, onions, cabbages, *dodo,* tomatoes, carrots, other vegetables, other fruits, and other crops. Unfortunately, estimates of production of livestock and fishery products are not included in the crop survey. Considering that most of the poor rely primarily on cropping for a living, the impact of the exclusion of livestock and fishery products on poverty measures is minimal.

---

20. Appleton (2001) has reported poverty rates only at the regional level.

LAND.   The land variable refers to agricultural land, which is taken from the Crop Survey of UBOS.

FERTILIZER.   Fertilizer refers to the aggregate value of fertilizer used by farmers for crop production. The data are from the Crop Survey of UBOS.

EMPLOYMENT.   The household socioeconomic survey reports the activity status as well as the codes for industry and occupation. Based on this information, we estimated the total labor force, employment rate, and share of farming and nonfarm employment in total employment.

WAGES.   Farming and nonfarm wage rates for men and women at the district level are aggregated from the community survey, expressed as shillings per month.

HEALTH OUTCOMES.   The household socioeconomic survey reports data on household members who had fallen ill in the previous 30 days and on how many days were lost. Based on this information, we created two indicators at the district level: percentage of residents who had fallen ill and average days of work lost due to illness over the past 30 days.

EDUCATION LEVEL.   The literacy rate is from the household socioeconomic survey and is defined as the share of the population over the age of 15 who can read and write.

ROADS.   Average distances in kilometers to the nearest feeder road and all-season *murram* and tarred (or tarmac) roads are generated from the community survey.

AGRICULTURAL RESEARCH AND EXTENSION.   Agricultural research expenditures are available only at the national level. After the mid-1990s, agricultural extension expenditures were available for most of the districts. The expenditures were available only for selected districts in the early 1990s. For earlier years, we aggregated the district-level expenditures into regions and used regional aggregate expenditures for all districts within a region, assuming that extension services spill into each district equally. Finally we allocated national agricultural research expenditures by district in proportion to their extension expenditures.

Uganda: Model Estimation and Results

We used double-log functional forms for all equations in the system (Table 3A.7). The observations with missing or zero values (e.g., in the case of fertilizer) were deleted from our sample during the estimation. As a result, we had 90 observations (3 years and 30 districts). More flexible functional forms (such as translog or quadratic equations) impose fewer restrictions on estimated parameters, but many coefficients are not statistically significant because of multicollinearity problems. The estimates were made using the FIML technique.

TABLE 3A.7 Estimates from system equations

Eqn. no.			Estimated equations					
1	P	=	−0.266AOUTPC (−4.04)*	−0.183 RWAGE (−0.98)	−0.270 NFE (−2.75)*			R² = 0.407
2	AOUTPC	=	0.126 LANDP (3.65)*	+0.161 FERTP (2.99)*	+0.189 AGEXT (1.75)*	+0.332 RLITER (1.80)*	−0.139 DFROAD (−1.94)*	R² = 0.675
			+0.245DMROAD (1.39)	−0.09 DTROAD (−1.04)	−0.465PSICK (−2.04)			
3	RWAGE	=	−0.088Y (−1.52)	+0.133 RLITER (1.00)	+0.23 DFROAD (0.63)	−0.068 DMROAD (−0.63)	−0.048 DTROAD (−1.12)	R² = 0.418
			−0.216 PSICK (−2.32)*					
4	NFE	=	−0.172Y (−0.78)	−0.152 RLITER (−0.81)	−0.53 DFROAD (−0.78)	−0.216 DMROAD (−2.25)*	−0.234 DTROIAD (−3.05)*	R² = 0.315
			−0.104 PSICK (−0.62)					

SOURCE: Fan, Zhang, and Rao (2004).

NOTES: * indicates that coefficients are statistically significant at the 10 percent level, based on the statistics reported in respective parentheses. The coefficients of regional dummies are not reported.

References

Adams, R., Jr. 1999. Nonfarm income, inequality and land in rural Egypt. World Bank Policy Research Working Paper 2178. Washington, D.C.: World Bank.

Ahluwalia, M. S. 1978a. Rural poverty and agricultural performance in India. *Journal of Development Studies* 14 (3): 298–324.

———. 1978b. Rural poverty in India: 1956/57 to 1973/74. In India: Occasional Papers. World Bank Staff Working Paper 279. Washington, D.C.: World Bank.

Alston, J. M., C. Chan-Kang, M. Marra, P. Pardey, and T. Wyatt. 2000. *A meta-analysis of rates of return to agricultural R&D: Ex pede Herculem?* Environment and Production Technology Division Research Report 113. Washington, D.C.: International Food Policy Research Institute.

Appleton, S. 2001. Changes in poverty in Uganda, 1999/2000: Preliminary estimates from UNHS (Uganda National Household Survey). University of Nottingham, Nottingham, England.

Bagachwa, M. S. D., and F. Stewart. 1992. Rural industries and rural linkages. In *Alternative development strategies in Sub-Saharan Africa,* ed. F. Stewart, S. Lall, and S. Wangwe. London: Macmillan.

Bell, C., and R. Rich. 1994. Rural poverty and aggregate agricultural performance in post-independence India. *Oxford Bulletin of Economics and Statistics* 56 (2): 111–133.

Benefo, K. D., and T. P. Schultz. 1994. Determinants of fertility and child mortality in Côte d'Ivore and Ghana. Living Standards Measurement Study Working Paper 103. Washington, D.C.: World Bank.

Besley, T., and A. Case. 1994. Unnatural experiments? Estimating the incidence of endogenous policies. NBER Working Paper 4956. Cambridge, Mass.: National Bureau for Economic Research.

Binswanger, H., S. Khandker, and M. Rosenzweig. 1989. How infrastructure and financial institutions affect agricultural output and investment in India. World Bank Working Paper 163. Washington, D.C.: World Bank.

Canagarajah, S., C. Newman, and R. Bhattamishra. 2001. Non-farm income, gender, and inequality: Evidence from rural Ghana and Uganda. *Food Policy* 26 (4): 405–420.

Canning, D., and E. Bennathan. 2000. The social rate of return on infrastructure investments. Policy Research Working Paper 2390. Washington, D.C.: World Bank.

China, Ministry of Agriculture. 2005. *China agricultural development report.* Beijing: Agricultural Publishing House of China.

———. 1998a. Farm productivity and rural poverty in India. *Journal of Development Studies* 34 (4): 62–85.

———. Various years. *China agricultural yearbook.* Beijing: Agricultural Publishing House of China.

———. Various years. *China rural energy yearbook.* Beijing: Agricultural Publishing House of China.

———. Various years. *China rural statistical yearbook.* Beijing: Agricultural Publishing House of China.

China, Ministry of Education. Various years. *China education yearbook.* Beijing: China Statistical Publishing House.

———. Various years. *China education expenditure yearbook.* Beijing: China Statistical Publishing House.

China, Ministry of Electric Power. Various years. *China power yearbook.* Beijing: China Statistical Publishing House.

China, Ministry of Transportation. Various years. *China transportation yearbook.* Beijing: China Statistical Publishing House.

China. Ministry of Water Conservancy. 1980. *Thirty years of water conservancy statistical materials.* Beijing: Water and Power Publishing House.

———. Various years. *China water conservancy yearbook.* Beijing: Water and Power Publishing House.

China, National Bureau of Statistics. 1997. *The gross domestic product of China.* Beijing: China Statistical Publishing House.

———. Various years. *China statistical yearbook.* Beijing: Statistical Publishing House.

China, State Statistical Bureau. 1997. *Calculation and methods of China's annual GDP.* Beijing: China Statistical Publishing House.

———. Various years. *China fixed asset investment statistical materials.* Beijing: Statistical Publishing House.

———. Various years. Historical statistical materials for provinces, autonomous regions, and municipalities, 1949–1989. Beijing: China Statistical Publishing House.

Datt, G., and M. Ravallion. 1998b. Why have some Indian states done better than others at reducing poverty? *Economica* 65: 17–38.

David, C., and K. Otsuka, eds. 1994. *Modern rice technology and income distribution.* Boulder, Colo.: Reinner.

Davidson, R., and J. MacKinnon. 1993. *Estimation and inference in econometrics.* New York: Oxford University Press.

De Janvry, A., and E. Sadoulet. 1993. Rural development in Latin America: Relinking poverty reduction to growth. In *Including the poor,* ed. M. Lipton and J. van der Gaag. Proceedings of a symposium organized by the World Bank and the International Food Policy Research Institute. Washington, D.C.: World Bank.

———. 2001. Income strategies among rural households in Mexico: The role of off-farm activities. *World Development* 29 (3): 467–480.

Diao, X., P. Hazell, D. Resnick, and J. Thurlow. 2006. The role of agriculture in development: Implications for Sub-Saharan Africa. Discussion paper Series DSGD, Discussion Paper 29. Washington, D.C.: International Food Policy Research Institute.

Dollar, D., and A. Kraay. 2001. Growth is good for the poor. Manuscript, World Bank, Washington, D.C.

Elbers, C., and P. Lanjouw. 2001. Intersectoral transfer, growth, and inequality in rural Ecuador. *World Development* 29 (3): 481–496.

Fabrizio, B., G. Feder, D. Gilligan, H. Jacoby, T. Onchan, and J. Quizon. 2000. The impact of the financial crisis on the farm sector in Thailand. Working paper, World Bank, Washington, D.C.

Fan, S., and C. Chan-Kang. 2005. Returns to investment in less-favored areas in developing countries: A synthesis of evidence and implications for Africa. *Food Policy* 29: 431–444.

Fan, S., and P. Hazell. 2000. Should developing countries invest more in less-favoured areas? An empirical analysis of rural India. *Economic and Political Weekly,* April 22, 1455–1464.

Fan, S., C. Fang, and X. Zhang. 2003. Agricultural research and urban poverty: The case of China. *World Development* 31 (4): 733–741.

Fan, S., P. Hazell, and S. Thorat. 1999. *Linkages between government spending and poverty in rural India.* Research Report 110. Washington, D.C.: International Food Policy Research Institute.

———. 2000. Government spending, agricultural growth and poverty in rural India. *American Journal of Agricultural Economics* 82 (4): 1038–1051.

Fan, S., S. Jitsuchon, and N. Methakunnavut. 2004. The importance of public investment for reducing rural poverty in middle-income countries: The case of Thailand. DSGD Discussion Paper 7. Washington, D.C.: International Food Policy Research Institute.

Fan, S., X. Zhang, and N. Rao. 2004. Public expenditure, growth and poverty reduction in rural Uganda. DSG Discussion Paper 4. Washington, D.C.: International Food Policy Research Institute.

Fan, S., L. Zhang, and X. Zhang. 2002. *Growth, inequality, and poverty in rural China: The role of public investment.* IFPRI Research Report 125. Washington, D.C.: International Food Policy Research Institute.

———. 2004. Reforms, investment and poverty in rural China. *Economic Development and Cultural Change* 52 (2): 395–422.

Ferreira, F., and P. Lanjouw. 2001. Rural nonfarm activities and poverty in the Brazil northeast. *World Development* 29 (3): 509–528.

Gaiha, R. 1989. Poverty, agricultural production and prices in rural India—A reformulation. *Cambridge Journal of Economics* 13 (2): 333–352.

Greene, W. H. 1993. *Econometric analysis.* Hemel Hempstead, England: Prentice-Hall.

Haggblade, S., P. Hazell, and J. Brown. 1989. Farm–nonfarm linkages in rural Sub-Saharan Africa. *World Development* 17 (8): 1173–1201.

Irz, X., C. Thirtle, and S. Wiggins. 2001. Agricultural productivity growth and poverty alleviation. *Development Policy Review* 19 (4): 449–466.

Jitsuchon, S. 2001. What is poverty and how to measure it? *TDRI (Thailand Development Research Institute) Quarterly Review* 16 (4): 7–12.

Kerr, J., and S. Kolavalli. 1999. Impact of agricultural research on poverty alleviation: Conceptual framework with illustrations from the literature. Mimeo of a paper prepared for the Workshop on the Impact of Agricultural Research on Poverty Alleviation, International Food Policy Research Institute, Washington, D.C., May 12–14.

Kohli, Ulrich. 1982. A gross national product function and the derived demand for imports and supply of exports. *Canadian Journal of Economics* 18: 369–386.

Lavy, V., J. Strauss, and P. DeVreyer. 1995. *The impact of the quality of health care on children's nutrition and survival in Ghana.* Living Standards Measurement Papers 106. Washington, D.C.: World Bank.

Mukherjee, A. 1996. Poverty and unemployment in urban India: Trends, issues and perspectives. In *Poverty and unemployment,* ed. K. Raghav and Leena Sekhar. New Delhi: New Age International.

Mundlak, Y. 1981. On the concept of non-significant functions and its implications for regression analysis. *Journal of Econometrics* 16: 139–149.

Newman, C., and S. Canagarajah. 2000. Gender, poverty, and nonfarm employment in Ghana and Uganda. Working Paper 2367. Washington, D.C.: World Bank.

NSSO (National Sample Survey Organisation). 1973. *Employment and unemployment survey.* 27th Round. New Delhi: NSSO Department of Statistics.

Ravallion, M., and B. Bidani. 1994. How robust is a poverty line? *World Bank Economic Review* 8 (1): 75–102.

Ravallion, M., and G. Datt. 1995. Growth and poverty in rural India. World Bank Policy Research Working Paper 1405. Washington, D.C.: World Bank.

Reserve Bank of India. Various years. *Finances of State Governments.* Mumbai.

Rosegrant, M., and P. B. R. Hazell. 2000. *Transforming the rural Asia economy: The unfinished revolution.* Hong Kong: Oxford University Press for the Asian Development Bank.

Saith, A. 1981. Production, prices and poverty in rural India. *Journal of Development Studies* 19 (2): 196–214.

Scobie, G. M., and R. T. Posada. 1978. The impact of technical change on income distribution: The case of rice in Colombia. *American Journal of Agricultural Economics* 60 (1): 85–92.

Sen, A. 1997. Agricultural growth and rural poverty. In *Growth, employment and poverty: Change and continuity in rural India,* ed. G. K. Chadha and A. N. Sharma. New Delhi: Indian Society of Labour Economics.

Tendulkar, S. D., and L. K. Jain. 1995. Economic reforms and poverty. *Economic and Political Weekly,* June 10, 1374–1377.

Thiesenhusen, W. C., and J. Melmed-Sanjack. 1990. Brazil's agrarian structure: Changes from 1970 through 1980. *World Development* 18 (3): 393–415.

Torero, M., and J. von Braun. 2005. Information and communication technologies for the poor. Brief, International Food Policy Research Institute, Washington, D.C.

Van de Walle, D. 1985. Population growth and poverty: Another look at the Indian time series data. *Journal of Development Studies* 21 (3): 429–439.

———. 1998. Assessing welfare impacts of public spending. *World Development* 26 (3): 365–379.

Warr, P. 2001. Poverty reduction and economic growth: The Asian experience. Paper presented at the Asia and Pacific Forum on Poverty: Reforming Policies and Institutions for Poverty Reduction, Asian Development Bank, Manila, February 5–9.

Westley, J. R. 1986. *Agriculture and equitable growth: The case of Punjab–Haryana.* Westview Special Studies in Agriculture Science and Policy. Boulder, Colo.: Westview Press.

World Bank. 1994. *World development report: Infrastructure.* Washington, D.C.

———. 1997. The India Project: Poverty and growth in India, 1951–94. Available at <http://web.worldbank.org/WBSITE/EXTERNAL/TOPICS/EXTPOVERTY/0,,contentMDK:20289089~menuPK:497971~pagePK:148956~piPK:216618~theSitePK:336992,00.html> (accessed November 2007).

———. 2001. *World development report: Attacking poverty.* Washington, D.C.

Yang, D. 1997. Education and off-farm work. *Economic Development and Cultural Change* 45: 613–632.

Yúnez-Naude, A., and J. E. Taylor. 2001. The determinants of nonfarm activities and incomes of rural households in Mexico, with emphasis on education. *World Development* 29 (3): 561–572.

Zhang, X., and S. Fan. 2004. How productive is infrastructure? New approach and evidence from rural India. *American Journal of Agricultural Economics* 86 (2): 492–501.

Zhang, X., S. Fan, L. Zhang, and J. Huang. 2004. Local governance and public goods provision in rural China. *Journal of Public Economics* 88 (12): 2857–2871.

Zhao, Y. 1999. Labor migration and earnings difference: The case of rural China. *Economic Development and Cultural Change* 47 (4): 767–782.

4 Human Capital Expenditures for the Poor

DAVID COADY

Over the past decade there has been increasing evidence and acceptance of the important role played by human capital in the development process, from both macroeconomic (Barro and Sala-i-Martin 1995) and microeconomic (Strauss and Thomas 1995) studies. In addition to generating higher rates of aggregate growth, widespread access to basic health and education services also results in greater economic equality through a more participatory or broader growth process (Drèze and Sen 1989). Chapters 2 and 3 discussed the relative importance of these public expenditures in the government budget as well as their impacts on growth and poverty. However, understanding the empirical relationships between these public expenditures and growth–poverty outcomes requires a more detailed analysis of the various components of these expenditures and of how the relevant programs are designed and implemented. This is particularly important when attempting to translate observed relationships into policy conclusions.

This chapter focuses primarily on the distribution of human capital outcomes and on identifying policy interventions that improve outcomes for poor households. The emphasis is therefore on program design rather than on program implementation and service delivery mechanisms. This is not meant to suggest that service delivery is relatively unimportant. On the contrary, identifying effective service delivery mechanisms is now widely recognized as a key factor in improving human capital outcomes for the poor. However, an adequate review of this issue is beyond the scope of this chapter. A comprehensive review of service delivery mechanisms is available in World Bank (2004) and Shah (2005). In addition, throughout the chapter the focus is on the design issues that need to be addressed, so the discussion of empirical evidence is intended to be illustrative and representative and not, by any means, exhaustive.

As seen in Chapter 2, nearly all developing countries allocate a very substantial proportion of their public expenditures to the social sectors, that is, to the education and health budgets. There are a number of motivations for public expenditures to provide such services. From an efficiency perspective, it is argued that the private sector in isolation would undersupply such services and that imperfect credit markets and information constraints lead households to underinvest in their human capital. To the extent that these market failures are worse for the poor, efficiency requires that the incidence of public expenditures be progressive, and this is reinforced when both income distribution and social justice considerations are taken into account. When the issue is viewed from these perspectives, there is a growing concern that social expenditures are undesirably regressive, reflecting the fact that higher-income households have greater access to and make better use of these resources. Here we are specifically concerned with this aspect of social expenditures, measuring how the benefits flowing from these resources are distributed across income groups as well as identifying particular types of expenditures within these sectors that are more pro-poor. More particularly, we want to identify specific public policies that are cost-effective in increasing utilization rates among the poor.

The structure of the chapter is as follows. In the next four sections we examine nutrition, health, and education interventions in more detail. We start by providing a brief summary of the rationale for public policy interventions aimed at influencing human capital outcomes and the implications for choice of policy instrument. In the subsequent two sections we synthesize the literature on nutrition and health and on education, respectively. Within each of these sections we (1) examine empirical evidence regarding the human capital impacts of these social expenditures and their distribution and (2) summarize and conclude by drawing implications for policy and research, with particular emphasis on the implications for the research agenda at the International Food Policy Research Institute (IFPRI).

The Rationale for Public Policy

Because the underlying motivations for public intervention can be expected to determine the most appropriate policy response, it is important to have a clear understanding of the nature of these motivations. Public policies to influence human capital outcomes, especially for poor households, are typically justified on the grounds that the presence of numerous "market failures" will result in an inefficient demand for and supply of human capital services. A range of market failures are commonly identified, including information failures, external effects, and credit and insurance market failures. The presence of these market failures often provides a strong efficiency argument for subsidizing household investments in human capital. Where these failures are thought to be especially relevant for poor households, this also provides an efficiency argument for targeting interventions at poor populations. Where income poverty itself is seen as the cause of low investments in human capital, targeted income transfers may also be desirable. We will discuss each of these types of market failure and poverty in turn.

Because market failures are often more relevant for poor households and poverty itself is often the source of insufficient investments in human capital, the effectiveness of public expenditures can be greatly enhanced both by more explicitly targeting transfers at those in need and by linking (or conditioning) benefit entitlements to household behaviors that enhance the human capital status of household members. The synergies between education, nutrition, and health outcomes also mean that the effectiveness of public policy can be enhanced by the integration and coordination of investments across the health sector. However, having a good program design is not enough. For programs to have actual impact they must be well implemented, and this requires both allocating sufficient resources to planning and operations activities and recognizing the economic, social, and political incentives faced by the planning, financing, and implementing agencies in developing countries.

Information Failures

In the context of education, parents and individuals, particularly in poor households, may have poor information regarding the private benefits of investments in these sectors. In the context of nutrition and health, because both preventive and curative health services involve the supply and demand of information regarding the prevention and treatment of disease and illness, not surprisingly a key motivation for government intervention is the existence of information failures. For example, with regard to preventive care, individuals often have inadequate information about the link between their behavior and the health status of various family members, especially infants and children (e.g., information about more nutritious diets, better food preparation, and improved hygiene practices in the home; the health consequences of alcohol and drugs; the benefits of family planning and immunizations; the importance of chimneys or protection against AIDs). With regard to curative care, individuals are often unable to identify early on the symptoms of disease and illness, lack information about appropriate actions to take to address these illnesses (e.g., simple oral rehydration therapy for diarrhea), are unable to determine when professional treatment is required, and may not follow the prescribed treatment.

On the supply side, the asymmetry of information between those seeking the information and those supplying the information means that competitive private provision will not necessarily result in efficient outcomes. Individuals are unable to determine the quality of the advice, others' experiences are not necessarily informative given the heterogeneous and individual-specific nature of many health services, and the costs of searching for information (for example, in terms of resources and health status) can be very high, especially in the case of emergencies. The fixed costs of specialized training also mean that demand in sparsely populated areas may not be sufficient to ensure an adequate private return, and this also raises important questions regarding the most efficient technology for providing health services (for example, the use of mobile clinics). For all these reasons, in most countries the public sector plays a crucial role in determining the supply of healthcare services.

Where information failures are seen as an important reason underlying insufficient investment in human capital information and where information can be transferred at low cost (e.g., information regarding less serious illnesses or nutrition or regarding the benefits of education), the best solution to remedy this failure is obviously to provide individuals with sufficient information, for example, through public information campaigns. Where it is difficult for households to effectively absorb information, subsidies for human capital investments are warranted. To the extent that this is a particular problem among poor households with low levels of education, this provides a strong argument for targeted subsidies.

Externalities

In the context of health, an important motivation for public sector intervention is market failure arising from the externalities associated with some forms of healthcare, for example, vaccination programs to lower the incidence of contagious disease such as tuberculosis or smallpox or the use of insecticide-treated mosquito nets. Because of the external effects associated with immunization against infectious diseases, even in the presence of full information, individuals faced with costly treatment may not seek medical care quickly enough to avoid spreading the disease, or they may fail to complete a full course of treatment, which may lead to a resurgence of their illness, further transmission, and increased risk of resistance to the drugs available for treatment. Infectious diseases are still responsible for a large proportion of deaths in developing countries, especially among the poor.

In the context of education, the perceived social externalities of greater aggregate productive efficiency and improved social cohesion are seen by many as a strong justification for subsidizing education, particularly primary and secondary education. Public supply is also often favored as a way of ensuring the development and implementation of a curriculum that reinforces a common national (as opposed to ethnic, religious, or regional) identity. It is also often argued that even where parents recognize the private benefits of education investments, the absence of complete altruism means that an inability to ensure that the present costs are recouped from the higher incomes their children could earn results in inefficiently low education investments.

Imperfect Credit and Insurance Markets

In the context of nutrition and health, if individuals have more information on their health risk characteristics, can influence their risks by adjusting their behavior, and do not have an incentive to reveal their risk type, problems of adverse selection and moral hazard are substantial. Gaps in insurance coverage are most problematic for chronic and congenital illness, for illnesses associated with old age, and for primary healthcare (for which problems of moral hazard are thought to be particularly severe). Compulsory insurance (for example, a subsidized public service financed by general revenues), which prevents individuals at low risk from opting out, can provide substantial welfare improvement in such cases. The provision of a package of primary healthcare services free of charge or at highly subsidized rates is also often justified by the insurance motive. Obtaining credit for household investments in the health and nutritional status of infants and young children is also often hampered by the long period between the improved health status and future economic returns as well as the uncertainty associated with such returns, both of which prevent the use of future higher incomes as collateral.

In the context of education, credit constraints may mean that households are unable to finance potentially profitable investments, especially human capital investments, because of the uncertainty involved in such long-term investments and the fact that education cannot be used as collateral. Similarly, the resulting lack of access to more efficient consumption-smoothing possibilities may cause children to be withdrawn from school, resulting in high dropout rates and slow progression rates. The poor are, virtually by definition, more constrained in terms of access to credit (e.g., due to low amounts of disposable income and savings and to lack of alternative collateral). Again, this introduces an efficiency argument for targeting interventions at the poor.

Poverty and Income Distribution

Income poverty is often a major cause of poor nutritional and health status, and governments alone possess the powers to implement policies that redistribute income toward the poor. Therefore, in the shorter term, effective social safety nets are likely to be an important component of the solution. In addition, because of the socioeconomic characteristics of the poor (e.g., remoteness, lack of basic infrastructure), they often face higher access costs and are least able to afford them. Although it may be more cost-effective, at least initially, to concentrate education expenditures in areas where the non-poor are likely to benefit disproportionately, issues of social justice (or horizontal equity) relating to the right to equal access regardless of income or location would point in the direction of equal access to some basic level of human capital services. Note also that such arguments may be totally consistent with allocation of a disproportionate share of the budget to more costly expansion to more remote areas. However, the issue of alternative, more cost-effective approaches to expanding to these areas also deserves attention.

Poverty may cause poor nutrition and thus lower returns to education, reflecting both higher absentee rates and lower cognitive ability among the poor. Inferior health outcomes may reflect the absence of complementary public investments in areas such as the provision of clean water and sanitation, and the poor may be politically weak in lobbying for such investments. Therefore, lack of coordination of public investments leads to low human capital investments by households—an example of policy failure. Similarly, low education levels may reflect the low quality of schooling in poor and remote areas, reflecting the absence of appropriate incentives (e.g., teachers' not turning up for school, lack of teacher motivation, or low-quality facilities). Of course, where poverty is an important source of the problem, effective policy interventions will require alleviation of this resource constraint, for instance, increasing the consumption and nutrition levels of the poor as well as strengthening their capacity to monitor and acquire quality schooling. For example, subsidies targeted at poor households should aim at not only meeting the extra private costs of education but also providing an additional increment for increasing consumption. Similarly, in such environments compulsory education policies not only may be regressive (e.g., through making poor households incur the private costs of schooling while losing the earning potential of young adults) but are likely to be totally ineffective.

Analytical Approaches

The so-called human capital approach, or the *production function approach,* is the workhorse of the profession when it comes to modeling human capital outcomes. Based on such a model, a "reduced-form" empirically estimable "health outcome" or "health demand" function can be derived and then estimated using regression analysis based on individual-, household-, community-, and facility-level survey data. This approach has the advantage of having a strong theoretical foundation and thus an associated conceptual clarity. However, in practice, the data requirements are obviously very demanding, requiring information from a wide range of sources. For this reason one needs to be very cautious when differentiating between correlation and cause and effect and thus drawing policy conclusions from results (Glewwe 2002).

The nature and severity of the empirical problems when using cross-section household data depend on the specific policy issue being addressed, but invariably include potential estimation bias due to omitted variables, self-selection on the part of households, endogenous program placement, endogenous explanatory variables, and measurement error. One of the attractions of the regression-based modeling approach is that it helps researchers to understand the nature of the estimation problems. Both instrumental variable and panel data approaches can help them to overcome many of these problems, but access to good instrumental variables or quality panel data is rare. Therefore, even in the case of the better studies, the results should be treated as being suggestive of underlying causal relationships. Many researchers believe that we have learned as much as we can from such "conventional studies" (Glewwe 2002). However, where the data available are of reasonable quality, the results from these studies can help to provide evidence on relationships that can be examined using more focused studies.

Because of the myriad estimation problems associated with using cross-section data to analyze the determinants of education outcomes, evidence from randomized trials, which avoid many of these problems, is particularly valuable (Kremer 1995; Glewwe 2002). Better estimates also substantially improve the credibility of cost-effectiveness analyses, which is the issue of most interest to policymakers. In addition, because regression approaches identify average impacts, evidence from carefully targeted programs (e.g., supply interventions where supply is below very basic investments targeted at poor areas, where the factors determining education outcomes may be very different than elsewhere) can help to provide more relevant information for policymakers. Also, from the policy perspective, results from randomized trials also have the advantage that (unlike the production function approach) they are "reduced form effects" in that they incorporate household responses. However, although the fact that one does not require knowledge of the structural relationships generating net program impacts can be seen as an advantage of this approach from the perspective of identifying impacts, for policy purposes it can be seen as a weakness because such knowledge can be crucial for identifying how programs can be redesigned to improve program impacts.

An alternative analytical approach is the *benefit incidence approach,* which is particularly useful when evaluating the distributional impact of public expenditures. This approach combines household surveys for gathering data on access to or use of public services with surveys for collecting data on the level and pattern of public expenditures. Public expenditures are allocated to households on the basis of their use of public facilities; usually these are allocated on a cost-per-student or cost-per-visit basis. For example, the cost allocated to each household can be derived as

$$T^h = \frac{A^h}{\sum_{h=1}^{H} A^h} E = A^h \frac{E}{\sum_{h=1}^{H} A^h},$$

where A^h is the number of times the household accesses the facility (e.g., the number of children attending primary school or visiting health clinics), with the summation in the denominator taken over all households (i.e., the total enrollment or visit numbers nationally), and E is the total amount of the relevant expenditure. Therefore, the transfer allocated to the household is its share in total access (T^H) times the total budget or, equivalently, the average expenditure per unit times the household's level of access.

In principle, costs should be defined at the lowest level possible (e.g., by facility). However, in practice, costs are typically available only at a very aggregate (e.g., national) level. These cost allocations are then treated as "in-kind transfers" and aggregated across households and income deciles. The analysis then focuses on the proportion of the total transfers accruing to each decile. It is also common to analyze the distributional impact of different components of the total separately, such as primary versus secondary education expenditures, as well as the allocation across different groupings (e.g., by region, ethnic group, or gender).

This approach was first employed for developing countries by Meerman (1979) for Malaysia and by Selowsky (1979) for Colombia. With the reemphasis by the World Bank on interventions to help the poor, there has recently been a resurgence in the application of this approach (van de Walle 1995; Demery 2003). It is perceived as being less demanding in terms of data requirements, but as simultaneously having a shortcoming in that it ignores behavioral responses that may have an important impact on distributional outcomes. Also, in practice, data limitations on the levels and distribution of expenditures often mean that access patterns drive the results, with variations in expenditure playing a secondary role.

Benefit incidence studies are primarily concerned with determining whether the distribution of benefits from human capital expenditures, either on average or on the margin, is progressive or regressive. Progressivity is typically determined by reference to one of two reference distributions: (1) the distribution of income or (2) the distribution of the population. For example, based on 1, if the poor's share of benefits is greater than their share of income, the benefit distribution is progressive. In other words, a transfer that is proportional to income is seen as the neutral reference distribution. This, however, would appear to be an unattractive reference because it would simply reinforce existing inequalities. Based on 2, a benefit distribution is progressive if the poor's share of benefits exceeds their share of the population. In other words, a uniform transfer is seen as the reference distribution. Note that from the perspective of benefit distribution, the latter is a stricter reference because a uniform transfer will always be progressive under 1, whereas a proportional transfer will be regressive under 2. When referring to progressivity and regressivity later, we take note of these distinctions.

Nutrition and Health Expenditures

In this section we discuss the relationship between public expenditures in the nutrition and health sectors in developing countries and the welfare of the poor. It is now widely accepted that one of the most important constraints on poverty reduction and growth in developing countries is the high burden of malnutrition and disease (WHO 2001). As one would expect, then, there is also much evidence that reducing this burden will not only substantially improve human development, but will also generate large economic returns (Strauss and Thomas 1998). For example, the World Health Organization (WHO 2001, 103) calculated that the provision of basic primary healthcare for all in low-income countries would have a (lower-bound) benefit-cost ratio of around 2.8, which is very high by any standard. The high prevalence of malnutrition is often singled out as being directly or indirectly responsible for a substantial proportion of the existing high levels of preventable morbidity and mortality, especially among women and children. For example, it has been estimated that over 20 percent of worldwide disability-adjusted life years (DALYs) due to mortality and morbidity can be attributed to malnutrition, with some more speculative estimates putting the proportion at around one-half (Gillespie and Haddad 2001).[1]

The high correlation between poverty and poor nutrition and health outcomes, both across and within countries, is well documented and reflects the fact that low-income households have little access to quality public healthcare facilities and other health-related investments (e.g., clean water and sanitation). For example, the infant mortality rate (IMR) and under-5 mortality rate (U5MR) in the least developed countries are 100 and 159 (per 1,000 live births) compared to 35 and 39, respectively, in lower-middle-income countries and 6 and 6, respectively, in high-income countries (WHO 2001). Similar biases exist within countries across income groups (Gwatkin 2000).[2] For example, in Bangladesh, the IMR and U5MR are 96 and 141 in the poorest income quintile compared to just 57 and 76 in the highest. There is also clear evidence that malnutrition rates are disproportionately concentrated among the poor (Wagstaff and Watanabe 2000). Therefore, because the poor account for a substantial proportion of the total malnutrition and disease burden in most developing countries, achieving substantial reductions in morbidity and mortality will also require a much greater emphasis on improving the nutrition and health status of poor households, and thus also a more progressive allocation of the public health budget in favor of health issues of most importance to this group. Addressing this issue will be a key factor in stopping the intergenerational transmission of poverty.

It is widely accepted that renewed growth and poverty reduction are important components of any strategy for reducing malnutrition and poor health (Strauss and Thomas 1998). But the evidence also suggests that even improved economic performance in isolation will not be enough to, for example, reach the targets set by the Millennium Development Goals (MDGs) (Haddad et al. 2003).[3] Reaching this target will thus require some fundamental changes in the level and

---

1. DALYs are a commonly used estimate of the number of years of life lost due to premature death, adjusting for years lived with less than full health. One DALY represents the loss of the equivalent of one year of full health.

2. See also the May 2005 issue of *Development Outreach,* published by the World Bank, which looks at the issue of nutrition and health interventions that benefit the poor (Coady, Filmer, and Gwatkin 2005).

3. The MDG health targets include (1) a reduction in child mortality by two-thirds of the 1990 level by 2015, (2) a reduction in maternal mortality ratios by three-fourths of the 1990 ratio by 2015, and (3) the end of rising HIV/AIDS and other major disease prevalence no later than 2015.

use of resources in the health and nutrition sectors. The high prevalence of malnutrition in many countries (especially South Asia, East Asia, and Sub-Saharan Africa) means that achieving these goals will require direct nutrition interventions that are well designed, coordinated, and implemented. Research has shown that such effective health and nutrition interventions are available and that most of these services can be effectively delivered through health centers, smaller health posts, or even outreach services within communities. But such services are not always used or implemented efficiently (World Bank 1993; Allen and Gillespie 2001). Therefore, achieving the desired nutrition and health improvements will require both extra resources and a better use of total resources (WHO 2001).

Empirical Evidence

In this section we summarize the literature on the relationship between public health expenditures and health outcomes. This section is therefore meant to supplement the related discussions in Chapters 2 and 3, which suggested that in aggregate this relationship was weak. The purpose of this chapter is thus to look behind this aggregate relationship with the intention of identifying how the relationship can be enhanced.

CROSS-COUNTRY/REGIONAL ANALYSES.   Some recent *cross-country* empirical studies of the relationship between countries' public expenditures on health and health outcomes provide very little support for an independent effect of these expenditures. For example, using an instrumental variables approach to deal with problems of endogeneity, Filmer and Pritchett (1999) found that the effect of public health expenditures as a share of GDP on child mortality is both statistically insignificant and of small magnitude. They found that variations in public spending account for less than one-sixth of 1 percent of the variation in infant mortality across countries. Their estimates suggest that doubling spending from 3 percent to 6 percent of GDP will result in only a 9–13 percent decrease in mortality. In spite of contrary evidence of a positive relationship (Anand and Ravallion 1993; Hojman 1996), the evidence of Filmer and Pritchett has raised some concerns regarding the role and effectiveness of public health expenditures.

Studies analyzing the relationship between health outcomes and public health expenditures using *cross-regional* (e.g., district-level) data also provide little support for the effectiveness of such interventions as increasing proximity to health centers, hospitals, doctors, or other health workers. Of course, because of program placement bias (e.g., clinics' being placed in areas with poor health outcomes), interpreting associations in the raw data as demonstrating cause and effect is a hazardous task. But even studies that attempt to correct for such biases provide little support for any impacts.

Three factors that can be expected to determine the effectiveness of public expenditures in terms of improved health outcomes are

- the allocation of these expenditures across the different levels of health-care (e.g., between primary healthcare and "higher" levels of care) and their different services and client profiles,
- the composition of inputs purchased by these expenditures (e.g., between salaries, drugs, and infrastructure), and
- the efficiency with which these inputs are transformed into effective health services (e.g., reflecting the effectiveness of monitoring and incentive systems).

Therefore, the absence of a strong relationship between total public health expenditures and health outcomes (or access) may reflect inappropriate composition of expenditures (e.g., too much being spent on services adequately supplied by the private sector to specific populations), inefficient delivery of services (e.g., due to lack of sufficient monitoring or poor incentive structures), or use of expenditures to finance such things as higher salaries without any return in terms of service quality.

Gupta, Verhoeven, and Tiongson (1999) suggest that the lack of any strong relationship can be partly attributed to an inappropriate composition of expenditures, with too little being allocated to primary healthcare services. Their results indicate that both the share of spending on primary healthcare and total healthcare spending have a statistically significant effect on infant and child mortality rates (the latter only when an explanatory variable capturing measles immunization rates is dropped). Their estimates suggest that primary healthcare spending variables explain as much as an additional 4 percent of cross-country variation in health status and that increasing its share by 5 percentage points (from a mean of 18 percent to 23 percent of total spending) would decrease child mortality rates by 4.9 and infant mortality rates by 2.3 (both per 1,000 children and from levels of 65 and 55, respectively).

In a more recent paper, Rajkumar and Swaroop (2002) found that the link between public health expenditures and health outcomes (i.e., infant and child mortality) is positively related to the level of governance. These results hold up when public health expenditures are instrumented to deal with endogeneity concerns. There is also evidence that the effectiveness of public health expenditures depends on the incidence of healthcare across poor and non-poor households. Bidani and Ravallion (1997) found that public expenditures have a large impact on the health status of the poor, in spite of having only a small impact on the population as a whole. This suggests that better targeting of expenditures at poor households should prove more effective at generating improvements in health status. It is also important to recognize that other factors besides these expenditures (e.g., incomes, education, access to safe water and sanitation, culture, and location) also matter. Therefore, other policy levers exist that may be important complements in determining the overall effectiveness of public health expenditures. This also suggests that generating the desired improvements in health status will require a more integrated approach.

    HOUSEHOLD CROSS-SECTION ANALYSES.   The dominant paradigm among international development institutions and policymakers in the late 1970s and early 1980s was that poor heath service quality was the binding constraint and that this, for the most part, reflected budgetary constraints (WHO/UNICEF 1978; World Bank 1987). Therefore, it was argued that the appropriate policy response was to allocate resources to improving the quality of services provided by public facilities and to finance this through the introduction or increase of user fees. African health ministers promoted this policy strategy explicitly in 1988 through the Bamako initiative, which depends on community financing of recurrent costs to improve the accessibility and quality of primary health services (McPake, Hanson, and A. Mills 1993). This approach led to much debate, in particular regarding the equity implications of such policies (Russel and Gilson 1997) and also regarding an increasing research effort to empirically identify the relative importance of the different factors affecting health outcomes and facility utilization rates.

    The push toward introducing user fees to finance higher-quality health services was undoubtedly influenced by the early research on this issue, which found little price sensitivity in demand. However, it is now widely believed that the perverse results of the earlier body of research were due mainly to poor-quality data and/or to the misspecification of the estimation equation (Gertler and van der Gaag 1990). More recent studies that have attempted to address these problems have found that prices are an important determinant of health demand in developing countries, with statistically significant negative price elasticities, which are also much higher for poorer households. Although the higher price elasticities for the poor imply that price increases are less regressive than they would otherwise be, they also imply that higher prices will result in a utilization pattern that is even further biased toward the non-poor. On the other hand, this also suggests that higher subsidies may be a very effective way of increasing demand by poor households. Also, simulations undertaken by Gertler and van der Gaag (1990), based on their estimates, suggest that extensive expansion may not be a cost-effective option for increasing access, especially if it needs to be financed through user fees.

    Increasing the access of poor households to quality private healthcare is obviously a necessary (if not sufficient) condition for improving their health status. Various studies have focused on the relationship between quality care and health facility access or use. Most of these studies have found that variation in quality is an important determinant of health demand.[4] Typically there is a high level of multicollinearity between the quality variables used, so only their joint

---

4. See World Bank (2004) and Shah (2005) for more detailed discussions of these studies.

effect, as opposed to the effect of individual quality dimensions, can be identified with sufficient statistical precision. In any case, arguably supply-side structural and process variables are better interpreted as proxies for some unobservable quality variables, so one needs to be careful when turning empirical results into policy prescriptions. Yet the perceived importance of quality remains, and recent research output by Filmer, Hammer, and Pritchett (2000) has argued that the ineffectiveness of increasing public spending in improving health status is largely due to the failure of public facilities to deliver effective services. These findings are obviously important in determining what constitutes the appropriate policy response.

Quality has to do not just with resources; it also has to do with how effectively these resources are transformed into health services. There is now emerging evidence that the delivery of quality healthcare is a major problem in many countries, with reports of a severe lack of drugs combined with black market availability widespread (World Bank 1994). In 1984 more than 70 percent of the government supply of drugs disappeared in Guinea. Various studies in Cameroon, Tanzania, and Uganda have estimated that about 30 percent of publicly supplied drugs have been misappropriated. In one case, as much as 30–40 percent of the public supply was "withdrawn for private use" by staff. In the Dominican Republic only 12 percent of the allocated funds were reaching patients as services. There is also substantial evidence of individuals' "bypassing" the nearest clinics for private care given the shortage of public drugs and equipment, appropriate health workers, poor care, or inconvenient open hours.

PROGRAM EVALUATIONS. Although the myriad estimation problems inherent in the use of cross-section data suggest that special significance should be given to the results of studies that use social experimental data, these studies are still very rare and this undoubtedly constitutes a large research gap. Here we discuss the results of a few of such experiments.

Evaluations of a social experiment in Indonesia (Dow et al. 2001) found that the increasing prices of health services led to a substantial decline in healthcare utilization and also in labor force participation. These effects were also found to be much greater for the lowest-income households. In 1997, in Bangladesh, Filmer, Hammer, and Pritchett (2000, 207) studied the introduction of an intensive maternal and child health and family planning program, where pregnant and lactating women were visited every 15 days by a female health worker who provided guidance on family planning. They found that this program had little effect on child mortality; although the mortality rate among children did fall, this was attributed almost exclusively to measles immunization (Menken and Phillips 1990; Koenig, Faveau, and Wojtyniak 1991).

As we pointed out earlier, one of the major concerns regarding the effectiveness of existing nutrition interventions is their poor record in reaching the poorest and most vulnerable households of society. Such households typically live in remote rural areas and have low incomes, and health services are not easily accessible. Low incomes result in both low levels of food consumption and low-quality diets. These households are often exposed to relatively more disease- and infection-prone environments while simultaneously lacking adequate access to curative health services. Lower education levels and an inability to acquire nutrition information compound problems with lack of access to preventive services. It is widely believed that effective action to deal with this situation requires an integrated approach that addresses all of these concerns simultaneously.

This is the motivation underlying an integrated program, PROGRESA (now called Oportunidades), introduced in Mexico, and similar programs that have been introduced, or are being seriously considered, in a number of other Latin American countries, such as Brazil (BA), Honduras (PRAF), and Nicaragua (RED). These programs attempt to address the issues of economic poverty, poor nutrition, and lack of access to quality health services within a single program.

The evaluation of the PROGRESA, introduced in Mexico on a national scale in 1997, is probably the most comprehensive evaluation of the impact of a public health intervention in a developing country based on social experimental techniques (Skoufias 2000; Gertler 2004). Poor households in very remote rural communities receive cash transfers conditioned on family members' (particularly pregnant women and children) making regular trips to clinics for preventive check-ups (essentially a standard basic primary healthcare package, including nutrition and growth monitoring as well as immunization) and for nutritional and hygiene education lectures. Nutritional supplements are given to children between the ages of 4 months and 2 years and to pregnant and breast-feeding women on a monthly basis (equivalent to one dose per day). They are also given to children between the ages of 2 and 5 if they have any signs of malnutrition. The nutritional supplements provide 100 percent of required vitamins and 20 percent of the recommended amount of protein. Additional resources are allocated to health centers in order to improve access to crucial inputs, timely services, and quality healthcare.

The evaluation results indicate that the program led to a 53–61 percent increase in visits to public clinics without a corresponding fall in visits to private providers. In terms of health outcomes, it resulted in a substantial decrease in the incidence of illness (25 percent for newborns, 19 percent for children aged 0–2 years, and 22 percent for children 3–5 years), increases in child height and weight (children were 1–4 percent taller, the percentage increasing with age, and 3.5 percent heavier), a 19 percent reduction in anemia for children aged 24–48 months, and improvements in the health status of adults (16 percent fewer days of difficulty with daily activities due to illness, 17 percent fewer days incapacitated due to illness, 18 percent fewer days in bed due to illness, ability to walk 7 percent farther without getting tired). The transfers constitute roughly a 25 percent increase in the incomes of those in extreme poverty, and 70 percent of this has been used to increase both the quantity and the quality of food available in the household (Hoddinott, Skoufias, and Washburn 2000). The substantial and wide-ranging impact of the program, which combines cash transfers with increased access to preventive and curative health services of good quality, is evidence that a comprehensive approach to health services can be very effective in poor populations.[5]

The lack of other such studies is a major constraint on the policy debate in other developing countries. An important question is this: To what extent are these programs transferable to other countries with much higher disease burdens and greater resource constraints, such as Sub-Saharan Africa and Asia? The early results emerging from a multicountry evaluation program seem promising in this regard (WHO 2001). One of these evaluations is taking place in Tanzania, which has a per capita GDP of $210 and one of the highest burdens of disease in the world. For example, 94 percent of its population is at risk of being affected by malaria; half are affected at least once each year, and 100,000 (out of a population of 35 million) die from it. In addition, 80–90 percent of children are anemic, and the U5MR stands at 180–190 per 1,000 population. The design of the program reflects the reality that resources are scarce, so to have a large-scale national impact one needs to identify the main health and nutrition problems as well as cost-effective interventions that bring about a substantial reduction in this burden at low cost.

This pilot program offers an additional U.S. $2 per capita per year (the average nationally is U.S. $8 per capita per year, including annualized personnel training and building costs); in fact, the regions with the program absorbed only 80 cents per capita in the first year. The only conditions attached were that the money be used to address health problems relevant to the population (e.g., malaria, pneumonia, diarrhea, measles, and malnutrition) using cost-effective methods.[6] Facility staff were trained in implementing the "integrated management of childhood illnesses," which focuses on improving case management, health systems, and community and family practices, as well as implementing a "safe-motherhood initiative" focusing on family planning and pre- and postnatal care. The program was implemented in the context of a decentralized health delivery system, with districts responsible for identifying the relevant health burdens and determining program responses.

The early results are encouraging; the IMR decreased by 28 percent between 1999 and 2000 (from 100 to 72 per 1,000 persons), and the U5MR decreased by 14 percent (from 140 to 120 per 1,000 persons). However, at this stage it is unclear how much of this is due to an underlying trend reflecting other socioeconomic factors as opposed to a direct effect of the intervention. Similar pilot interventions and evaluations are underway (or planned) in Bangla-

---

5. Similarly impressive results have been found for Nicaragua (Maluccio and Flores 2006).

6. For example, by encouraging the use of breastfeeding, vitamin A tablets, insecticide-treated mosquito nets, and rehydration salts to deal with diarrhea, as well as greater use of nurses and paramedics.

desh, Peru, Uganda, Kazakhstan, northeast Brazil, Cambodia, and an as-yet-unidentified country in francophone Africa. The results from such evaluations should substantially improve our understanding of the potential effectiveness of various health services in a wide variety of socioeconomic settings.

BENEFIT INCIDENCE APPROACHES.   Analysis of benefit incidence involves the merging of household survey data with public expenditure data. The household surveys typically gather information on households' health-seeking behavior, such as whether they seek treatment and where. Public expenditure incidence is obviously particularly focused on utilization of public facilities, for instance, in terms of whether households visit such facilities and/or the frequency of visits. Typically, information relates to the number of visits in the past 1–3 months, from which a binary access variable is created. One obvious concern is that because the poor are thought to underreport illness episodes, they also underreport the frequency of access, thus biasing the degree of progressiveness downward. However, it is not clear whether this latter effect is important.

Where possible, treatment facilities are divided into those offering private traditional care or private modern care, public health facilities, and hospital in- or outpatient care. Ideally one would want to collect public expenditure data that could be disaggregated by facility. However, this level of disaggregation is rarely, if ever, available. It is even very rare for public expenditure data to be available at a regional level. Typically only disaggregation across primary healthcare and hospitals is available. So the availability of cost data varies widely. In some cases one has access to virtually nothing, so one needs to perform "mini–public expenditure reviews." In other cases, costs can be broken down by facility type (hospital or health center) as well as by different levels of the hospital system (central, provincial, district, or branch level). Data on spending are available from both municipal and central budgets for many regions. However, the norm would appear to be that aggregates are available only by facility type.

The disaggregation of the cost side is thus usually the binding dimension of such studies, and unit costs (e.g., expenditures per unit of access) are calculated at these levels. As pointed out earlier, it is thus very important to identify separately the contributions of access behavior and public expenditure allocations to the overall distributional impact of expenditures. It is also important to separate out recurrent and capital expenditures because these probably relate to different interventions. For example, recurrent expenditures would include those for intensive expansion or maintaining quality, while capital expenditures would likely capture more extensive expansion; these are likely to have very different distributional impacts on the margin. However, even this separation is often not available.

Most of these studies have found that the poor either do not seek treatment or use private traditional sources of treatment, and that the rich demonstrate greater utilization of modern private treatment and hospital care (presumably partly because these are more often available in urban areas, which tend to have higher average incomes). Overall, total health expenditures are regressive, and this typically reflects the high per unit expenditures on hospitals and the fact that the rich disproportionately frequent these facilities.

Figure 4.1 presents the proportion of health expenditures accruing to the bottom 20 percent and 40 percent of the population across 12 countries. The benefits of public expenditures were found to be progressive in only 3 or 4 out of the 12 countries analyzed (i.e., Argentina, Uruguay, Malaysia, and Chile), with the percentage of benefits accruing to the bottom 20 percent and 40 percent of the population in the other countries falling below 20 percent and 40 percent. Even a uniform (i.e., random or nontargeted) transfer would have a greater distributional impact, and food subsidies typically have been found to be slightly progressive (Alderman and Lindert 1998). However, because the distribution of benefits tends to be more progressive than the underlying distribution of income, financing such expenditures through proportional taxation would tend to be more progressive. If crowding-out of private health services is less prevalent for the poor, the distribution of the incremental health impacts is also likely to be more progressive. Also, because the poor suffer more from infectious diseases, expenditures in such areas as vector control, immunization, and sanitation are likely to be relatively progressive compared to many other components of total health-related expenditures (World Bank 1998; Bonilla-Chacin and Hammer 1999). Still, by any standard, the distributional impact of these expenditures is low.

FIGURE 4.1 Proportion of public health expenditures accruing to the bottom 20 percent and 40 percent of the population in 12 countries

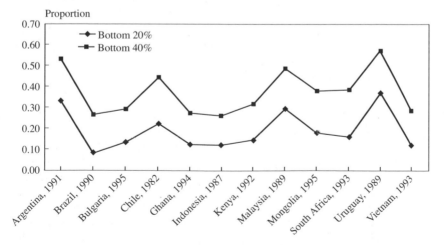

SOURCE: Filmer, Pritchett, and Hammer (2000).

FIGURE 4.2 Proportion of public health expenditures accruing to the bottom 20 percent of the population in 10 countries

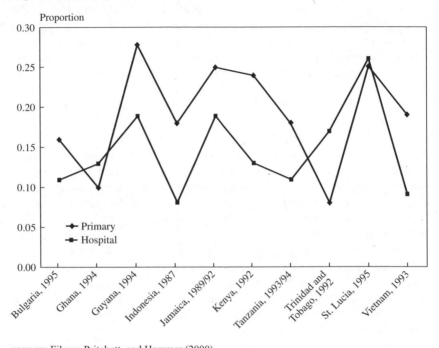

SOURCE: Filmer, Pritchett, and Hammer (2000).

Figure 4.2 shows that expenditures on primary healthcare tend to be more progressive than those on hospitals, but only because the latter are so regressive. Even then, whether primary healthcare is progressive or regressive often tends to depend on the reference for neutrality; it is only slightly progressive when proportional transfers are taken as one's reference for neutrality. Low gender and ethnic access rates tend to increase the degree of regressivity. Analyses of benefit incidence over time (e.g., van de Walle 1995; Lanjouw et al. 2000) tend to show very little improvement in progressivity over time.

Therefore, the picture is essentially one that reinforces our prior sense that the bulk of the benefits generated by public health expenditures are captured by the non-poor. It also reinforces the view that the commonly observed outcome is one in which the most regressive forms of health expenditures (i.e., on hospitals) absorb a disproportionate amount of the budget. It further suggests that sole reliance on the conventional approach of extensive expansion, although more progressive on the margin, is unlikely to have any significant impact on the overall progress of health expenditures. Next we address the issue of the types of reforms necessary to change the current picture.

Concluding Remarks

Both within the public health community and among donors, there is a strong consensus that investing in primary healthcare systems is a cost-effective method of improving health status in developing countries. However, in spite of this consensus, the current view is that the returns from public health expenditures have been, at best, disappointing. This is particularly so in terms of their impact on the health status of the poorest households.

Returns from a given total level of public health expenditures depend simultaneously on three key elements: (1) the composition of expenditures, (2) the delivery of health services, and (3) the use of services by individuals. Although there is some evidence that health expenditures decreased in the early 1980s, in many cases these have recovered, so that by the late 1990s they were at or above 1980 levels. However, it may be that the problem lies with an inappropriate composition of health expenditures. There is some evidence that the emphasis on providing and subsidizing inexpensive curative care through the primary health network is likely to have a large "crowding-out" impact on private provision, resulting in a substantially smaller net health impact. To the extent that this is true, reducing public subsidies (i.e., introducing fees) should not have adverse health consequences and would help to mobilize valuable resources for further expansion. However, there is also strong evidence that reducing subsidies will result in even more inequity in access to health services and in health outcomes. The poorest households already face higher private costs of access (e.g., reflecting the greater distances they have to travel to health clinics), and reducing subsidies will exacerbate this situation further. The fact that market failures have a greater impact both on poor households and on their poverty provides a strong rationale for maintaining subsidies for this group. Therefore, if it is not to be self-defeating, the introduction of fees needs to be selective, for instance, applying only to better-off households and to inexpensive curative care.

Even with public subsidies, generating improved health status requires the provision of quality care. This issue is now beginning to receive much attention. The lack of quality healthcare is a problem, particularly for poor households without access to affordable private provision. But it should be recognized that the provision of an effective integrated network of primary health facilities to all sections of the population is likely to be a capacity-intensive endeavor, because poverty and inadequate capacity often go hand in hand. There is therefore a need to find ways to deliver these services to poor populations in a cost-effective manner and to understand the potential roles of community actors.

Improving quality alone is unlikely to have any substantial impact on health outcomes unless ways are found to substantially increase access for poor households. The fact that public health expenditures have been found not to be very progressive in practice reflects (1) that a substantial proportion of these resources are absorbed by hospitals that tend to be used much less by poor households, (2) that it is much more cost-effective to locate health facilities in relatively densely populated areas, (3) that health service quality is often particularly bad in poor areas, and (4) that the poor do not fully appreciate the benefits of preventive health check-ups and cannot afford even inexpensive curative care. Improving the distributional impact of health expenditures therefore requires both a reallocation of resources toward primary healthcare and an increase of access to quality health services for the poor, that is, both resource mobilization and resource reallocation.

There is an emerging consensus that although there may be some role for the introduction of fees for some services and income groups, such an approach is not consistent with improving the nutritional and health status of poor households. An alternative complementary reform strategy is to look for more cost-effective ways of increasing access for the poor. Because of economies of scale, at least with respect to existing health service delivery through health clinics, it is unlikely that an extensive expansion is a cost-effective way of improving access for the poor. Another alternative is to focus more on the demand side (i.e., on bringing the poor to the health services rather than vice versa). Recent experience with targeted health subsidies suggests that these conditioned transfers can be very effective at increasing the access of the poor to health services as well as addressing poverty and malnutrition. The results from Mexico's PROGRESA program (and similar programs elsewhere) suggest that an integrated approach that addresses access, information, quality, and poverty provides great potential.

However, the PROGRESA evaluation is but one program evaluation. The recently completed evaluations of other similar programs in Latin America (i.e., PRAF in Honduras, RPS in Nicaragua, and BA in Brazil), which were carried out at IFPRI, have also made important contributions toward filling the existing research gaps. The relevance of such policy options for lower-income developing countries is also an issue, especially because the capacity requirements of such a comprehensive approach may be too demanding for the lowest-income countries. For these, budgets and administrative capacity are relatively more constraining, so the issues of transfer size and the most effective mechanism for delivering quality services need to be addressed. More research is needed here to evaluate the relative cost-effectiveness of alternative expansion strategies, including greater use of nurses, paramedics, and community workers supported by community organizations. Again, there is little if any evidence of the availability or cost-effectiveness of such alternative strategies. In this respect, the ongoing evaluations of pilot programs in Africa and Asia should be very informative.

Education Expenditures

A wide range of benefits has been attributed to investments in education and improved education outcomes (Schultz 1988). Consistent with this, many economists have argued that investment in education should be a high policy priority for governments in developing countries (Becker 1995; World Bank 2001). There is also a vast body of macroeconomic and microeconomic evidence that expansion of formal education is a key component of successful development strategies (Psacharopoulos 1994; Barro and Sala-i-Martin 1995; World Bank 1995). But recent empirical evidence suggests that the impact of expanding education on growth is less than expected, with little evidence of substantial positive externalities (Pritchett 2001; Bloom and Canning 2003).

Pritchett (2001) provides three possible reasons for the absence of any empirical externality effect. First, it could be that the educated labor force has been severely misallocated to sectors with high private but low social returns, such as the public sector or inefficient industries. Second, in the absence of sufficient demand to absorb this greater skill base, private returns may have diminished, so the average returns from micro data were substantial overestimates of the marginal return. But although there is evidence that returns are highest in growing economies, there is little evidence of a general downward trend in returns. Third, it is possible that the extra schooling was of very poor quality. However, the evidence that the substantial returns observed in micro studies reflect economic productivity (as opposed to just signaling returns) does not in general support this argument

In spite of any strong support for economic externalities from education investments, it is almost universally the case, in developed and developing countries alike, that the public sector plays a dominant role in both the provision and the financing of education. This undoubtedly reflects the substantial noneconomic returns from education. For example, empirical evidence consistently supports the existence of the strong beneficial impact of maternal schooling on child mortality and fertility outcomes in developing countries (Pritchett and Summers 1996). In addition, public provision of education, especially at lower levels, is seen as crucial to promoting social cohesion. In this respect, universal access to basic education is seen as desirable. However, in developing countries there is growing concern that most of the benefits from public education expenditures has been captured by the non-poor.

In this section we focus on the distributional impact of public expenditures in the education sector. We start by examining the empirical literature from the perspective of the distributional impact of public expenditures, discussing in turn evidence from the production function and benefit incidence approaches. We finish with a discussion of the policy reforms needed to substantially increase the progressivity of public expenditures and the implications for the research agenda.

Empirical Evidence

CROSS-COUNTRY / REGION ANALYSES.   In spite of the strong emphasis on the importance of education accumulation in the economic growth process and the role of government in this accumulation process, there are numerous *cross-*

country studies that question the relationship between public education expenditures and education outcomes (Landau 1986; Noss 1991; Flug, Spilimbergo, and Wachtenheim 1998; Mingat and Tan 1998). As in the case of health, discussed earlier, this absence of a strong relationship between public education expenditures and education outcomes could reflect (1) an inappropriate allocation of expenditures across education levels (i.e., across primary, secondary, and tertiary education), (2) an inappropriate composition of inputs purchased by existing expenditures (e.g., across salaries, teaching materials, and infrastructure), or (3) an inefficient use of existing inputs (e.g., reflecting inadequate monitoring and incentive systems).

For example, Gupta, Verhoeven, and Tiongson (1999) found that when one controls for the composition of expenditures across education levels, one generally finds a statistically significant positive relationship between total education expenditures and both enrollment (in primary and secondary school combined) and grade achievement. A percentage point of GDP increase in spending on education increases gross secondary enrollment by more than 3 percentage points. The authors also found that a 5 percentage point increase in the share of primary and secondary expenditures increases gross secondary enrollment by 1 percentage point. The finding that impact increases with the share of primary and secondary expenditures is also consistent with the belief that market failures are most important at these levels, that is, the crowding-out of private expenditures by government spending is less of a problem in these areas. To the extent that increasing primary and secondary expenditures reflects extensive expansion into poorer rural areas, this is also consistent with the fact that the poor are more constrained by market failures and low incomes. In terms of use of expenditures, Gallagher (1993) found that education expenditures did have a positive impact on education outcomes once one controlled for its quality and efficiency. In a more recent paper, Rajkumar and Swaroop (2002) found that the link between education expenditures and education attainment is greater in countries with better governance.

Taken together, these findings suggest that the lack of any strong association between public education expenditures and education outcomes in part reflects the inappropriate use of these expenditures, with too much allocated to tertiary (and possibly secondary) levels and an inefficient use of resources. But it is also clear that other factors, such as demographics, urbanization, initial education levels, and income, are also very important determinants of education outcomes, suggesting that other policy levers are also important and that these may be complementary to direct education interventions.

An interesting policy question is whether private education provision is more efficient. Jimenez and Lockheed (1989) assessed the relative efficiency of public versus private education in several developing countries by comparing the ratio of their test scores to their average cost per pupil and found that the public sector is always more costly. However, this may reflect self-selection bias, with the private schools locating in areas where education provision is cheaper (e.g., urban areas), or the best pupils (e.g., those with greater ability or socioeconomic conditions conducive to learning) may self-select into private schools. One therefore needs to be careful when interpreting these results in terms of efficiency.

There is some evidence on expenditure effectiveness from cross-regional data. Pitt, Rosenzweig, and Gibbons (1995), using Indonesian household-level survey and census data together with sub-district-level program data for two points in time (i.e., 1980 and 1985), estimated the effect of access to schools on attendance rates for boys and girls aged 10–14 years and 15–18 years. They found that the presence of grade schools and middle schools has significant effects on attendance rates, which are significantly higher for households where the mother has little or no schooling.

HOUSEHOLD CROSS-SECTION ANALYSES.　Most often, the policy debate in education is couched in terms of the competing goals of quality versus access, that is, improving the quality of existing schools versus increasing access by building more schools. We can take as our starting point in this debate survey of empirical literature on education by Hanushek (1995), who identified quality as the important constraint in relation to increasing education levels. Based on his review, he argued that there is no systematic relationship between inputs and outcomes and that our inability to explain much of the variation in outcomes reflects our poor understanding of a complex education process. For this reason he argued for a shift in emphasis toward the decentralization of "process" and "resource" decisions to schools, backed up by a system of carrots and sticks linked to performance. Such an approach requires the specification of desirable goals and a mechanism for measuring performance. Because we have little experience of such systems, even in developed countries, it is necessary to allow and monitor experiments in these directions in an attempt to identify better organizational forms. However, it is important to keep in mind that decentralizing education decisions on the basis of a narrow set of incentives may have perverse consequences. For example, if schools are judged by results, they may respond by promoting only the best students and force others to repeat grades.

On the other hand, based on the same literature, Kremer (1995) argues that when one weights empirical studies according to the quality of their analyses, the evidence suggests that expenditures on basic inputs such as radio education and textbooks will improve school quality. Indeed, it is accepted that the provision of such basic inputs as a decent building, a teacher, textbooks, a blackboard, and so on is necessary to provide quality education. Although Kremer accepts that reducing class size is a lower priority, he argues that once a minimum level of quality is achieved, higher priority should be given to either extensive expansion or subsidization of schooling, both of which tend to promote increased enrollments among poorer households. He also argues that although it may be desirable to decentralize spending on education, as long as school systems are centralized, policymakers should allocate resources on the basis of the average impact. Even though the impact of additional resources varies with circumstances (e.g., with management capability), textbooks should be provided to all schools, even though the may go to waste in some of them.

When evaluating the role of quality, where possible one needs to include information not only on "resources" but also on the "process" of education. For example, Glewwe et al. (1995) reviewed a wide range of inputs, capturing both resource and process factors in the context of Jamaican primary schools in 1990. Over 40 school and teacher characteristics were examined, including pedagogical processes and management structures. However, most variables had statistically insignificant effects. Their results suggest that student achievement also responds to various pedagogical factors, such as the amount of time devoted to instruction and the use of written assignments. The largest impact was found for textbook use for instructional purposes, which raised reading scores by 1.6 standard deviations.

Some studies have looked at the impact of decentralization on decision-making. Jimenez and Sawada (1999) found that schools in El Salvador, which are run by parent committees that can purchase school equipment and hire and fire teachers, outperform other schools in terms of reading skills (by as much as 1.3 standard deviations) and daily attendance (by 3–4 days in the past 4 weeks). In another paper, King and Ozler (2000) examined the relative performance of autonomous primary schools in Nicaragua that use teacher, parent, and student councils to select textbooks, set school fees, and hire and fire the school principal. They found that de facto autonomy is associated with higher scores only for math and only at the 10 percent level. However, Glewwe (2002) highlights the important shortcomings in the strategy used in both these studies for dealing with self-selection issues. Eskeland and Filmer (2000) also provide evidence that the combination of school autonomy and parental participation is positively associated with test scores for children in grades 6 and 7 in Argentina. However, from the perspective of improving educational outcomes for the poorest households, one could argue that autonomy is likely to work only in areas where parents and teachers already are more motivated and enrollment is likely to be high. It is arguable, then, whether such policies are really relevant for schools in the poorest areas.

Since the mid-1990s, motivated by research from developed countries (Angrist and Lavy 1999; Krueger 1999), attempts have been made to reassess the issue of the causal relationship between school inputs (in particular, teacher-pupil ratios) and education outcomes. Case and Deaton (1999) examined the effects of pupil-teacher ratios and school facilities on educational outcomes in South Africa, including school attendance, educational attainment, and test scores. They found strong and significant effects of pupil-teacher ratios on enrollment, educational achievement, and test scores for numeracy, with these impacts important mainly at low resource levels. In the context of rural Bolivia, Urquiola (2001) also found that class size has a negative and significant impact on test scores. In their analysis of enrollment and performance outcomes in primary schools in India, Drèze and Kingdon (2001) also found that class size is important. But so are a whole range of factors proxying resource and process issues, highlighting the importance of a comprehensive view of the determinants of education outcomes. Of particular interest is a finding regarding the strong positive impact of school meals on female school participation; the provision of a mid-day meal in the local school roughly halves the proportion of girls excluded from the schooling system. This finding highlights the impact that such conditioned transfers (i.e., conditioned on attendance) can have on education outcomes, an issue that we will return to later.

Most would accept that improving quality to basic levels, including teacher-student ratios, is likely to have an impact. In this respect, recent policies in India are of special interest. In spite of an aggressive school-building program in the 1970s, primary school attendance has remained low, and many argue that poor school quality lies at the root of this problem, especially in the poorest areas (PROBE Team 1999). In response to this, the government of India introduced "Operation Blackboard" in 1987, under which it was to provide a second teacher to all single-teacher primary schools and a teaching-learning equipment set to all primary schools. Results of a study by Chin (2000) indicate that the program significantly increased primary school completion and literacy for girls, by 3–4 and 2–3 percentage points, respectively, but had no effect on boys.

As indicated earlier, because of the myriad estimation difficulties associated with cross-section studies, one needs to be very careful how one interprets empirical findings and individual coefficients. For example, a positive coefficient on quality variables may best be interpreted as meaning "quality matters" without attaching any cause-and-effect interpretation to the individual variable used. The issue of interpretation of empirical results is brought strongly to the fore when considering the related issue of cost-effectiveness. Undertaking cost-effectiveness analysis makes sense only when one is confident that one can identify a precise set of inputs, which can be costed out and lead to a precisely identified average impact. Although there are strong reservations on these grounds, because the issue of cost-effectiveness is of more policy importance, a small number of studies have either calculated cost-effectiveness ratios for alternative interventions or provided sufficient information for such ratios to be calculated. Generally speaking, these results suggest that expenditures on instructional materials are substantially more cost-effective than those on infrastructure, which in turn are slightly more cost-effective than those on teachers' salaries (Pritchett and Filmer 1999, 227–229; Glewwe 2002).

There is also some evidence that extensive expansion (i.e., school-building) is a cost-effective strategy for increasing enrollments from a relatively low base. Handa and Simler (2000) found that extensive expansion is much more cost-effective than intensive expansion in increasing school enrollment, whereas it is only slightly more cost-effective in increasing student achievement. Intensive expansion came out as marginally more cost-effective than is extensive expansion in improving the average number of years successfully completed, but they argue that even this might be reversed if one were to add in the cost of training more teachers. Duflo (2001) analyzed the impact of the extensive expansion (school construction) program in Indonesia between 1973 and 1978. The results indicate that each primary school constructed per 1,000 children led to an average increase of 0.12–0.19 years of education. Of course, extensive expansion also requires that the expansion be of a certain minimum quality to be effective in generating the desired education outcomes.

Because improving access to private schooling is often perceived as a mechanism for reducing pressures on the public education budget and possibly more cost-effective than public education in providing education, it is also important to understand how effective such a strategy can be. One of the few studies in this area was by Angrist et al. (2001), who evaluated the impact of a voucher system for private schooling in urban Colombia. They found that access to vouchers did not increase the probability of enrollment, although there could have been an indirect effect on enrollment in that those taking a voucher may have released a place in overcrowded public schools, which were frequently turning away students for lack of places. (This is less likely to be a problem in lower-income developing countries.) But access did reduce grade repetition by 5–6 percentage points (from about 20 percent), resulting in around an additional 0.12–0.16 years of schooling (from around an average of 7.5 years). However, there is some concern that private schools may have had an incentive to promote students with vouchers even if their performance did not meet normal promotional standards. In addition, beneficiaries scored 0.13–0.2 standard deviations higher on standardized tests for math, reading, and writing, but only the impact for reading was significant at even the 10 percent level. There is also evidence that these effects were larger for girls than for boys.

PROGRAM EVALUATIONS.   As indicated earlier in the case of health, because of the myriad estimation problems associated with using cross-section data to analyze the determinants of education outcomes, evidence from randomized trials is of particular interest. One of the first program evaluation studies for developing countries was that by Jamison et al. (1981) for Nicaragua. The results indicated that investments in radio instruction raised test scores by 1.2 standard deviations, while textbook investments raised scores by a third of a standard deviation. Unfortunately, no cost-effectiveness analysis was undertaken. Heyneman, Jamison, and Montenegro (1984) evaluated a similar program in the Philippines for students in grades 1 and 2 of primary school. The results indicate that investments in textbooks for science, math, and languages increased average test scores by 0.4 standard deviations, although there was no difference in outcomes when books were shared, one for every two students. In the context of Kenya, Kremer et al. (1997) and Glewwe, Kremer, and Moulin (2007) found that textbooks improved test scores only for better students.

Tan, Lane, and Lassibille (1997) also evaluated the impact of a program in the Philippines by comparing the impacts of school feeding, learning materials for teachers, and each combined with structured parent-teacher partnerships. Their study looked at the impacts on both dropout rates and test scores, but the former were found to be negligible. School feeding combined with parent-teacher partnerships had significant impacts, ranging from 0.28 to 0.44 standard deviations for math, Filipino, and English test scores. The combined learning materials and parent-teacher partnerships had substantial impacts, ranging between 0.23 and 1.05 standard deviations, but only for languages. School feeding had statistically significant impacts on English and math scores, while learning materials had only small and insignificant impacts.

More recently, three important detailed program evaluations have become available, namely the evaluation of Bangladesh's "food-for-education" (FFE) program and evaluations of both Mexico's and Nicaragua's "cash-for-education" (CFE) programs.[7] In 1993, Bangladesh introduced its FFE program, which provides a free monthly ration of foodgrains to poor families if their children attend primary school. Based on data collected after the implementation of the program and using nearby villages as "controls," Ahmed and del Ninno (2001) found that enrollment increased by 5 to 10 percent. Using matching techniques, Ravallion and Wodon (1999) estimated that enrollment increased by 17 percent.

The recent evaluation of Mexico's CFE program (PROGRESA) is especially important because it allowed analysts to overcome many of the estimation problems encountered in previous evaluations. The program was introduced in August 1997 in rural areas. Beneficiaries receive payments for each child enrolled in grades 3–6 of primary and grades 7–9 of junior secondary school, with the transfer levels increasing by grade and being slightly higher for females at the secondary level. Because of the relatively high enrollments that already existed over the primary grades, most of the program impact was seen over the secondary grades, where it was heavily concentrated at the transition from primary to secondary school (Schultz 2000a,b; Skoufias 2000). The program increased enrollments by 7.2–9.3 percentage points for girls (from an initial enrollment rate of 67 percent) and by a lower 3.5–5.8 percentage points for boys (from an initial enrollment rate of 73 percent). If children were to participate in the program between the ages of 6 and 14 years, this would result in 19 percent more children attending secondary school (Behrman, Sengupta, and Todd 2001). As a result of the program, the differences in education outcomes between the poor and the non-poor were also substantially reduced. Coady and Parker (2001) show that the use of conditional transfers (i.e., education subsi-

7. See Morley and Coady (2004) for a more detailed description of these and similar programs.

dies) was a substantially more cost-effective policy instrument (i.e., around 10 times more cost-effective) than the extensive expansion that took place simultaneous with the program. These results suggest that, subject to the provision of a minimum quality of education, well-targeted education subsidies constitute a very cost-effective approach to improving the education status of children from poor families.

A similar program (the RPS) was introduced in Nicaragua in 2000, but with substantially lower transfers (in terms of U.S. dollars) and focusing only on the first four grades of primary school. The education impacts have been very impressive. Enrollment rates in the affected communities were around 69 percent before the program, and the program increased this by 22 percentage points, to 91 percent. There is also evidence that the educational impact was greatest for the poorest households, for which enrollment rates increased by 30 percentage points from an enrollment rate of 66 percent before the program. The impact of the program on progression rates also looks substantial. On average, the program increased progression rates by 8.5 percentage points from a base of around 85 percent, but again, there is evidence that this increase was greatest, 9.3 percentage points, for the poorest households. It is also clear that, as in PROGRESA, this impact was the greatest for the higher grades in primary school, with the progression rate from grade 4 to grade 5 increasing from around 80 percent to 92 percent, an increase of 12 percentage points. The success of this program is all the more important because Nicaragua is substantially poorer than Mexico, with characteristics closer to those of lower-income countries. The findings thus provide some optimism that such programs can be successful in these lower-income countries, although country-specific circumstances should obviously influence specific design features (e.g., the emphasis on supply versus demand).

Results from an ongoing evaluation of a series of supply-side interventions in Kenyan primary schools are also now becoming available. Seven randomized trials have been conducted in rural Kenyan primary schools, measuring the impacts of (1) a standard package of inputs, including textbooks and construction materials; (2) textbooks only; (3) block grants; (4) flip charts; (5) a package of teacher incentives; (6) treatment of intestinal parasites; and (7) a standard package of preschool assistance. Kremer et al. (1997) examined the impact of the standard package. No statistically significant impact on test scores was found, but dropout rates decreased and enrollment levels increased by 35 percent (compared to a 10 percent decline in the control group).

A study by Glewwe, Kremer, and Moulin (1997) looked at the provision of textbooks. In 1996 textbooks were provided to students from grades 3 to 8 from a starting point at which very few students had access to textbooks. However, after 5 years there is little evidence of a sizable impact on test scores, except those of the better students. The lack of impact was attributed to teachers' not being trained to use the textbooks and the fact that textbooks were probably too difficult for the average student. There was also no evidence of an increase in enrollment levels. Glewwe, Jacoby, and King (2000) examined the impact of using flip charts (i.e., large poster-sized charts with instructional materials that can be mounted on walls or placed on easels) covering science, math, geography, and health. However, they found no evidence of any impact on test scores after two years, although ordinary least squares estimates indicated an impact of 0.2 standard deviations, 5–10 times greater than estimates based on the randomized trial. The most recent Kenyan study looked at the impact of a program implemented in 1998 that tries to reduce the incidence of intestinal parasites, which are endemic in rural areas (Miguel and Kremer 2001). Although attendance rates increased and dropouts decreased, there has been no significant increase on test scores.

BENEFIT INCIDENCE APPROACHES.   Because many of the issues regarding data availability closely mirror those for health, they will not be repeated here. Typically one finds that unit subsidies at the tertiary level are substantially higher than at other levels and that enrollment rates at the tertiary level are substantially higher for higher-income households. As a result, expenditures on tertiary-level education are highly regressive, and the high share of this component in total education expenditures causes total expenditures to also be highly regressive.

Of total expenditures, primary expenditures tend to be slightly progressive, secondary expenditures regressive, and tertiary expenditures very regressive (Figures 4.3–4.5). However, for primary expenditures, whether they are progressive often depends on whether one uses equal proportional or absolute transfers as one's reference for neutrality. Similarly, it makes a difference whether one focuses on children or households as the unit of analysis, because poor households tend to have more children, so focusing on children is more likely to make primary expenditures appear more progressive. But the empirical evidence strongly indicates that the distribution of primary expenditures is more or less neutral. In fact, for the lowest-income developing countries, where average primary enrollment rates are relatively low, primary expenditures are also likely to be regressive. Again, when different methodologies are employed, one needs to take great care when comparing results across countries.

Where school fees are charged, one needs to adjust expenditure allocations accordingly, taking into account that higher fees may be buying higher quality. However, rarely does one see adjustments for cost recovery from households. Although the rich have substantially higher per capita education expenditures, proportionally these are usually higher for poor households. Also, it is unclear whether the higher expenditures of the rich buy higher quality or are only tenuously related to quality (e.g., better uniforms). The existence of a private education option is also important, because the rich disproportionately take this option, and this tends to make public expenditures more progressive. For example, Selden and Wasylenko (1995) found that in both urban and rural areas,

FIGURE 4.3 Quintile shares of total education subsidies in six countries

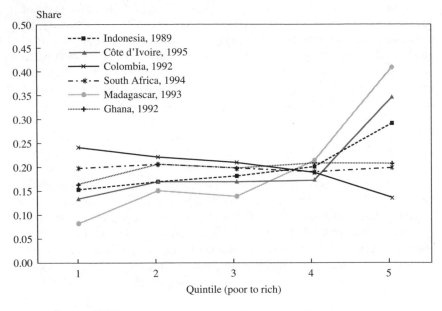

SOURCE: Demery (2003).

FIGURE 4.4 Quintile shares of primary education subsidies in six countries

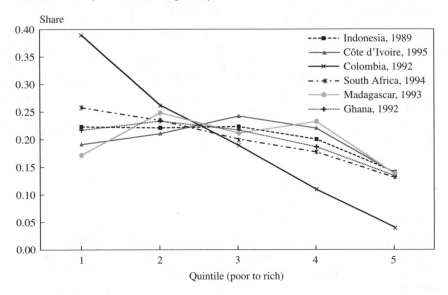

SOURCE: Demery (2003).

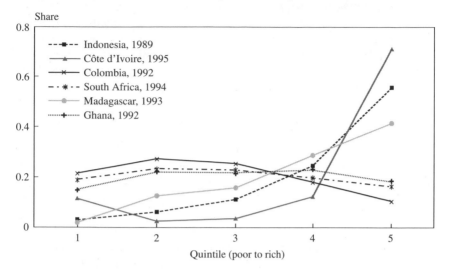

FIGURE 4.5 Quintile shares of secondary education expenditures in six countries

SOURCE: Demery (2003).

per capita expenditures for secondary school have an inverted-U pattern, starting off low for the poorest households (reflecting low enrollment rates), rising for middle-income groups, and falling to low levels again for higher-income groups (reflecting greater enrollment in private schools). In such situations, whether one views secondary expenditures as progressive or regressive will depend on the relative weights attached to low- and middle-income groups.

Analyses of expenditures over time (e.g., Lanjouw et al. 2000) have found very little change in the degree of progression in either total education expenditures or their components. This is not surprising, because one rarely sees major policy changes regarding how expenditures are allocated, and although extensive expansion is likely to be more progressive on the margin (compared to the average), the low rates of expansion observed in practice are unlikely to change the average to any great degree. When comparing results across time it is also important to control for demographic changes, because with population growth and fixed enrollment rates, primary education is more heavily weighted, which tends to make total expenditures more progressive. But increasing enrollment rates have also been found to be an important determinant of greater progressivity.

Concluding Remarks

From the preceding discussion it is clear that although there is a strong consensus regarding the need for government intervention in the education sector, there is still much debate about how best to allocate scarce public resources across competing uses within this sector. One can consider three alternative types of government education investment strategy: (1) intensive expansion (i.e., improving the quality of existing schools), (2) extensive expansion (i.e., building more schools), and (3) the provision of education subsidies (i.e., transfers conditioned on attending school). What constitutes an appropriate distribution of scarce resources across these competing uses will depend on the precise policy objectives, such as increasing average enrollment or performance versus ensuring more equal access. For the most part, we are concerned here with identifying policies that improve access or performance for the poorest households.

The available evidence suggests the following stylized conclusions. First, public expenditures on education in developing countries are typically regressive, reflecting the large budget share of expenditures going to tertiary-level education. But even expenditures on primary education are at best only slightly progressive. Second, extensive expansion is worthwhile only if basic quality is maintained (e.g., access to basic infrastructure and instructional resources, including teachers or instructors who turn up and are motivated to teach). Third, once a basic level of quality is attained, intensive expansion is more likely to have an effect on improving student performance than on increasing enrollment and is thus likely to be only slightly progressive even if confined to primary education. Fourth, although extensive expansion is likely to be more progressive on the margin, when initial enrollment levels are relatively high it is unlikely to be a cost-effective way of improving the equality of access relative to better-targeted expenditures. In such circumstances, targeted education subsidies may be a relatively cost-effective way of making education more accessible to children from the poorest households. Finally, reflecting the nature of the underlying market failures in this sector, better targeting of expenditures, both to children at lower levels of education (i.e., in primary and secondary school) and to poorer households, is likely not only to improve the distributional impact of these expenditures but also to increase their overall effectiveness in terms of improved aggregate education outcomes.

It is clear, though, that our detailed knowledge regarding public education expenditures, education resources, the education process, and education outcomes is still very limited. This suggests several important areas for research. First, we need to improve our understanding of the relationship between the education process and outcomes. In particular, we need to be more open to alternative, possibly very cost-effective, ways of providing education to children (e.g., education technologies using radio and television communication or other means requiring smaller investments, such as public transport). Second, we need to improve our understanding of the role that community and other nongovernment organizations can play in enhancing the effectiveness of public expenditures, particularly in the context of decentralization of budgeting and service delivery in low-income countries with low capacity in these areas. But it is important to realize that these issues are still debated even in developed countries, and because consensus on best practice may take some time, policymakers need to better use what we know in order to achieve their objectives.

Building up knowledge in these areas requires a shift in emphasis in the allocation of research resources. First, there should be a greater recognition of the need for experimental evaluation designs given the extreme difficulty associated with getting credible results using cross-sectional and household-, regional-, and country-level data sets. Second, there is a need for a greater emphasis on extending impact analyses to incorporate the need for cost-effectiveness analyses, which are of important policy relevance for low-income countries with very scarce resources. It is also important to set investment programs within the context of public finances, because expansion requires either a reallocation of existing resources or the raising of new resources through reforming pricing policies or increasing taxation. Third, given our limited knowledge of the education process, particularly with respect to enhancing the education of the poorest segments of society, it is important to combine both quantitative and qualitative analytical approaches in order to better understand how program inputs translate into program impacts.

For a research program to have much added value, it is necessary that it address all of these issues. The recent research work at IFPRI has been a major step in this direction. The research into the impacts of targeted education subsidies in Bangladesh (FFE), Mexico (PROGRESA), Honduras (PRAF), and Nicaragua (RPS) has emphasized the use of experimental evaluation techniques, the issue of operational capacity, the use of a combination of quantitative and qualitative research methods, and the examination of their relative cost-effectiveness and the general-equilibrium implications for government budgets and the distribution of tax incidence. It is important, however, that these analyses be extended to address the issues of the education process as well as the potential role of community and other nongovernmental organizations in enhancing the effectiveness of public education expenditures and the implications for the decentralization of budgets and the choice and/or implementation of delivery mechanisms. Experimentation alone is unlikely to provide useful insights in the absence of a carefully designed evaluation of effectiveness.

References

Ahmed, A., and C. del Ninno. 2001. Food for education program in Bangladesh: An evaluation of its impact on educational attainment and food security. Mimeo, International Food Policy Research Institute, Washington, D.C.

Alderman, H., and K. Lindert. 1998. The potential and limitations of self-targeted food subsidies. *World Bank Research Observer* 13 (2): 213–229.

Allen, L., and S. Gillespie. 2001. *What works? A review of the efficacy and effectiveness of nutrition interventions.* Asian Development Bank. Washington, D.C.: International Food Policy Research Institute.

Anand, S., and M. Ravallion 1993. Human development in poor countries: On the role of private incomes and public services. *Journal of Economic Perspectives* 7 (1): 133–150.

Angrist, J., and V. Lavy. 1999. Using Maimonides' rule to estimate the effects of class size on scholastic achievement. *Quarterly Journal of Economics* 114: 533–575.

Angrist, J., E. Bettinger, E. Bloom, E. King, and M. Kremer. 2001. Vouchers for private schooling in Colombia: Evidence from a randomized natural experiment. NBER Working Paper 8343. Cambridge, Mass.: National Bureau of Economic Research.

Barro, R., and X. Sala-i-Martin. 1995. *Economic growth.* Cambridge, Mass.: MIT Press.

Becker, G. 1995. Human capital and poverty alleviation. Human Capital Development Operations, Policy Working Paper 52. Washington, D.C.: World Bank.

Behrman, J., M. Sengupta, and P. Todd. 2001. Progressing through PROGRESA: An impact assessment of a school subsidy experiment in Mexico. Mimeo, University of Pennsylvania, Philadelphia.

Bidani, B., and M. Ravallion. 1997. Decomposing social indicators using distributional data. *Journal of Econometrics* 77 (1): 125–139.

Bloom, D., and D. Canning. 2003. The health and poverty of nations: From theory to practice. *Journal of Human Development* 4 (1): 47–71.

Bonilla-Chacin, M., and J. Hammer. 1999: Life and death among the poor. The Johns Hopkins University and the World Bank Development Research Group, Baltimore and Washington, D.C. Mimeo.

Case, A., and A. Deaton. 1999. School inputs and educational outcomes in South Africa. *Quarterly Journal of Economics* 114 (3): 1047–1084.

Chin, A. 2000. The returns to school quality when school quality is very low: Evidence from Operation Blackboard in India. University of Houston, November. Mimeo.

Coady, D., and S. Parker. 2001. A cost-effectiveness analysis of demand- and supply-side education interventions: The case of PROGRESA in Mexico. *Review of Development Economics* 8 (3): 440–451.

Coady, D. P., D. P. Filmer, and D. R. Gwatkin. 2005. PROGRESA for Progress: Mexico's health, nutrition, and education program. *Development Outreach,* May (Special Issue). Available at <www1.worldbank.org/devoutreach/may05/article .asp?id=296> (accessed November 2007).

Demery, L. 2003. Analyzing the incidence of public spending. In *The impact of economic policies on poverty and income distribution: Evaluation techniques and tools,* ed. F. Bourguignon and L. Pereira da Silva. Washington, D.C.: World Bank.

Dow, W., P. Gertler, R. Schoeni, J. Strauss, and D. Thomas. 2001. Health care prices, health and labor outcomes: Experimental evidence. Labor and Population Program Working Paper 97–01. Santa Monica, Calif.: RAND Corporation.

Drèze, J., and G. Kingdon. 2001. School participation in rural India. *Review of Development Economics* 5 (1): 1–24.

Drèze , J., and A. Sen. 1989. *Hunger and public action.* Oxford, England: Oxford University Press.

Duflo, Esther. 2000. Child health and household resources in South Africa: Evidence from the Old Age Pension program. *American Economic Review* 90 (2): 393–398.

Eskeland, G., and D. Filmer. 2000. Autonomy, participation and learning in Argentine schools: Findings and their implications for decentralization. World Bank, Washington, D.C.

Filmer, D., and L. Pritchett 1999. The impact of public spending on health: Does money matter? *Social Science and Medicine* 49: 1309–1323.

Filmer, D., J. Hammer, and L. Pritchett. 2000. Weak links in the chain: A diagnosis of health policy in poor countries. *World Bank Research Observer* 15 (2): 199–224.

Flug, K., A. Spilimbergo, and E. Wachtenheim. 1998. Investment in education: Do economic volatility and credit constraints matter? *Journal of Development Economics* 55: 465–481.

Gallagher, M. 1993. A public choice theory of budgets: Implications for education in less developed countries. *Comparative Education Review* 37 (2): 90–106.

Gertler, P. 2004. Do conditional cash transfers improve child health? Evidence from PROGRESA's controlled randomized experiment. AER Papers and Proceedings. *American Economic Review* 94 (2): 336–341.

Gertler, P., and J. van der Gaag. 1990. *The willingness to pay for medical care: Evidence from two developing countries.* Baltimore, Md.: The Johns Hopkins University Press.

Gillespie, S., and L. Haddad. 2001. Attacking the double burden of malnutrition in Asia and the Pacific. ADB Nutrition and Development Series 4. Manila: Asian Development Bank.

Glewwe, P. 2002. Schools and skills in developing countries: Education policies and socioeconomic outcomes. *Journal of Economic Literature* 40: 436–482.

Glewwe, P., H. Jacoby, and E. King. 2000. Early childhood nutrition and academic achievement: A longitudinal analysis. *Journal of Public Economics* 81 (3): 345–368.

Glewwe, P., M. Kremer, and S. Moulin. 2007. Textbooks and test scores: Evidence from a prospective evaluation in Kenya. Working Paper 169, August. Cambridge, Mass.: Harvard University.

Glewwe, P., M. Grosh, H. Jacoby, and M. Lockheed. 1995. An eclectic approach to estimating the determinants of achievement in Jamaican primary education. *World Bank Economic Review* 9 (2): 231–258.

Gupta, S., M. Verhoeven, and E. Tiongson. 1999. Does higher government spending buy better results in education and health care? Working Paper 99/21. Washington, D.C.: International Monetary Fund.

Gwatkin, D. 2000. Health inequalities and the health of the poor: What do we know? What can we do? *Bulletin of the World Health Organization* 78 (1): 48–54.

Haddad, L., H. Alderman, S. Appleton, and L. Song. 2003. Reducing child malnutrition: How far does income growth take us? *World Bank Economic Review* 17 (1): 107–131.

Handa, A., and K. Simler. 2000. Quality or quantity? The supply-side determinants of primary schooling in rural Mozambique. Discussion Paper 83. Food Consumption Nutrition Division. Washington, D.C.: International Food Policy Research Institute.

Hanushek, E. 1995. Interpreting recent research on schooling in developing countries. *World Bank Research Observer* 10 (2): 227–246.

Heyneman, S., D. Jamison, and X. Montenegro. 1984. Textbooks in the Philippines: Evaluation of the pedagogical impact of a nationwide investment. *Education Evaluation Policy Analysis* 6 (2): 556–567.

Hoddinott, J., E. Skoufias, and R. Washburn. 2000. Final report: The impact of PROGRESA on consumption. August. International Food Policy Research Institute, Washington, D.C.

Hojman, D. 1996. Economic and other determinants of infant and child mortality in small developing countries: The case of Central America and the Caribbean. *Applied Economics* 28 (3): 281–290.

Jamison, D., B. Searle, K. Galda, and S. Heyneman. 1981. Improving elementary mathematics in Nicaragua: An experimental study of the impact of textbooks and radio on achievement. *Journal of Educational Psychology* 73 (4): 556–567.

Jimenez, E., and M. Lockeed. 1989. Enhancing girls' learning through single-sex education: Evidence and a policy conundrum. *Educational Evaluation and Policy Analysis* 11 (2): 117–142.

Jimenez, E., and Y. Sawada. 1999. Do community-managed schools work? An evaluation of El Salvador's EDUCO Program. *World Bank Economic Review* 13 (3): 415–441.

King, E., and B. Ozler. 2000. What's decentralization got to do with learning? Endogenous school quality and student performance in Nicaragua. Development Research Group, World Bank, Washington, D.C.

Koenig M., V. Faveau, and B. Wojtyniak. 1991. Mortality reductions from health interventions: The case of immunization in Bangladesh. *Population and Development Review* 17: 87–104.

Kremer, M. 1995. Research on schooling: What we know and what we don't (A comment on Hanushek). *World Bank Research Observer* 10 (2): 247–254.

Kremer, M., S. Moulin, R. Namunyu, and D. Myatt. 1997. The quantity-quality trade-off in education: Evidence from a prospective evaluation in Kenya. Mimeo, Harvard University, Cambridge, Mass.

Krueger, A. 1999. Experimental estimates of education production functions. *Quarterly Journal of Economics* 114: 479–532.

Landau, D. 1986. Government and economic growth in less developed countries: An empirical study for 1960–80. *Economic Development and Cultural Change* 35 (1): 35–75.

Lanjouw, P., M. Pradhan, F. Saadah, H. Sayed, and R. Sparrow. 2000. Poverty, education and health in Indonesia: Who benefits from public spending. November. Mimeo, World Bank, Washington, D.C.

Maluccio, J., and R. Flores. 2006. *Impact evaluation of a conditional cash transfer program: The Nicaraguan Red de Proteccion Social.* Research Report 141. Washington, D.C. International Food Policy Research Institute.

McPake, B., K. Hanson, and A. Mills. 1993. Community financing of health care in Africa: An evaluation of the Bamako initiative. *Social Science Medicine* 36 (11): 1383–1395.

Meerman, J. 1979. *Public expenditures in Malaysia: Who benefits and why?* New York: Oxford University Press.

Menken, J., and J. Phillips. 1990. Population change in a rural area of Bangladesh, 1967–87. *The Annals* 510: 87–101.

Miguel, E., and M. Kremer. 2001. Worms: Education and health externalities in Kenya. NBER Working Paper 8481. Cambridge, Mass.: National Bureau of Economic Research.

Mingat, A., and J. - P. Tan. 1998. The mechanics of progress in education: Evidence from cross-country data. Policy Research Working Paper 2015. Washington, D.C.: World Bank.

Morley, S., and D. Coady. 2004. *From social assistance to social development.* Washington, D.C.: Center for Global Development and International Food Policy Research Institute.

Noss, A. 1991. Education and adjustment: A review of the literature. PREM Working Paper 701. Washington, D.C.: World Bank.

Pitt, M., M. Rosenzweig, and D. Gibbons. 1995. The determinants and consequences of the placement of government programs in Indonesia. In *Public spending and the poor: Theory and evidence,* ed. D. van de Walle and K. Nead. Baltimore, Md.: The Johns Hopkins University Press.

Pritchett, L. 2001. Where has all the education gone? *World Bank Economic Review* 15 (3): 367–391.

Pritchett, L., and D. Filmer. 1999. What education production functions really show: A positive theory of education expenditures. *Economic Education Review* 18 (2): 223–239.

Pritchett, L., and L. Summers. 1996. Where has all the education gone? Policy Research Paper 1581. Washington, D.C.: World Bank.

PROBE Team. 1999. *Public report on basic education in India.* New Delhi: Oxford University Press.

Psacharopoulos, G. 1994. Returns to investment in education: A global update. *World Development* 22 (9): 1325–1343.

Rajkumar, A., and V. Swaroop. 2002. Public spending and outcomes: Does governance matter? Working Paper 2840; Washington, D.C.: World Bank.

Ravallion, M., and Q. Wodon. 1999. Does child labor displace schooling? Evidence on behavioral responses to an enrollment subsidy. World Bank Policy Research Working Paper 2118. Washington, D.C.: World Bank.

Russel, S., and L. Gilson. 1997. User fee policies to promote health service access for the poor: A wolf in sheep's clothing. *International Journal of Health Series* 27 (2): 359–379.

Schultz, T. P. 2000a. Final report: The impact of PROGRESA on school enrollments. April. International Food Policy Research Institute, Washington, D.C.

———. 2000b. School subsidies for the poor: Evaluating a Mexican strategy for reducing poverty. Final report submitted to PROGRESA (Mexico). International Food Policy Research Institute, Washington, D.C. Available at <www.ifpri.org/themes/progresa/pdf/Schultz_schsubsidy.pdf> (accessed November 2007).

Selden, T., and M. Wasylenko. 1995. Measuring the distributional effects of public education in Peru. In *Public spending and the poor: Theory and evidence,* ed. D. van de Walle and K. Nead. Baltimore, Md.: The John Hopkins University Press.

Selowsky, M. 1979. *Who benefits from government expenditures? A case study of Colombia.* New York: Oxford University Press.

Shah, A. 2005. *Public expenditure analysis.* Public Sector Governance and Accountability Series. Washington, D.C.: World Bank.

Skoufias, E. 2000. Is PROGRESA working? Summary of the results of an evaluation by IFPRI. Discussion Paper 118, Food Consumption Nutrition Division. Washington, D.C.: International Food Policy Research Institute.

Strauss, J., and D. Thomas. 1998. Health, nutrition and economic development. *Journal of Economic Literature* 36 (2): 766–817.

———. 1995. Human resources: Empirical modeling of household and family decisions. In *Handbook of development economics,* Vol. 3A, ed. J. R. Behrman and T. N. Srinivasan. Amsterdam: North-Holland Publishing, 1883–2024.

Tan, J., J. Lane, and P. Lassibille. 1997. Putting inputs to work in elementary schools: What can be done in the Philippines? *Economic Development and Cultural Change* 45: 857–879.

Urquiola, M. 2001. Identifying class-size effects in developing countries: Evidence from rural schools in Bolivia. Mimeo, World Bank, Washington, D.C.

van de Walle, D. 1995. The distribution of subsidies through public health services in Indonesia, 1978–87. In *Public spending and the poor: Theory and evidence,* ed. D. van de Walle and K. Nead. Baltimore, Md.: The John Hopkins University Press.

Wagstaff, A., and N. Watanbe. 2000. Socioeconomic inequalities in child malnutrition in the developing world. Policy Research Working Paper 2434. Washington, D.C.: World Bank.

WHO (World Health Organization). 2001. Macroeconomics and health: Investing in health for economic development. Report of the Commission on Macroeconomics and Health, Geneva. Background papers available at <www.cmhealth.org/ cmh_papers&reports.htm> (accessed March 2003).

WHO/UNICEF (World Health Organization / United Nations Children's Fund). 1978. *International Conference on Primary Health Care,* Alma-Ata, UDDR.

World Bank. 1987. *Financing health services in developing countries: An agenda for reform.* Washington, D.C.

———. 1993. *World development report 1993.* New York: Oxford University Press.

———. 1994. *Better health in Africa: Lessons and experiences learned.* Washington, D.C.

———. 1995. Priorities and strategies for education: A World Bank review. Development in Practice Series. Washington, D.C.

———. 1998. Handbook on economic analysis of investment operations. Draft. Washington, D.C.

———. 2001. *World development report.* Washington, D.C.

———. 2004. *World development report.* Washington, D.C.

5 Social Safety Nets

DAVID COADY

Although there has been an emerging consensus that renewed "broad-based" economic growth is a necessary condition for alleviating poverty within an acceptable time frame, in isolation it is not sufficient (World Bank 1997).[1] In particular, it is now widely accepted that effective social safety nets are an important component of an effective poverty alleviation strategy. In fact, public safety net programs are the only hope of many of the world's poor for a life free from chronic poverty, malnutrition, and disease. The importance of these transfers is magnified insofar as informal private networks (e.g., based on kinship or community) are thought to become less effective in environments that experience extensive economic and political reforms, tighter budget constraints, and increasing commercialization and urbanization.

In spite of the growing recognition of the importance of social safety nets in the development and poverty alleviation process, as practiced these transfer programs often have a number of shortcomings that undermine their effectiveness.[2] First, the transfers often fail to reach the most vulnerable groups. Second, transfer programs are often not very cost-effective in that much of the poverty alleviation budget is eaten up by unnecessarily large administrative costs. In addition, many programs are rife with corruption and operational inefficiencies, resulting in theft or other losses that reduce the resources available to be distributed to vulnerable households. Third, social safety net systems are often made up of myriad uncoordinated components that need to be better integrated in pursuit of a common set of objectives in order to be more effective. Fourth, social safety net programs usually have a short-term focus on alleviating only current poverty and thus generally fail to generate a sustained decrease in poverty independent of the transfers themselves. In fact, their design can of-

The views expressed in this chapter are those of the author and should not be attributed to the International Monetary Fund, its executive board, or its management.

1. See Sahn and Stifel (2000) and Haddad et al. (2002) for a more detailed cross-country discussion.

2. For more detail see Smith and Subbarao (2000) and Coady, Grosh, and Hoddinott (2004a,b).

148   *David Coady*

ten introduce perverse incentives in order to meet eligibility criteria (e.g., in terms of reducing labor supply and earned income, replacing private transfers with public ones, or reducing savings and asset accumulation). Achieving the right balance between incentives and public support is difficult but important.

In this chapter we evaluate the distributional impact of typical social safety net expenditures, which are usually incorporated under "social security expenditures" in government accounts. In Chapter 2 we saw that these expenditures account for a sizable proportion of total government expenditures (similar to the size of health expenditures in many countries), especially in Latin America, where in 1998 they accounted for over 25 percent of total public expenditures. These expenditures are also often referred to as "social assistance," reflecting their primary objective of increasing the current welfare of poor households. We first look at food subsidies, including both universal and administratively targeted food subsidies. We then discuss public works schemes that aim to employ the poor on projects that maintain or create community assets.[3] More recently, social fund projects have become very popular, especially in Latin America.[4] Finally, we discuss human capital subsidies (i.e., transfers conditioned on children of the poor attending school or health clinics), which have recently become popular, again especially in Latin America. Invariably, household-level data from many developing countries show that the poorest households are poor not only in terms of income and consumption levels, but also in terms of human capital status (i.e., nutrition, health, and education). This discussion also provides a useful link with Chapter 4 on human capital expenditures.

Reflecting the conceptual methodology set out in Chapter 1, we take as the objective of these expenditures the improvement of the short-run and long-run welfare of the poorest households through direct transfers (either cash or in-kind). A transfer itself is intended to increase current welfare through an immediate increase in consumption of goods and services, but also to increase long-term welfare through providing incentives for the accumulation of physical or human capital. The latter is typically accomplished by conditioning the transfers on household or community behavior that enhances the accumulation of human or physical capital. While the need for transfers is motivated by a pure redistributive objective and the recognition that many households will not benefit from growth in the short run, the conditioning of transfers is typically rationalized by appealing to the existence of market failures that result in investment levels by poor households that are well below optimal (e.g., the existence of

---

3. Traditionally, although these projects involve the construction of infrastructure that can enhance future incomes, it has usually been the transfer component through wages that has been emphasized, especially in Asia and Africa.

4. Social funds usually differ from public works in that they put more emphasis on the asset creation side and are demand driven insofar as they require communities to identify and propose projects as well as to provide some matching financing.

credit or information constraints). An ability to identify poor households and efficiently deliver to them transfers and other complementary services (e.g., well-managed public works or nutrition, health, and education services) is, of course, crucial to the cost-effectiveness of these policy instruments.

For each of the different expenditure types, in turn, we identify the design issues that need to be addressed in order to rectify the shortcomings commonly found in practice. The institutional features determining implementation effectiveness are also discussed. Although the chapter focuses primarily on the contribution of research undertaken at or through the International Food Policy Research Institute (IFPRI), this contribution is placed within the literature more generally. However, the discussion of the literature more generally is intended to identify the relevant analytical and policy issues that arise and is thus not meant to be a comprehensive review. In addition, although the expenditures discussed here under social safety net expenditures are by no means exhaustive of the myriad components one finds in these systems, together they do tend to account for a very large proportion of total social safety net expenditures, and many of the issues raised apply equally to these other expenditures. Table 5.1 provides an overview of the issues discussed.[5]

Food Subsidies

We start by discussing the distributional impact of universal food subsidies, subsidized rationed food, and food stamps. All of these involve transfers to households that are essentially conditioned on households' consuming the subsidized food. A universal food subsidy involves the government's fixing the food price below the market (or world) price, and households are free to consume as much of the food as they wish. Subsidized rationing of food involves the sale of a fixed amount of food at a subsidized price through publicly designated ration shops. Food stamps involve the transfer of a coupon of a certain monetary value to households, and this coupon can be exchanged in private outlets for certain foods at market prices up to the value of the coupon.

The expressed objectives of such subsidies have varied across countries and time, but typically include increasing the purchasing power of low-income households, reducing calorie and micronutrient deficiencies, maintaining low urban wages, and ensuring social and political stability. Here we are interested primarily in the first of these; that is, we are interested in discussing their distributional power as measured by their ability to get a large amount of a poverty alleviation budget into the hands of the poorest households. The nutrition

---

5. See Coady (2004) for details on the theoretical framework used to guide our discussion of the empirical literature. For a fuller discussion of these and related issues, see Drèze and Stern (1987) and Coady and Drèze (2002).

TABLE 5.1 The design and effectiveness of social safety net programs

Intervention type	Description	What do they do?	How do they perform?
Cash transfers	Typically take the form of transfers to households based on the number of children or of transfers to elderly. Targeting is usually done by a combination of means or proxy means testing plus categorical targeting (e.g., based on age).	In the presence of market failures (e.g., liquidity constraints), cash transfers can generate multiplier effects from increased investments. But this requires not only that households lack access to credit but also that they have investment opportunities that they are capable of exploiting. To the extent that food consumption increases, the resulting improvement in nutritional and health status helps maintain human capital and future incomes. This effect is thus more likely for very poor households vulnerable to malnutrition. For beneficiaries, transfers provide stable source of income and can prevent costly depletion of human and physical assets in the event of adverse shocks. A more stable source of income may encourage participation in more risky but higher-income activities.	Transfers need to be targeted to maximize impact from a constrained budget. There is evidence of good targeting on average, with a median performance index of 1.4, implying a cost ratio of $2.20. But there is a lot of variability, with median cost ratios of the top and bottom five programs ranging from $3.40 to $1.20. Nearly all these programs are in Latin America and Eastern–Central Europe. The design of the targeting system needs to avoid disincentive effects (e.g., reduced labor supply and income in order to meet eligibility conditions). These can be minimized by avoiding finely graduated transfers, capping transfer levels, and linking transfers to household characteristics that are hard to manipulate. Programs' effectiveness in addressing vulnerability depends on how flexible eligibility rules are and how targeting criteria can be adjusted to precisely identify "new poor."

| Universal food subsidies | Subsidy of a commodity that is in principle available to all households in unlimited amounts. Targeting is usually done by self-selection of households based on a decision to consume and how much to consume, so it should subsidize commodities with very high or negative income elasticities. | As with cash transfers, the income effects can lead to multiplier effects through asset accumulation when households are liquidity constrained. To the extent that food consumption helps improve nutritional status, future labor productivities and income are enhanced. Households can switch to subsidized commodities when income decreases. And subsidies can be increased in response to national economic shocks. | Subsidies introduce inefficiencies, and these increase exponentially with subsidy levels. So universal subsidies can be a very costly and inefficient way of transferring income to the poor, even when they target the right commodities. When financed through low producer prices, they can lead to large production inefficiencies, especially in agriculture. On the whole, universal food subsidies are rarely progressive. Median targeting performance is 0.93, ranging from medians of 0.60 to 1.00 for the top and bottom five programs, implying cost ratios of $3.30 and $5.00–$3.00, respectively. So such subsidies are usually seen as stopgap measures until more efficient transfer mechanisms can be developed. |
| Ration food subsidies | Subsidy of a commodity available to households but in limited amounts. Subsidies can be universally available as above, but typically are targeted | As with cash transfers, the income effects can lead to multiplier effects through asset accumulation when households are liquidity constrained. To the extent that food consumption helps improve nutritional status, | Rationing at low levels avoids inefficiencies arising from substitution effects. Focusing only on leakage to the non-poor, the median targeting performance is 1.3, with medians for the top and |

(Continued)

TABLE 5.1 *Continued*

Intervention type	Description	What do they do?	How do they perform?
	using a combination of means or proxy means tests or categorical (e.g., geographic, household size) methods.	future labor productivities and income are enhanced. Households can switch to subsidized commodities when income decreases. Subsidies and ration levels can be increased in response to national economic shocks.	bottom five programs of 1.0 and 1.6, implying a median cost ratio of $2.40, ranging from $2.90 to $1.90, respectively. When rations are administratively targeted, their ability to address vulnerability efficiently depends on the flexibility of eligibility rules and how targeting criteria can be adjusted to precisely identify "new poor." But administrative targeting usually is not flexible enough to adapt easily to crises. However, greater reliance on self-selection and geographic targeting may help.
Public works	Employment at a low wage on programs that enhance community assets. (Public works tend to emphasize the former.) The requirement to work is also often seen as something that is individually and socially desirable. Targeting is based on self-selection (by willingness	Future income streams from community assets can help address persistent poverty. Higher current income from wages helps to protect nutritional and health status and thus future incomes. Seen as an effective way of addressing vulnerability. Households can self-select into programs when hit with adverse income shocks (except in the case of disability or poor health).	To be cost-effective in increasing the current income of the poor, programs should be very labor-intensive, use low wages, be located in poor areas, and be flexible in terms of employment rules. This restricts outputs that can be sensibly produced. There can be a strong trade-off between asset creation and cost-effectiveness in decreasing current

to accept a low wage) and geographic targeting through program placement in poor areas.

In the absence of a low wage, rationing of jobs is often based on categorical methods (gender, age, etc.).

Programs can expand in times of local, regional, or national crises. Assets themselves (e.g., irrigation and road programs) can help to stabilize incomes.

poverty. Programs perform better when communities participate in selecting assets and managing the programs.

Focusing on wages, median targeting performance is 1.85, ranging from 1.5 to 4 for best and worst. These imply cost ratios of $1.60, ranging from $1.25 to $2.00. Forgone earnings have been found to account for between 25 percent and 50 percent of wage transfers; using lower bound rates increases the median cost ratio to $2.18. Similarly, if nonwage costs are (a low) 20 percent of total project costs, these increase the cost ratio to $3.20. So it is important to create assets valued by the community. Community involvement has been found to be important in increasing overall effectiveness.

To be effective in addressing vulnerability, programs need to be able to expand to meet demand during local or regional downturns, again suggesting labor-intensive programs.

(Continued)

TABLE 5.1 *Continued*

Intervention type	Description	What do they do?	How do they perform?
			Such programs are most effective in crises (e.g., natural or manmade disasters) where there is a need to build up community assets and a very low current demand for labor. Evidence is needed on valuing benefits due to increased consumption-smoothing opportunities and the potential for increasing unskilled wages.
Social funds	Funds distributed to communities subject to project approval. (Projects involve construction or maintenance of community assets, with emphasis on gains from asset creation rather than from employment.) Often involve communities' providing matching funds. Demand-driven in the sense that communities must submit a proposal.	The focus on creating valuable community assets (e.g., construction and maintenance of health clinics, schools, and community infrastructure) helps build up the asset base of the poor. Where the emphasis is on assets, such programs are unlikely to be suitable for addressing vulnerability, although some assets themselves (e.g. irrigation and road programs) can help to stabilize incomes. The need to develop projects and bid for funds means that project access or expansion is usually not flexible	For a large poverty impact, projects need to be located in poor areas. There has been a median targeting performance of 1.20, ranging from 1.07 to 1.05 (medians of the top and bottom three programs). This implies a median cost ratio of $2.75, ranging from $2.40 to $2.80. But relatively high nonwage costs will increase the cost ratio substantially (to $3.60 for nonwage costs of 30 percent). Effective geographic targeting of poor areas requires that resources be devoted to aiding the poorest

	Targeting is done by geographic targeting and actively encouraging proposals from poor communities.	enough to expand to include new poor during crises.	communities to develop projects, bid for funds, and develop management capabilities.
Human capital subsidies	Transfers to households conditioned on investment in the human capital of children (i.e., through school enrollment and preventive health checks). Targeting is done by a combination of individual and categorical targeting methods.	Improved nutrition, health, and education status helps break the intra- and intergenerational transmission of poverty and facilitates future participation in the development process. Improved human capital can result in more stable income flows.	The attraction of these subsidies is that they can simultaneously address current poverty and structural poverty in the medium to long run. The approach to targeting needs to address the issue of entry and exit. Effectiveness in addressing vulnerability depends on the flexibility of eligibility rules and how the targeting criteria can be adjusted to precisely identify "new poor." The overall design of such programs needs to reflect the local context (e.g., the quality of the supply side, education/health profiles, capacity to implement and monitor, and the potential role for community actors).

SOURCE: Numbers are taken from Coady, Grosh, and Hoddinott (2004b).

NOTES: Targeting performance is measured as the ratio of the proportion of transfers going to the poor to what they would receive without targeting. Cost ratios are the budget cost of getting $1.00 into the hands of the poor.

objective was discussed in the previous chapter under our discussion of nutrition interventions.

During the 1960s and 1970s, universal food subsidies formed a major component of the poverty alleviation strategies in many developing countries. Countries such as Bangladesh, Egypt, India, Pakistan, Sri Lanka, and Tunisia introduced universal food subsidies in the early 1950s. These typically took the form of a combination of implicit and explicit taxes on agricultural outputs (e.g., import subsidies, export taxes, and low, domestically controlled procurement prices).

Two events combined to highlight the shortcomings of such an approach. First, the large increase in world prices in the mid-1970s meant that the cost of subsidies became enormous, often leading governments to absorb the higher costs through higher public expenditures and budget deficits. For example, in the early 1980s the cost of such programs was as high as 4–5 percent of GDP in Sri Lanka and Tunisia. Second, the stabilization and structural adjustment programs introduced in the early 1980s emphasized the need to cut back on ineffective government expenditures in an attempt to reduce budget deficits and inflation. Universal food subsidies were seen as being inefficient because (1) a large proportion of the benefits leaked to the non-poor and (2) the price manipulations inherent in such an approach were often highly distortionary.

One of the first substantial pieces of research into the role and implications of food subsidies was an edited volume by Pinstrup-Andersen (1988).[6] This summarized the results of the early research at IFPRI in the late 1970s (on South Asia) and early 1980s (on Egypt), which focused on analyzing the trade-offs between the distributional implications of universal food subsidies and the efficiency costs of the price distortions imposed to finance such transfers. This research emphasized the important role played by food subsidies in increasing food consumption and nutrition in poor households. However, it also emphasized the need to minimize any adverse impact on agricultural production, a point also emphasized by Mellor and Ahmed (1988), and that budgetary pressures on public expenditures necessitated a greater effort to target these subsidies at the poor. Such an approach was entirely consistent with the emphasis in the structural adjustment programs of the early 1980s.

The output of this research, in particular the work on Egypt (Alderman and von Braun 1984), also highlighted important research priorities and provided some initial steps toward filling these gaps, including the need to (1) develop a conceptual and methodological framework to guide the research agenda, (2) collect adequate data to facilitate the research, (3) focus on the nutritional implications of policies as well as on the implications for income distribution, (4) incorporate the macroeconomic environment in which these policies are imple-

---

6. Note that many of the issues discussed here also apply to maintaining lower food prices through exempting foods from value-added taxes.

mented, and (5) keep the focus on policy implications, and in particular to take account of the administrative, political, and social environments in which such policies were formulated.

In the late 1980s, the conceptual framework for the analysis of pricing policy in developing countries was developed based on standard taxation theory (Ahmad and Stern 1984; Drèze and Stern 1987; Newbery and Stern 1987). The increasing availability of household data sets for many developing countries also facilitated the empirical application of this theory (Newbery and Stern 1987; Ahmad and Stern 1991; Coady 1997). The welfare impact of raising (spending) a unit of revenue by taxing (or subsidizing) good i (i.e., λ_i) can be derived, according to Coady (2004, 9) as

$$\lambda_i = \frac{\theta_p}{E_i},$$

where θ_p is the share of transfers going to "poor" households (which equals their share in the total consumption of i) and captures the equity (or distributional) implications of the tax or subsidy. E_i is the elasticity of revenue with respect to this tax and captures the efficiency implications. For a tax, the welfare impact on households is negative and $E_i < 1$ when demand decreases with the tax, thus magnifying the welfare losses. The inverse of the revenue elasticity captures the fact that taxes have to be increased by more to raise a unit of revenue when households can switch away from the taxed commodity. For a subsidy, the welfare impact on households is positive and $E_i > 1$ when demand increases, with the subsidy thus reducing the welfare gains. Crudely speaking, one can think of E_i as being closer to unity when efficiency costs, which are due to substitution effects, are small.

The standard result in the empirical literature relates to the trade-off between equity and efficiency when setting tax and subsidy rates. Efficiency concerns require taxes to be inversely related to commodity price elasticities (the so-called inverse elasticity rule). But because elasticities are typically relatively low for necessities such as food, which account for a relatively substantial proportion of the expenditures of the poor, efficient taxes are highly inequitable. However, the corollary of this is that such commodities are good candidates for transfers through universal subsidies because they are consumed disproportionately by low-income households and their low price elasticities imply low efficiency costs.

In the context of developing countries, the "inverse elasticity rule" relates to net trade elasticities (i.e., the elasticity of marketed surplus). Many households consume a substantial proportion of their food production on-farm, so net market trades are often only a small proportion of their total consumption or production. For example, using the price controls existing in Pakistan in the mid-1970s, Coady (1997) showed that fixing producer prices for such commodities as wheat below world prices could be a very powerful redistribution policy instrument, because the poorest households are net consumers and the richer households are net producers, implying a high θ_p. Therefore, low prices are simultaneously a subsidy to the poor financed by a tax on the rich.

However, the large proportion of consumption out of households' own production means that net trade elasticities are very high (even if consumption and/or production elasticities are relatively low), so producer price controls are highly inefficient. Thus the standard trade-off between equity and efficiency is magnified in developing countries. Schiff and Valdes (1992) provided an in-depth analysis of the economic effects of agricultural price manipulations in 18 developing countries for the period 1960–85. Their analysis highlighted the large transfer of resources out of agriculture, with indirect taxes on agriculture standing at around 22 percent, and the fact that "the modernization of agriculture was being sacrificed at the alter of industrialization" (from the foreword to their book by T. W. Schultz). The importance of political economy in shaping the form this extractive approach took, and in determining the possibilities for reform, was discussed in Krueger (1992).

From the perspective of structural adjustment, the required policy response was seen as obvious: price liberalization implied shifting the burden of transfers to the public sector (i.e., away from agricultural producers) by financing these out of general revenues, while cost-effectiveness required targeting public expenditures more directly at the poor. Better targeting could then be achieved in a number of ways,[7] including

- selecting commodities consumed disproportionately by the poor (i.e., inferior goods or those with low income elasticities),
- placing ration shops in the poorest areas and subjecting people to queuing, and
- explicitly targeting ration coupons or food stamps at the poorest households.

The first of these involves the targeting of universal subsidies using "self-selection" targeting methods. The second involves a combination of geographic targeting and self-selection. The last involves finer administrative targeting methods and thus probably higher administrative costs. The welfare impact of subsidies can be adapted to incorporate these administrative costs as follows:

$$\lambda_i = \frac{\theta_p \theta_t}{E_i},$$

---

7. See Grosh (1994) and Coady, Grosh, and Hoddinott (2004b) for a discussion of alternative targeting methods and a review of targeting practice.

where θ_t is the share of transfers in total costs, that is, one minus the share of administrative costs in the total budget. However, all else equal, the lower θ_t the lower the welfare impact, one should keep in mind that one generally expects a lower θ_t due to costs associated with finer targeting to lead to a higher θ_p.

Even when the right commodity is selected, universal food subsidies are rarely very progressive, and are often slightly regressive. This partly reflects the fact that it is difficult to identify commodities that are inferior and whose price can also be easily manipulated by government controls. In addition, the amount of the transfer is limited by the commodity's budget share (Pinstrup-Andersen 1988; Alderman and Lindert 1998), and the associated inefficiencies (e.g., feeding inexpensive foods to cattle) tend to increase with the size of the subsidy. Expanding the set of commodities that are subsidized in order to facilitate larger transfers will usually involve a large trade-off in terms of lower progressivity. Keeping the transfer budget constant, spreading subsidies across a number of commodities should help to keep the efficiency cost of price distortions lower than it otherwise would be. But including more commodities may also substantially increase administrative costs.

Based on the review of Coady, Grosh, and Hoddinott (2004b), which focuses on the share of transfers going to the poor (i.e., θ_p), it appears that universal food subsidies are rarely progressive. Median targeting performance (defined as the share of transfers going to the poor divided by their population share) is 0.93, ranging from 0.6 to 1.0 across all universal subsidy programs considered. Assuming that the poor account for 30 percent of the population, the leakage to the non-poor population implies that the median cost of getting $1.00 to the poor through universal subsidies (i.e., the inverse of θ_p) would be $3.30, ranging from $5.00 to $3.00.[8] Incorporating efficiency and administrative costs would obviously increase this cost even further. For these reasons, universal subsidies are typically seen as a short-term solution until better targeting mechanisms are developed.

The second and third targeting methods mentioned earlier (i.e., ration shops and food coupons) potentially have more distributional power as well as being more efficient. There are many examples of attempts to target subsidized food at poor households. These can take a number of forms,[9] including the following:

- Universal access can be provided to subsidized food sold through a public distribution center (or designated private outlet) on a first-come, first-served basis. Outlets are often located in poorer areas, are open at inconvenient times, and can require lengthy queuing times, with individuals often queuing well before opening time. The sum of cash plus time costs

8. All monetary values in this chapter are in U.S. dollars at the official exchange rate.
9. See Alderman (2002) for a detailed discussion of the pros and cons of these alternatives.

effectively clears the market. Although access is universal in principle, it is argued that because non-poor households have higher opportunity costs of time and there may be some social stigma costs, they have lower take-up rates. As with universal subsidies sold through private markets, this is a form of targeting through self-selection.

- Universal access can be provided to a fixed quantity ration of food sold at subsidized prices through public ration shops, which may also be located in poor areas, only open at inconvenient times and often requiring lengthy queuing times.[10]

- Ration cards can be targeted at poor households using means tests or other forms of administrative targeting. Targeted households receive a ration card that entitles them to a certain amount of food at a subsidized price. The progressiveness of transfers will depend on how well they are targeted, as well as on the time and stigma costs described earlier.

- Rationed food stamps are often used instead of ration cards; the difference is that they usually entitle the holder to a fixed amount of food denominated in money (as opposed to quantity) units free of charge and can be redeemed at private outlets or even sold to others. Private traders can then redeem them at face value at a bank. Again, the progressiveness of transfers will depend on how well they are targeted.

A number of countries have switched from universal to targeted food subsidies, including Bangladesh, Honduras, Jamaica, Jordan, Mexico, Sri Lanka, and Tunisia.

Providing universal access to unrestricted consumption of subsidized food has both income and substitution effects. However, if ration transfers are fixed below existing household consumption levels or if resale is possible at low transaction costs, these subsidized rations are approximately equivalent to cash transfers and thus have only income effects. Thus, from the perspective of income poverty, (equivalent) cash transfers are always superior to food subsidies because the latter typically have an additional inefficiency (i.e., a deadweight loss) associated with their substitution effects.

There are many examples of targeting and rationing systems in developing countries. For example, the public distribution system in India has a long history (Ahluwalia 1993; Radhakrishna and Subbarao 1997). However, the performance of these systems has not always been great, typically because of a combination of a lack of political will, corruption, and the high costs associated

---

10. An important policy issue raised by research on the public distribution system in India and the food rationing system in Egypt is the importance of not setting ration levels too high. If the poorest households have liquidity constraints that limit their ability to take up the full transfer, this reduces its degree of progressivity (Alderman and von Braun 1984; Rao 2000).

with distributing food. Focusing only on leakage to the non-poor, median targeting performance is 1.3, with medians for the top and bottom five programs of 1.0 and 1.6, respectively, implying a median cost ratio of $2.40, with ratios ranging from $2.90 to $1.90, respectively.

Many of the practical difficulties associated with reforming ration systems were discussed by Pinstrup-Andersen (1988). The work of Ahmed et al. (2001) on the reform of the Egyptian rationing system also provides an example of these difficulties. This research identified and analyzed the economic impacts of a range of alternative policy options, with special emphasis on the administrative, political, and social implications of each option. In order to facilitate better targeting of the subsidized ration program, an easily implementable "proxy means test" was developed that was based on a thorough poverty analysis that identified the characteristics of poor households (or "poverty correlates"). Staff at the Ministry of Trade and Supply were also trained to implement the system, and a field test was carried out to demonstrate its effectiveness. However, in spite of the strong emphasis from the very beginning on building domestic capacity and political support, a change in government prevented the implementation of policy reforms.

While the above difficulties are recognized, there is a strong consensus that better targeting of food transfers can substantially increase their distributional power and thus also their ability to alleviate poverty. For example, as indicated earlier, the median universal food subsidy program was slightly regressive (i.e., performed worse than without targeting), whereas the median administratively targeted rationed food subsidy program increased the proportion of the transfer budget going to "the poor" by 30 percentage points more than they would have received without targeting. However, the available empirical evidence does raise concerns regarding the tendency for substantial leakage of the food transfers through both transport losses and corruption (Ahmed and del Ninno 2001; Ahmed et al. 2001, Chap. 6). To the extent that such inefficiencies are inherently linked to the use of food as a benefit, there may be a strong argument for switching to cash transfers. This is an area in which more policy research is urgently needed.

Finally, the targeting method chosen must be appropriate within the existing social, political, and administrative context of the country. The existence or reform of food subsidy systems affects a number of competing groups in society, and their relative power often determines outcomes (Bienen and Gersovitz 1986; Adams 1988, 2000; Alderman 1988; Tuck and Lindert 1998). But informing the public of the costs and benefits of these programs seems to play a crucial role in determining the acceptance of these reforms and in neutralizing small but vocal power groups. Similarly, it is usually easier to reform subsidy systems when market food prices are low or when vocal groups are otherwise distracted.

Public Works

One of the common criticisms of food subsidies and other cash or in-kind transfers is that their effect persists only as long as the transfers themselves persist. Such a strategy is typically seen as undesirable both in terms of the dependency culture it creates and because of the pressure it puts on public finances, thus raising concerns regarding its sustainability. Longer-term measures that address persistent poverty require policies that help poor households build up their asset base in order to promote their participation in the development process, that is, a "more developmental" approach. Public works provide one such alternative because they can have both features, with wage transfers addressing short-term poverty and the output from these projects potentially enhancing the asset base of the poor and thus helping to alleviate poverty in the medium to long run.

Public works are also often perceived as an effective policy instrument for addressing vulnerability to poverty, especially when they allow households to self-select into existing programs in times of hardship or where programs are activated in areas where aggregate (as opposed to idiosyncratic) shocks occur. But some shocks (e.g., illness or disability) may preclude some households' participation in such programs, so other interventions are also required.

Public works programs are seen to include several advantages: (1) the existence of a work requirement can be an effective way of targeting transfers (i.e., wages) at poor households, (2) the benefits from output also often accrue disproportionately to poor households, and (3) the work experience can also enhance the future productivity of workers through on-the-job training. In spite of the potential for 3, usually it is the output side that is seen as transforming such programs into development expenditures. These programs are typically intended to provide only a temporary safety net, allowing participants to escape poverty with, for example, temporary employment during the off season.

Public works programs have been around for decades, constituting an important component of India's famine relief during the nineteenth century and existing in South Africa and Bangladesh since the nineteenth century and the 1960s, respectively.[11] But they became more widespread and more focused in the late 1980s and early 1990s, especially in Asia and Africa. Public works programs often account for a substantial proportion of employment generated nationally, for instance, 21 percent of the labor force in Botswana in 1985–86 and 13 percent in Chile in 1983. The recent emphasis on "social funds" is part of this trend (Rawlings, Sherburne-Benz, and van Domelen 2004). But these programs differ from the traditional approach insofar as they put greater emphasis on the output side and typically are demand driven because they require communities to identify and propose programs as well as to provide matching funds.

---

11. For more detailed discussion of public works see Subbarao et al. (1999) and Subbarao (2003) and references therein.

The immediate welfare impact on poor households comes from higher wage earnings. I have shown (Coady 2004, 10–12) that if we ignore the output benefits and assume that forgone income due to the existence of a work requirement is a fixed proportion (α) of the public wage, this welfare impact is given by

$$\lambda_p = (1 - \alpha)\theta_w\theta_p,$$

where θ_w is the share of wage payments in total program costs (i.e., wage plus nonwage costs) and θ_p is the share of total wage payments received by poor households. The welfare gains per unit of expenditure are therefore greater the higher the proportion of the labor employed that comes from poor households, the greater the gap between project and market wages (or, more generally, forgone earnings), and the greater the share of wages in total program costs. However, there is typically a trade-off between the first two components; the higher the project wage, the more attractive is employment on public works to the nonpoor. This effectively puts a practical limit on the amount of resources that can be efficiently transferred to the poor under such schemes. One way around this is to combine higher wages with, for example, an administrative targeting method to ration employment. Timing projects during periods of slack (e.g., during the rainy season) or placing them in the poorest areas may also enhance their welfare impact. Of course, such strategies may also have important implications for the type of output that can be sensibly produced by the project.

A useful starting point in the literature is a paper by Ravallion (1990a).[12] There he argues that as of the late 1980s there was surprisingly little quantitative evidence on the gains from targeting and the performance of incentive schemes for self-targeting, with most attempts at doing so involving simulations using ad hoc assumptions. The paper refers to evidence on the targeting performance of two specific programs:

- The Employment Guarantee Scheme (EGS) in Maharashtra, India, which was the single largest poverty alleviation scheme of any state in India in the late 1980s. This scheme provided work on small-scale rural public works projects, such as roads, irrigation facilities, and reforestation, at wage rates on a par with prevailing agricultural wages.
- The Food for Work (FFW) program in Bangladesh, which provided employment for construction and maintenance of irrigation, drainage, and embankment projects.

The available evidence suggested that the targeting performance of these schemes was very good, although there is still a need for more rigorous targeting analyses based on random samples. However, rough estimates also suggest

---

12. See also Ravallion (1991a,b, 2000).

that forgone earnings constitute around half of the transfer from participation in the program, and this substantially reduces the efficiency of the program in transferring income to the poor.[13] Adopting piecework schemes may be a way of addressing these problems if it enables participants to undertake other work; such flexibility is often thought to be more conducive to female participation because of the demand that housework places on their time. In addition, the wage bill accounted for around 70 percent of total government outlays on the EGS, while only about 70 percent of the food aid used to finance the FFW went to beneficiaries. In fact, both programs have a rule that wage costs should account for at least 60 percent of variable costs.

Based on the these numbers, we can calculate the cost of transferring income to the poor under these schemes as the inverse of λ_p. For every 100 rupees transferred to beneficiaries, the beneficiaries have an average net gain of about 50 (i.e., net of forgone earnings), and non–transfer program costs are around 43 rupees (i.e., three-sevenths of the 100 rupees). So, making the very optimistic assumption that all of the benefits accrue to the target group (i.e., the "poor"), these figures for forgone earnings and nontransfer costs suggest that it costs 143 rupees to get 50 rupees to the poor (i.e., a ratio of nearly 2.9 to 1!). Although one needs to factor in the output benefits accruing to the poor, these programs would appear to be very expensive ways of transferring income to the poor.

However, one would also need to adjust for any general-equilibrium wage effects, which may be substantial. Higher wages may also have beneficial second-round welfare effects if they help to reduce employers' power in monopolistic labor markets.[14] Even in competitive labor markets, higher wages may be desirable from an equity perspective, although this comes at an efficiency cost. The little evidence that exists suggests that these general-equilibrium wage effects may be substantial, for instance, as much as doubling the direct transfer benefit (Ravallion 1990b). But additional research is needed on the nature and magnitude of these general-equilibrium effects, including the possibly adverse effect of the displacement of private transfers.

Similarly, providing a guarantee of employment at a fixed wage has additional welfare impacts when it helps to stabilize the incomes and consumption of households that are unable to smooth consumption optimally over time; the gains essentially come from providing income in periods when income is oth-

---

13. Ravallion and Datt (1995) provided an estimate of forgone earnings for the EGS of 25 percent of wages, although there was substantial spatial variation, and the proportion was higher for men than for women.

14. There is some evidence that large landowners may have monopsony power, manifested as discriminatory wage rate differentials (e.g., between men and women or migrants and local workers or across castes). For discussion see, for example, PEO (1980), Dandekar (1983), Binswanger et al. (1984), Hirway et al. (1990), and Subbarao et al. (1999).

erwise very low. Such a safety net feature requires the program to expand and contract in response to (anticipated and unanticipated) income shocks experienced by households. For example, experience with both the EGS and the FFW shows that employment increases substantially during the dry summer season and also during periods of widespread drought (e.g., during the severe drought in Maharashtra in 1987 following a sequence of poor monsoons and during potentially famine-producing situations in Bangladesh in 1988).

The additional opportunity for smoothing provided by public works may prevent households from engaging in distress land sales or in running down their asset base in bad times, for instance, by slaughtering cattle or pulling children out of school (Cain and Lieberman 1983). Because such benefits may be substantial, they should not be overlooked. It has been argued that substantial improvements along these lines can be made in Bangladesh's FFW program, for example, by choosing outputs that are sensible in periods of drought and generally increasing program flexibility (Hossain 1985, 1987). The outputs (e.g., more effective irrigation or soil conservation systems) can also generate additional gains in terms of reducing fluctuations in incomes (i.e., in addition to their impact in terms of higher average incomes). Therefore, it may be that the comparative advantage of such programs lies in their ability to deal with vulnerability and crises rather than with structural poverty.

Another important contribution to the literature was the edited volume produced by IFPRI in 1995 (von Braun 1995), also covering the programs discussed earlier and echoing similar issues. This volume summarized the various outputs from research undertaken since the early 1980s, including (1) food-for-work programs run by the World Food Programme in Bangladesh (Chowdhury 1983); (2) the successful employment guarantee scheme in Maharashtra, India (Dev and Suryanarayana 1991); and (3) public works for relief and development in Africa (Hossain and Akash 1993). While emphasizing the important contribution of such programs to poverty alleviation, this work made clear that the effectiveness of such an approach depended on how well the programs were targeted and managed. However, targeting effectiveness depended on setting low wages, and this limited the potential impact on poverty. With higher wages, demand for employment exceeds the jobs available, so it is important to incorporate additional screening based on characteristics that are highly correlated with poverty (e.g., geographic targeting). Targeting with a work requirement also rules out transfers to those unable to work, and demand-led projects tend to exclude the poorest communities, which lack capacity. These effects are often exacerbated by political interference in the selection of projects.

There is also some evidence that in-kind transfers (e.g., food for work) may involve relatively high transaction costs (including illegal pilferage) and thus be less cost-effective than cash transfers. In the context of famine relief, Drèze and Sen (1989, 1990) argue that greater use of cash support (rather than the direct provision of food) should be considered because the difficult logistics of transporting food (especially through public distribution systems) often appears to cause delays that can be very costly in terms of lost lives. They also argue that previous experience during famine or near-famine situations has shown that where the demand exists, private markets can be more efficient in transporting food to famine areas at low cost. They further argue that "a plethora of recent studies has shown that the acquisition of cash (for subsequent conversion into food through the market) is now one of the most important survival strategies of vulnerable populations in famine prone countries" (Drèze and Sen 1990, 19). It is often argued that cash injections in the absence of a food injection will just lead to higher prices, thus benefiting private suppliers at the expense of famine-stricken households. This is likely to be the case only when substantially large areas of a country are famine stricken, but past experiences suggest that potential famine conditions often exist side by side with areas of large food market surpluses. But the main point to be taken from this discussion is that if cash support can work more effectively in famine conditions, surely such a strategy is even more likely to be effective during normal conditions.

On the output side, the potential for generating valuable output depends on good management and the selection of appropriate investments. Avoiding the types of corruption often witnessed in these schemes requires providing management with the appropriate incentives and capacity.[15] For relatively more capital-intensive projects, efficient provision requires good management skills and sufficient demand for output, suggesting that location in remote rural areas is often inappropriate. Therefore, for these programs there tends to be an important trade-off between targeting and productive efficiency, although this trade-off may be relaxed with greater intercommunity labor mobility. When short-term famine relief is the objective, targeting performance is viewed as being relatively more important than long-term asset creation, although the presence of productive inefficiency implies that such programs are not likely to be cost-effective in transferring income to the poor. There is also evidence that local involvement in the selection and delivery of projects improves outcomes. All of this evidence suggests that public works programs appropriate for alleviating poverty are likely to be those that use unskilled-labor-intensive technologies for producing outputs that are undersupplied by the market and located in poor areas. For such projects to fulfill their insurance function they need to be flexible enough to be expanded during off-peak seasons or slumps.

The choice of output may also be influenced by political considerations. For example, it has been argued that the fact that rich farmers benefited from the project output played an important role in generating support from these farm-

---

15. Dandekar (1983) and Echeverri-Gent (1988) discuss such problems and possible solutions in the case of the EGS, while Ahmed et al. (1985) and Bandyopadhyay (1988) do so in the context of the FFW.

ers for the EGS in Maharashtra, India, during the 1980s (Herring and Edwards 1983; Echeverri-Gent 1988). In contrast, if high project wages had put upward pressure on market wages for hired labor, this might have reduced their support for such schemes; this reinforces the need for better targeting by means of both choice of a lower project wage and the appropriate timing of projects so that they do not compete for labor in times of high demand. The desire for effective targeting and flexibility also has important implications for choice of output and mode of delivery; for example, when there is a requirement to put contracts out to tender to allow private sector participation, this may delay implementation.

One of the most thorough evaluations of a public works program is the recent evaluation of the Trabajar program introduced in 1997 by the government of Argentina, which was an expanded and reformed version of an earlier pilot program that was introduced in 1996 in response to a prevailing economic crisis and unemployment rates of over 17 percent.[16] The program was a reformed version of the pilot and put greater emphasis on geographic targeting using an explicit formula for allocating resources based on the number of poor unemployed workers in each province and also on the extent of poverty. There was also a greater emphasis on creating assets valued by these poor communities. Low wages were used to provide incentives for only the poorest households to participate; there was a specific objective of employing otherwise unemployed workers from poor families. Local governments and nongovernmental organizations propose projects, and these projects must cover the nonwage program costs.

It has been estimated that 60 percent of the beneficiaries are in the bottom 10 percent of the income distribution, with 80 percent in the bottom 20 percent of the distribution. In other words, the program transfers 4–6 times more to target households than it would without targeting. This performance is very impressive; this program had the best targeting performance among the targeted programs reviewed by Coady, Grosh, and Hoddinott (2004b), although targeting performance varied substantially across provinces. However, the program evaluation also found that forgone incomes accounted for roughly half of the average project wage. Assuming (1) that 80 percent of the transfers went to the target group, (2) that wages accounted for 70 percent of the total program budget, and (3) that forgone income was 50 percent of the wage,[17] we can calculate that the cost of transferring one unit of income to the target population

---

16. There are a large number of papers reporting evaluation results, including those of Jalan and Ravallion (2000), Ravallion (2000), Galasso, Ravallion, and Salvia (2001), and Ravallion et al. (2001).

17. Using matching methods, Jalan and Ravallion (2000) found that the average direct gain to participants was about half the gross program wage. Ravallion et al. (2001) found that those leaving the work program had incomes equal to 25 percent of the program wage after 6 months and 50 percent after 12 months.

was 3.6 (falling to our earlier estimate of 2.9 if all benefits accrued to the poor). Again, in spite of its excellent targeting performance, this program did not appear to be a cost-effective way of transferring income to the poor.

One of the objectives of Trabajar was to enable participants to eventually get off workfare (Galasso, Ravallion, and Salvia 2001). From a random sample of 848 participants, 354 were given a voucher entitling them to a wage subsidy paid to any private sector firm that provided them with regular employment, another 213 were given both a voucher and additional training, and the remaining 281 participants acted as the "control" group. It was found that 14 percent of those with vouchers got a private sector job, compared to 9 percent of the control group; the difference was statistically significant at the 5 percent level. The gain in wage employment was largely confined to women and younger workers. However, there was no additional impact for those who received the offer of training. Nor was there any evidence of a significant income gain for those with vouchers. The fact that very few (only three) of the private sector firms actually claimed the wage subsidy was interpreted as the employment effect arising from the fact that those with vouchers were more confident with respect to their job search and/or that employers interpreted the vouchers as a quality signal.

Haddad and Adato (2001), using a combination of actual data and simulations, recently evaluated the performance of 101 public works projects in the Western Cape province of South Africa, which were introduced in the early 1990s to combat large-scale unemployment. They found a large amount of variability in performance as measured by the cost of transferring income to the poor, which highlights the point that performance depends on the detailed design and management of the program. Much of the bad targeting performance was due to bad geographic targeting. Choosing labor-intensive projects, preferably in poor areas, was also found to be crucial to performance when the output is not of major benefit to the poor. Based on the same data, Hoddinott et al. (2001) found that community participation is generally associated with improved project cost-effectiveness and better targeting.

Adato and Haddad (2001) provide an example of how qualitative studies can help build up a much richer picture of the forces that determine project design and implementation in practice. They point out that because the criteria used to target projects were often not based on targeting performance but rather on the output objectives of the program (e.g., ecological impacts or the need for infrastructure), a narrow evaluation of performance may give a misleading picture of the impact and role of these programs. They also point out the difficulty of imposing low wage rates without community backing, because once the project has been set up the threat of withdrawing labor is a powerful weapon. This is especially the case when similar work earns higher wages in the private sector. Enhancing the sense of community ownership may help to counteract such forces, as may additional design features such as fixing the wage budget so that there is a visible trade-off between higher wages and employment levels. The authors highlight the importance of active information and coordination efforts for targeting outcomes when participation is demand driven given the lower capacity of poorer communities in these areas. But transparency and community participation are often strong forces working to achieve poverty alleviation objectives.

Human Capital Subsidies

In large part due to the shortcomings identified regarding existing approaches to social safety nets, developing countries and donors have recently experimented with and promoted the implementation of a relatively new approach to social safety nets that combines their traditional "preventive" roles with a "promotional" role. The former addresses the problem of current poverty, while the latter attempts to promote a sustained decrease in poverty through improving the nutrition, health, and education status within households. In particular, investing in the nutritional, health, and education status of children is seen as playing a key role in breaking the intergenerational transmission of poverty and destitution. In this sense, such programs are particularly focused on the "structurally poor" (as opposed to those just vulnerable) whose poverty persists over time. This dual role of providing shorter-term "social assistance" combined with longer-term "social development" (Morley and Coady 2003) introduces a clear link between these programs and the policy objectives addressed in the previous chapter.

Two design features are especially important in achieving these objectives. First, the programs use a range of targeting methods (e.g., geographic, household proxy means, and community targeting methods) to ensure that program benefits reach the poorest households. Second, the continued eligibility to receive benefits is conditioned on various household members' regularly going to health clinics for nutrition and hygiene information sessions and preventive check-ups as well as attending school. Failure to meet these conditions leads to a loss of benefits, usually at first temporarily but eventually permanently.

The design of these programs thus recognizes the fundamental right of individuals to a basic level of nutrition, health, and education but also the responsibilities of individuals and households in achieving this end. It is also important to emphasize the catalytic role of nutrition and health status. Failure to ensure that infants and children are well nourished and in good health substantially compromises not only their physical capacities but also their mental capacities. In this sense, failure to address the high prevalence of malnutrition in developing countries means that the education battle is half lost even before it is begun.

While these programs exist in various forms in a number of countries, they have recently become increasingly popular in Latin America. Such programs exist or are in their planning stages in Brazil, Columbia, Honduras, Jamaica,

Mexico, Mozambique, Nicaragua, and Turkey. The growing interest in such programs reflects the fact that an unusually rigorous evaluation of Mexico's program (PROGRESA) has shown it to be very effective. But it is also the case that the Inter-American Development Bank has played a key role in promoting such an evaluation culture in support of these programs. Undoubtedly, development institutes and donors in other regions of the developing world can play a similar role.

IFPRI has been prominent in the evaluation of many these programs, including in Bangladesh (Food for Education, or FFE), Brazil (BA), Honduras (PRAF), Mexico (PROGRESA), and Nicaragua (RPS). These programs are being evaluated using varied and highly rigorous evaluation methods. In the rest of the chapter we will discuss in more detail the design and performance of three of the programs, namely those in Bangladesh, Mexico, and Nicaragua. The focus on these programs reflects the fact that at the time of this writing the other evaluations are at an earlier stage and performance results are not yet available. However, these three programs provide experience from countries at different levels of income and development. For a more comprehensive discussion of similar programs, see Rawlings and Rubio (2003).[18]

PROGRESA in Mexico

The PROGRESA program in Mexico, implemented in 1997, is a federally designed and administered program but with the active participation of the community through a "community promoter" elected by beneficiaries in each community (Skoufias 2001).[19] Although not the first such program to be created, it was one of the first to be so rigorously evaluated. The program targets the poorest households in marginal rural communities. To receive cash transfers, which are given to the mother, eligible households must meet two sets of conditions. First, family members (especially mothers and children) must regularly go to health clinics for preventive health checks as well as for information sessions regarding appropriate hygiene and nutrition practices within the household. Second, children 6–17 years old must meet an 85 percent attendance requirement in grades 3–6 (primary school) and grades 7–9 (middle school). In 1997, the transfer levels for health clinic visits were $12.50 per household per month, but households with children 6–24 months old (or with children deemed to be undernourished) also received a nutritional supplement. The transfer levels for education attendance increased by grade, and in middle school were higher for females. These ranged from $8.00–$16.50 per child per month in primary school

---

18. Consistent with the findings discussed later, Attanasio et al. (2005) report large improvements in human capital resulting from a similar conditional cash transfer program (Familias en Acción) in Colombia.

19. This program has since been renamed Opportunidades and expanded geographically.

(plus $15.50 annually per child for school supplies) to $24.00–$30.50 per child per month in middle school (plus $20.50 annually for school supplies).

To avoid promoting overdependence on public transfers, the maximum a single household could receive was $75 per household per month. The average transfer received by households was around $40 per month, equivalent to around 21 percent of household monthly total consumption; obviously for the poorest households this percentage was even more substantial.

The targeting methods used in PROGRESA to identify eligible households were relatively sophisticated, involving a two-step process and a combination of geographic targeting and a proxy means test applied universally at the local level (Skoufias, Davis, and de la Vega 2001). At the first stage (choosing the poorest communities), information from the national census on the demographic, housing, infrastructure, occupation, and education characteristics of communities was used to construct a "marginality index" (i.e., a community score) for each community in the country, and this was used to identify the most marginal communities to be included in the program. Once these were identified, a locality census was conducted, and the socioeconomic data on households from the census was used to calculate a proxy means score for each household (using discriminant analysis with income as the left-hand variable) and then to classify households as "poor" (or eligible for the program) and "nonpoor" (or not eligible). In all, 20 percent of households were deemed not eligible, and these were concentrated in the least marginal communities.

By 2000, 2.6 million households, equivalent to 40 percent of rural households and over 10 percent of all households in Mexico, had been incorporated into the program. The annual budget in 1999 was $777 million, equivalent to 0.2 percent of Mexico's GDP and accounting for 20 percent of the federal poverty alleviation budget. Over the first three years of the program, administrative costs accounted for less that 10 percent of the total budget, implying a budget cost of $1.10 for every $1.00 received by households. Out of this cost, costs associated with targeting the program accounted for 30 percent, costs associated with conditioning transfers for 26 percent, and the remaining 44 percent was accounted for by recurring operational costs. But it is important to also recognize that households incur additional private costs (e.g., time and financial costs) associated with going to health clinics and school as well as collecting transfers. The financial costs were estimated at around 30 percent of program costs, equivalent to program targeting costs.

Analyses of the targeting efficiency of the program show that it is very well targeted, with a high proportion of the transfers going to the poorest households. It is estimated that 87 percent of transfers go to households in the bottom 20 percent of the national income distribution and that over 97 percent go to the bottom 40 percent of the distribution (Coady 2006). In other words, based on the latter numbers, "poor" households receive 2.4 times as much as they would have received without targeting. It has also been estimated that 60 percent of these gains are due to geographic targeting, an additional 10 percent to household proxy means targeting, and a further 30 percent to demographic targeting by way of linking transfer levels to the number of children in the household. Although the gains from household proxy means targeting are relatively small, these increase substantially as the program expands into less marginal localities.

The potential for nutrition and health benefits arises partly from the size of the transfers, which are equivalent to a 25 percent increase in income for extremely poor households. It has been estimated that on average households allocated around 70 percent of this increase to increasing both the quantity and quality of their food (Hoddinott, Skoufias, and Washburn 2000). This, together with improved preventive care, improved information on hygiene and nutrition practices, and access to nutritional supplements, has led to a range of health improvements in the population (Behrman and Hoddinott 2000; Gertler 2004). There has been a substantial decrease in the incidence of illness, ranging from a 25 percent decrease among newborns to a 19 percent decrease for children 0–2 years old and a 22 percent decrease among children 3–5 years old. Child height has increased by 1–4 percent, and children are on average 3.5 percent heavier. The prevalence of anemia among children 24–48 months of age has decreased by 19 percent. In addition, there is evidence of improved adult health status, with adults reporting on average 16 percent fewer days with difficulties undertaking daily activities due to illness, 17 percent fewer days incapacitated due to illness, 18 percent fewer days in bed due to illness, and the ability to walk 7 percent farther without getting tired.

There is also evidence of substantial education benefits (Schultz 2000). In primary school, where enrollment rates were already around 95 percent, progression rates have improved. The largest impacts came in secondary school, where enrollment increased by 7.2–9.3 percentage points for girls (from a base of 67 percent) and 3.5–5.8 percentage points for boys (from a base of 73 percent). Simulations have shown that these education impacts are consistent with a long-term impact of 19 percent more children attending secondary school (Behrman, Sengupta, and Todd 2001). Further, using existing returns to education in rural Mexico, it has been estimated that the program has an internal rate of return of 8 percent (Schultz 2000). The demand-side grants were also estimated to be around 10 times more cost-effective than the accompanying school-building program in terms of getting more children into school (Coady and Parker 2004). Although these impacts are substantial, they are likely to be context-specific.

A potential indirect benefit from the relatively large cash transfers to households under PROGRESA is increased investment arising from the relaxation of households' credit or liquidity constraints (Ravallion 2003). Such benefits can be expected to be permanent, that is, they will exist even after the withdrawal of the program, because they result in an increase in household assets.

Gertler, Martinez, and Rubio (2006) have estimated that PROGRESA transfers have resulted in increased investments in microenterprises and agricultural production, with 25 percent of transfers invested by beneficiaries. These investments yielded returns of greater than 32 percent and resulted in a 1.2 percent permanent increase in consumption. These findings provide a promising basis for graduating beneficiaries from the program over time, thus avoiding a welfare dependency culture.

RPS in Nicaragua

The RPS program in Nicaragua, which in its current form was implemented in 2000, is also federally designed and administered with a "community promoter" as in PROGRESA (Maluccio 2007). Eligible households receive cash transfers on the conditions that household members go to health clinics and that children aged 7–13 years attend primary school over grades 1–4. For health visits, households receive $18.70 per household per month. The education transfer is also fixed at the household level at $9.20 per month, but all eligible children must attend. Each child also receives $21.00 per annum for school supplies as well as $4.60 per annum that must be turned over to the school. In principle, half of this school transfer is to be allocated to teachers' salaries and half to other school expenses.

The maximum transfer a household can receive accounts on average for 17 percent of the average consumption of beneficiary households, 17 percent of the moderate poverty line, and 26 percent of the extreme poverty line. It has been calculated that such a level of transfers is sufficient to reduce the average poverty gap by 70 percent (at a maximum), based on the moderate poverty line. The administrative costs of the program have been calculated as ranging from 9 percent to 33 percent of the total budget between 2000 and 2002, reducing over time. The lower percentage for later years most likely reflects recurring operational costs. This implies that the program costs $1.10–$1.50 per $1.00 transferred to beneficiaries.

In Nicaragua's RPS program, although municipality poverty indexes were calculated, the pilot nature of the program necessitated the selection of municipalities based on additional criteria regarding access to social infrastructure, accessibility, and organizational capacity. Therefore, two departments (or states) were chosen on the basis of need, implementation capacity, and supporting infrastructure. Within these two departments, 6 (out of 20) municipalities were chosen on the basis of poverty levels, access to education and health facilities, easy communication and access for operational purposes, and high capacity for local organization and participation. Within these 6 municipalities, a marginality index was calculated for all of the 59 rural communities (*comarcas*). The index was based on the following variables from the 1995 National Population and Housing Census: family size, access to potable water, access to latrines, and illiteracy rates. All households in the 42 poorest communities were eligible,[20] while only the poorest 80 percent (based on predicted consumption) in the 17 remaining communities were deemed eligible.

The targeting performance of the program has been quite impressive, especially considering that it was a pilot, so its geographic targeting also reflected operational concerns. It has been estimated that 42 percent of the transfers accrue to households below the extreme poverty line and 80 percent to those below the moderate poverty line; nationally 17 percent and 31 percent of the population are classified as extremely or moderately poor, respectively. The absence of much household targeting also means that most of this performance has been achieved through geographic targeting.

The education impacts of the program have been very impressive. Enrollment rates in treatment communities were around 69 percent before the program, and the program increased these by 22 percentage points, to 91 percent. There is also evidence that the educational impact was highest for the poorest households, for which enrollment rates increased by 30 percentage points from an enrollment rate of 66 percent before the program. The impact of the program on progression rates also looks substantial. On average, the program increased progression rates by 8.5 percentage points from a base of around 85 percent, but again, there is evidence that this increase was highest, at 9.3 percentage points, for the poorest households. It is also clear that, as in PROGRESA, this impact was largest for the higher grades in primary school, with the progression rate from grade 4 to grade 5 increasing from around 80 percent to 92 percent, an increase of 12 percentage points. This increase is particularly interesting because enrolled students beyond the fourth grade are not eligible for cash benefits. It may be that this large difference reflects changes in attitude toward education. Alternatively, it could reflect confusion among beneficiaries about program requirements. But it could also reflect parents' belief that once they have sent their children to grade 4 this investment really pays off only if the children complete the full primary education cycle. In any case, the cumulative impact on average education levels that is implied by these grade transitions is very large.

FFE in Bangladesh

The FFE program in Bangladesh was introduced in July 1993 in part as compensation for the withdrawal of a badly targeted rural rationing scheme. Under this new program, households receive 50 kilograms of foodgrains (mainly wheat) per month per child if they enroll their children in primary school. The maximum a household can receive is 20 kilograms of foodgrains. The average transfer received by beneficiaries was $2.40 per month, equivalent to 4 percent of the total monthly consumption of the poor. The total program budget was $77 million in

---

20. Except for 2 percent of these who were eliminated on the basis of owning a vehicle and having large landholdings.

2000, giving on average $36.00 to each beneficiary student per annum. It has been estimated that it cost $1.60 for every $1.00 delivered to beneficiaries. Although this is substantial relative to the programs discussed earlier, it is substantially better than the costs of many other programs in Bangladesh. It is possible that the logistics of transporting food is an important factor on the cost side, but more analysis is needed on this issue.

The program uses a two-stage targeting approach. At the first stage, in each of 460 rural provinces (*thanas*), 2–3 "unions" were selected on the basis of low income and literacy. Within the unions, households with primary school-children are eligible if they meet one of four criteria: the family is landless or nearly landless, the household head is a day laborer, the family head is a woman, or the head is in a low-income profession. Based on these targeting criteria, a local school management committee and compulsory primary education ward committee jointly prepare a list of FFE beneficiary households in every union at the beginning of each year. That list is recorded in a registration book that is maintained by the headmaster of the school.

Overall, the targeting of the program is moderately effective in that 60 percent of the transfers go to "poor" households, that is, those falling into the bottom half of the rural income distribution. However, most (if not all) of this performance is due to community targeting, with geographic targeting relatively neutral. Two aspects of the targeting could be improved. First, it is likely that the "sharing" of the program across all rural *thanas* substantially reduces the targeting efficiency, although it may reflect political realities. Second, the program should also be redesigned to make the second-stage community targeting more progressive. Better targeting of households with children not currently in school would probably increase not only targeting performance but also education impacts.

Education impacts seem to be high, especially given the relatively low transfer level. Ahmed and del Ninno (2001) found that attendance in FFE schools increased by 35 percent per school over the two-year period when the FFE program was first introduced. Enrollment of girls jumped by 44 percent. In non-FFE schools there was also an increase, but it was only 2.5 percent. Thus, based on these school data, it appears that the impact of the program was an increase in average enrollments over the first two years of 32.5 percent, which is a substantial impact. However, this may be a substantial overestimate if children previously enrolled in non-FFE schools switched to FFE schools in order to qualify for education transfers. Also, these impressive results declined somewhat in subsequent years, partly due to capacity constraints in participating schools. But even so, the FFE schools continued to have higher enrollment rates. Ahmed and del Ninno also found significantly higher attendance rates and significantly lower dropout rates in the FFE schools. Estimates based on regression analysis (using matching evaluation techniques) have found a program impact of 9 percentage points. This is smaller than the 17 percentage point increase found by Ravallion and Wodon (2000) for 1995–96, possibly because of the choice of years.

Summary and Conclusions

Empirical evidence clearly shows that universal food subsidies are not very effective ways of transferring resources to the poor. This reflects the fact that they are very rarely progressive and often have large consumption and production efficiency costs. Even ignoring the latter efficiency costs, because of leakage to non-poor households it can cost as much as $3.30 to transfer $1.00 to the poor. Including efficiency costs will obviously increase this amount further. For this reason, universal food subsidies are often viewed as stopgap policies until more cost-effective transfer instruments can be developed.

Although targeted subsidized food subsidies (e.g., those delivered through ration shops) can greatly increase their benefit incidence and reduce associated efficiencies, in practice their performance has not always been great, reflecting both high leakages to the non-poor and high costs associated with distributing food and corruption. Empirical evidence highlights the high costs often associated with such transfers. Focusing only on leakage costs, the typical scheme costs $2.40 to transfer $1.00 to the poor, with other schemes ranging from $1.90 to $2.90. Achieving good performance requires that adequate resources be devoted to the separate administrative tasks of screening, delivery, and monitoring, and the potential for research to contribute to the development of useful tools in these areas needs to be explored. In particular, continually reassessing entry and exit criteria for a program can be crucial in maintaining its targeting performance. If the transport costs associated with distributing food cannot be reduced substantially, it may be that use of cash will be a more attractive option. This is an area in which research is urgently needed, and IFPRI has been a key player in moving this research agenda forward. It is widely accepted that cost-effective targeted schemes are available and can work. But social and political factors need to be taken into account when managing the reform process, and the role played by these factors may be another fruitful area for research.

Although well-designed and -implemented public works programs appear to have great potential for targeting poor households, they also appear to be a relatively costly way of dealing with current poverty; the existence of high non-wage costs and forgone earnings means that the cost per unit (net) income transferred to poor households is relatively high. For example, for the typical program, allowing simply for leakages of wages to the non-poor, it cost $1.60 to transfer $1.00 to the poor, with this number ranging across programs from $1.25 to $2.00. Forgone earnings have been found to account for between 25 percent and 50 percent of wage transfers; using lower bound rates increases the median cost ratio to $2.18. Similarly, if nonwage costs are (a low) 20 percent of total project costs, these increase the cost ratio to $3.20. Thus certain design features can ensure that such costs are substantially reduced, including the use of low wages, good geographic targeting, and selection of labor-intensive projects. Evidence suggests that these issues are crucial to the effectiveness of public works in reducing current poverty.

When asset creation is seen as a crucial objective, because there is likely to be a trade-off with the objective of reducing current poverty, it is important that these assets actually be created and benefit the communities. In this respect, there is evidence that community participation in selecting assets and implementing programs may have high returns. However, there is also some evidence that seems to show that community involvement works well only when there are good governance structures and active participation of civil society in these structures.

Public works are particularly effective in addressing the issue of vulnerability to poverty (as opposed to structural poverty) and in crisis situations. This, of course, requires that such programs be flexible in expanding and contracting in response to economic conditions, and this, in turn, may have important implications for the outputs that can be sensibly produced. Thus the choice of labor-intensive projects requiring few management skills and paying relatively low wages would appear to be a precondition for public works to be effective in addressing both current poverty and vulnerability. The combined emphasis of such programs on short- and long-term poverty alleviation, through wages and infrastructure development, respectively, may also make these programs particularly appealing in postconflict situations. Such programs are also often attractive when a social value is attached to work itself; for example, it is often argued that enabling adults to work for a living helps them maintain their dignity and self-esteem. Similarly, it may be easier to obtain political support for programs that require the poor do something to help themselves. Social funds, which put more emphasis on asset creation and community involvement in designing, proposing, and implementing projects, are probably better at addressing structural poverty (through community asset creation), but good geographic targeting and active promotion of demand for these programs in the poorest communities are necessary for them to have a substantial impact on poverty.

Rigorous evaluations are currently available only for India and Argentina, so there is an obvious need for further evaluations, especially of programs designed to avoid some of the shortcomings of existing programs. Important research issues are the nature and magnitude of any general-equilibrium effects, the potential for substantially decreasing forgone incomes, the role of good management and project selection in decreasing nonwage costs, and the trade-offs between the longer-term output and shorter-term income objectives. Both quantitative and qualitative methods are required to identify and evaluate the range of impacts these programs have on poor households and the economic, social, and political factors that determine their performance. The potential for introducing some training dimension to these programs along the lines of workfare programs in developed countries, especially in urban areas, also needs to be explored further. IFPRI has been an active partner in generating the research that exists and is well placed to play a leading role in addressing this research agenda.

A recent program innovation in developing countries, particularly Latin America, is targeted human capital transfers (i.e., transfers conditioned on households' investing in their children's nutrition, health, and education). These provide a promising approach for addressing the issue of structural poverty, adding a "promotional" dimension to the traditional "prevention" role of social safety nets. Invariably, household-level data in many developing countries show that the poorest households are not only poor in terms of income and consumption levels, but also in terms of human capital (i.e., nutrition, health, and education). These new human capital programs are attractive because they address many of the shortcomings of existing social safety nets. For example, they can help integrate a range of existing programs into a more coherent poverty alleviation strategy. Also, by increasing human capital in poor households as well as facilitating the accumulation of a higher physical asset base (e.g., by relaxing the liquidity constraints faced by poor households) they can contribute significantly to breaking the intergenerational transmission of poverty over the longer term.

These programs have also been found to be very well targeted, using a combination of geographic, demographic, proxy means, and community targeting methods. It has been estimated that on average around 68 percent of the benefits accrue to poor households. This implies a cost of $1.40 per $1.00 transferred to the poor, slightly higher than the cost of the best public works programs. In addition, nontransfer costs appear to be relatively low, on average accounting for around 20 percent of the budget. Combining this performance with the targeting efficiency, human capital subsidies cost $1.80 to transfer $1.00 to the poor and outperform the best public works programs discussed earlier.

Targeted human capital subsidies also have been shown, through rigorous evaluations, to have a substantial impact on nutrition, health, and educational outcomes. For example, in Bangladesh it has been estimated that such transfers resulted in primary school enrollment increases from 9 percent to 17 percent. In Nicaragua, one of the poorest countries in Latin America, making transfers dependent on children's attending school increased primary enrollments from 69 percent to 91 percent, with larger impacts for girls and for the poorest households. In Mexico, the program has resulted in around 19 percent more children's attending secondary school, and evaluation results also show a wide range of nutrition and health improvements. It has also resulted in households' significantly enhancing their physical asset base, with a quarter of transfers invested in high-yielding assets.

The fact that these human capital programs have been successful in some poor countries (e.g., Bangladesh and Nicaragua) suggests that they have the po-

tential to be successful elsewhere. However, for these programs to be successful, their design will need to reflect local conditions, including, for example, the
quality of education and healthcare, the existing level of access to these services by poor households, the capacity to implement and monitor such programs, and the potential role of community actors. Other economic policies
must also be conducive to generating broad-based growth capable of productively absorbing more of the skilled labor force. Although in and of themselves
these programs do not provide a panacea for all development problems, we believe that their proven performance justifies serious consideration of such programs as important components of an overall poverty alleviation system.

References

Adams, R. 1988. The political economy of the food subsidy system in Bangladesh. *Journal of Development Studies* 35 (1): 66–88.

———. 2000. Self-targeted subsidies: The political and distributional impact of the
Egyptian food subsidy system. *Economic Development and Cultural Change* 49
(1): 115–136.

Adato, M., and L. Haddad. 2001. Targeting poverty through community-based public
works programs: A cross-disciplinary assessment of recent experience in South
Africa. FCND Discussion Paper 121. Washington, D.C.: International Food Policy Research Institute.

Ahluwalia, D. 1993. Public distribution of food in India: Coverage, targeting and leakages. *Food Policy* 18 (2): 33–54.

Ahmad, E., and N. Stern. 1984. Theory of reform and Indian indirect taxes. *Journal of
Public Economics* 25: 259–295.

———. 1991. *The theory and practice of tax reform in developing countries.* Cambridge, England: Cambridge University Press.

Ahmed, A., and C. del Ninno. 2001. Food for education program in Bangladesh: An evaluation of its impact on educational attainment and food security. Mimeo, International Food Policy Research Institute, Washington, D.C.

Ahmed, A., H. Bouis, T. Gutner, and H. Lofgren. 2001. *The Egyptian food subsidy system: Structure, performance and options for reform.* Research Report 119. Washington, D.C.: International Food Policy Research Institute.

Ahmed, R., O. Chowdhury, M. Hossain, S. Kumar, and M. Abul Quasem. 1985. *Development impact of the food for work program in Bangladesh.* Washington, D.C.: International Food Policy Research Institute.

Alderman, H. 1988. Food subsidies in Egypt: Benefit distribution and nutritional effect.
In *Food subsidies in developing countries: Costs, benefits and policy options,* ed.
P. Pinstrup-Andersen. Baltimore, Md.: The Johns Hopkins University Press.

———. 2002. Subsidies as a social safety net: Effectiveness and challenges. Social Protection Discussion Paper 0224. Washington, D.C.: World Bank.

Alderman, H., and K. Lindert. 1998. The potential and limitations of self-targeted food
subsidies. *World Bank Research Observer* 13 (2): 213–229.

Alderman, H., and J. von Braun. 1984. The effects of the Egyptian food ration and subsidy system on income distribution and welfare. Research Report 45. Washington, D.C.: International Food Policy Research Institute.

Attanasio, O., E. Battistin, E. Fitzsimons, A. Mesnard, and M. Vera-Hernandez. 2005. How effective are conditional cash transfers? Evidence from Colombia. Briefing Note 54. London: Institute of Fiscal Studies.

Bandyopadhyay, D. 1988. Direct intervention programmes for poverty alleviation: An appraisal. *Economic and Political Weekly* 22 (January 24): 23 (26): A77–A88.

Behrman, J., and J. Hoddinott. 2000. An evaluation of the impact of PROGRESA on pre-school child height. International Food Policy Research Institute, Washington, D.C.

Behrman, J., P. Sengupta, and P. Todd. 2001. Progressing through PROGRESA: An impact evaluation of a school subsidy experiment. International Food Policy Research Institute, Washington, D.C.

Bienen, H., and M. Gersovitz. 1986. Economic stabilization, conditionality, and political stability. *International Organization* 39 (4): 729–754.

Binswanger, H., V. Doherty, T. Balarmaiah, M. Bhende, K. Kshirsagar, V. Rao, and P. Raju. 1984. Common features and contrasts in labor relations in the semiarid tropic of India. In *Contractual arrangements, employment, and wages in rural labor markets in Asia*, ed. H. Binswanger and M. Rosenzweig. New Haven, Conn.: Yale University Press.

Cain, M., and S. Lieberman. 1983. Development policy and the prospects for fertility decline in Bangladesh. *Bangladesh Development Studies* 11: 1–38.

Chowdhury, O. 1983. Profile of workers in the food for work programme in Bangladesh. *Bangladesh Development Studies* 11: 111–134.

Coady, D., 1997. Agricultural pricing policies in developing countries: An application to Pakistan. *International Tax and Public Finance* 4: 39–57.

———. 2004. Designing and evaluating social safety nets: Theory, evidence and policy conclusions. Discussion Paper 172. Food Consumption Nutrition Division. Washington, D.C.: International Food Policy Research Institute.

———. 2006. The welfare returns from finer targeting: The case of PROGRESA in Mexico. *International Tax and Public Finance* 13 (2–3): 217–239.

Coady, D., and J. Drèze. 2002. Commodity taxation and social welfare: The generalized Ramsey rule. *International Tax and Public Finance* 9: 295–316.

Coady, D., and S. Parker. 2004. A cost-effectiveness analysis of demand- and supply-side education interventions: The case of PROGRESA in Mexico. *Review of Development Economics* 8 (3): 440–451.

Coady, D., M. Grosh, and J. Hoddinott. 2004a. Targeting outcomes redux. *World Bank Research Observer* 19 (1): 61–85.

———. 2004b. *The targeting of transfers in developing countries: Review of experience and lessons.* Regional and Sectoral Studies Series, World Bank, Washington, D.C.

Dandekar, K. 1983. *Employment Guarantee Scheme: An employment opportunity for women.* Gokhale Institute Studies 67. Bombay: Orient Longman.

Dev, S., and M. Suryanarayana. 1991. Is PDS urban biased and pro-rich: An evaluation. *Economic and Political Weekly* 26 (4): 2357–2366

Drèze, J., and A. Sen. 1989. *Hunger and public action.* Oxford, England: Oxford University Press.

————. 1990. *The political economy of hunger: Famine prevention.* Oxford, England: Clarendon.

Drèze, J., and N. Stern. 1987. The theory of cost-benefit analysis. In *Handbook of public economics* Vol. 2, ed. A. Auerbach and M. Feldstein. Amsterdam: North Holland.

Echeverri-Gent, J. 1988. Guaranteed employment in an Indian state: The Maharashtra experience. *Asian Survey* 28: 1294–1310.

Galasso, E., M. Ravallion, and A. Salvia. 2001. Assisting the transition from workfare to work: A randomized experiment in Argentina. Mimeo, World Bank, Washington, D.C.

Gertler, P. 2004. Do conditional cash transfers improve child health? Evidence from PROGRESA's controlled randomized experiment. *American Economic Review, Papers and Proceedings* 94 (2): 336–341.

Gertler, P., S. Martinez, and M. Rubio. 2006. Investing cash transfers to raise long-term living standards. World Bank Policy Research Working Paper 3994. Washington, D.C.: World Bank.

Grosh, M. 1994. *Administered targeted social programs in Latin America: From platitudes to practice.* World Bank Regional and Sector Studies Series. Washington, D.C.: World Bank. Available at <www-wds.worldbank.org/external/default/WDSContent Server/WDSP/IB/1994/01/01/000009265_3970128111710/Rendered/PDF/multi 0page.pdf> (accessed November 2007).

Haddad, L., and M. Adato. 2001. How efficiently do public works programs transfer benefits to the poor? Evidence from South Africa. FCND Discussion Paper 108. Washington, D.C.: International Food Policy Research Institute.

Haddad, L., H. Alderman, S. Appleton, L. Song, and Y. Yohannes. 2002. Reducing child undernutrition: How far does income growth take us? Discussion Paper 137, Food Consumption Nutrition Division. Washington, D.C.: International Food Policy Research Institute.

Herring, R., and R. Edwards. 1983. Guaranteeing employment to the rural poor: Social functions and class interests in employment guarantee scheme in Western India. *World Development* 11: 575–592.

Hirway, I., P. Rayappa, T. Shah, I. Khanna, N. Raj, and S. Acharay. 1990. *Report of the study group of anti-poverty programmes.* New Delhi: National Commission on Rural Labour.

Hoddinott, J., E. Skoufias, and R. Washburn. 2000. The impact of PROGRESA on consumption: A final report. International Food Policy Research Institute, Washington, D.C. Available at <www.ifpri.org/themes/progresa/pdf/hoddinott_consumption .pdf> (accessed November 2007).

Hoddinott, J., M. Adato, T. Besley, and L. Haddad. 2001. Participation and poverty reduction: Issues, theory and new evidence from South Africa. FCND Discussion Paper 98. Washington, D.C.: International Food Policy Research Institute.

Hossain, M. 1985. Labor market and employment effects. In *Development impact of the food-for-work program in Bangladesh,* ed. R. Ahmed, O. Chowdhury, M. Hossain, S. Kumar, and M. Abul Quasem. Washington, D.C.: International Food Policy Research Institute.

Hossain, M. 1987. *The assault that failed: A profile of absolute poverty in six villages in Bangladesh.* Geneva: United Nations Research Institute for Social Development.

Hossain, M., and M. Akash. 1993. Rural public works for relief and development: A review of Bangladesh experience. Working Papers on Food Subsidies 7. Washington, D.C.: International Food Policy Research Institute.

Jalan, J., and M. Ravallion. 2000. Estimating the benefit incidence of an antipoverty program by propensity score matching. *Journal of Business and Economic Statistics* (American Statistical Association) 21 (1): 19–30.

Krueger, A. 1992. *The political economy of agricultural pricing policy,* Vol. 5. Baltimore, Md.: The Johns Hopkins University Press.

Maluccio, J. A. 2007. Education and child labor: Experimental evidence from a Nicaraguan conditional cash transfer program. In *Child labor in Latin America,* ed. P. Orazem, G. Sedlaceck, and Z. Tzannatos. Washington, D.C.: Inter-American Development Bank and World Bank.

Mellor, J., and R. Ahmed, eds. 1988. *Agricultural price policy for developing countries.* Baltimore, Md.: The Johns Hopkins University Press.

Morley, S., and D. Coady. 2003. *From social assistance to social development.* Washington, D.C.: Center for Global Development and International Food Policy Research Institute.

Newbery, D., and N. Stern, eds. 1987. *The theory of taxation for developing countries.* Oxford, England: Oxford University Press.

Orazem, P., G. Sedlaceck, and Z. Tzannatos, eds. 2007. *Child labor in Latin America.* Washington, D.C.: Inter-American Development Bank and World Bank.

PEO (Programme Evaluation Organization). 1980. *Joint evaluation report on employment guarantee scheme in Maharashtra.* New Delhi: Programme Evaluation Organization, Planning Commission.

Pinstrup-Andersen, P., ed. 1988. *Food subsidies in developing countries: Costs, benefits and policy options.* Baltimore, Md.: The Johns Hopkins University Press.

Radhakrishna, R., and K. Subbarao 1997. India's public distribution system. Discussion Paper 380. Washington, D.C.: World Bank.

Rao, V. 2000. Price heterogeneity and "real" inequality: A case study of poverty and prices in rural south India. *Review of Income and Wealth* 46 (2): 201–211.

Ravallion, M. 1990a. Reaching the poor through rural public employment: A survey of theory and evidence. World Bank Discussion Paper 94. Washington, D.C.: World Bank.

———. 1990b. Market responses to anti-hunger policies: Wages, prices, and employment. In *The political economy of hunger: Famine prevention,* ed. J. Drèze and A. Sen. Oxford, England: Clarendon.

———. 1991a. On the coverage of public employment schemes for poverty alleviation. *Journal of Development Economics* 34: 57–79.

———. 1991b. Reaching the poor through public employment: Arguments, evidence and lessons from South Asia. *World Bank Research Observer* 6: 153–175.

———. Monitoring targeting performance when decentralized allocations to the poor are unobserved. *World Bank Economic Review* 14 (2): 331–345.

———. 2003 Targeted transfers in poor countries: Revisiting the trade-offs and policy options. Social Protection Discussion Paper 0314. Washington, D.C.: World Bank.

Ravallion, M., and G. Datt. 1995. Is targeting through a work requirement efficient? Some evidence from rural India. In *Public spending and the poor: Theory and evidence,* ed. D. van de Walle and K. Nead. Baltimore, Md.: The Johns Hopkins University Press.

Ravallion, M., and Q. Wodon. 2000. Does child labor displace schooling? Evidence from behavioral responses to an enrolment subsidy. *Economic Journal* 110: C158–C176.

Ravallion, M., E. Galasso, T. Lazo, and E. Philipp. 2001. Do workfare participants recover quickly from retrenchment? Mimeo, World Bank, Washington, D.C.

Rawlings, L., and G. Rubio 2003. Evaluating the impact of conditional cash transfer programs: Lessons from Latin America. Mimeo, World Bank, Washington, D.C.

Rawlings, L., L. Sherburne-Benz, and J. van Domelen. 2004. *Evaluating social funds: A cross-country analysis of community investments.* World Bank Regional and Sectoral Studies Series Report 27834. Washington, D.C.: World Bank. Available at <www.wds.worldbank.org/external/default/WDSContentServer/WDSP/IB/2004/02/13/000090341_20040213142553/Rendered/PDF/278340PAPER0Evaluating0 social.pdf> (accessed November 2007).

Sahn, D., and D. Stifel. 2000. Poverty comparisons across time and over countries in Africa. *World Development* 28 (12): 2123–2155.

Schiff, M., and A. Valdes. 1992. *The political economy of agricultural pricing policy.* Baltimore, Md.: The Johns Hopkins University Press.

Schultz, P. 2000. School subsidies for the poor: Evaluating a Mexican strategy for reducing poverty. Report submitted to PROGRESA. International Food Policy Research Institute, Washington, D.C.

Skoufias, E. 2001. Is PROGRESA working? Summary of the results of an evaluation by IFPRI. Discussion Paper 118. Food Consumption Nutrition Division. Washington, D.C.: International Food Policy Research Institute.

Skoufias, E., B. Davis, and S. de la Vega. 2001. Targeting the poor in Mexico: An evaluation of the selection of households into PROGRESA. *World Development* 29 (10): 1769–1784.

Smith, J., and K. Subbarao. 2000. What role for safety net transfers in very low income countries? Social Protection Discussion Paper 0301. Washington, D.C.: World Bank. Available at <http://siteresources.worldbank.org/SOCIALPROTECTION/Resources/SP-Discussion-papers/Safety-Nets-DP/0301.pdf> (accessed November 2007).

Subbarao, K. 2003. Systemic shocks and social protection: Role and effectiveness of public works programs. Social Safety Net Primer Series, World Bank, Washington, D.C.

Subbarao, K., K. Ezemerani, J. Randa, and G. Rubio. 1999. *Impact evaluation in FY98 Bank projects: A review.* Poverty Group, Poverty Reduction and Economic Management Network. World Bank, Washington, D.C. Mimeo.

Tuck, L., and K. Lindert. 1998. From universal food subsidies to a self-targeted program: A case study of Tunisian reform. Discussion Paper 351. Washington, D.C.: World Bank.

Von Braun, J., ed. 1995. Employment for poverty reduction and food security. Occasional Paper 32. Washington, D.C.: International Food Policy Research Institute.

World Bank. 1997. World development report 1997: The state in a changing world. New York: Oxford University Press.

6 Public Spending, Growth, and Poverty Alleviation in Sub-Saharan Africa: A Dynamic General-Equilibrium Analysis

HANS LOFGREN AND SHERMAN ROBINSON

This chapter explores the impact of government policies on long-run growth and poverty in Sub-Saharan Africa (SSA). It complements Chapters 3, 4, and 5, which often ignore the general-equilibrium effects of various types of public spending by using an economywide approach. It will answer an important question about whether ignoring the general-equilibrium effects will bias the estimated returns to the various types of public spending that are typically reported in the cases in the previous chapters.

Methodologically, we analyze growth in an archetype SSA country using a dynamic computable general equilibrium (CGE) model that is an extension of the static standard CGE model set out by Lofgren et al. (2002). In addition to incorporating time, the model extends the earlier static model by incorporating the influence of economic openness and government spending on factor productivity. The model is applied to a stylized database that captures structural characteristics of the economies of SSA and draws on insights from research on the effects of different public spending policies on economic performance. More specifically, the database reflects the structure of a real-world average Sub-Saharan economy. The economywide approach supports analysis of trade-offs and synergies between different public investment strategies.

The second section of the chapter provides a brief review of the literature on the determinants of growth and poverty reduction, with an emphasis on the role of public policy, which informs the subsequent sections of this study. The synthesis draws on a large body of econometrically based cross-country analysis. In the third section the model structure is explained and situated in the context of the literature on dynamic economywide policy models. We also present the stylized model database and the ability of the model to replicate stylized facts from the growth and development literature. In the fourth section we present and analyze a set of simulations that explore the links between growth,

The authors thank Moataz El-Said for professional research assistance.

184

poverty, and government policies. In the final section we summarize our findings and identify high-priority areas for future research.[1]

Growth, Poverty, and Public Policy

In recent decades, a considerable research effort has been made to untangle the determinants of growth and poverty, including public policy. Although there is a lack of consensus on many of its findings, this body of research nevertheless provides a valuable source of stylized facts and parameter estimates that are useful in the construction of a CGE model and its database.[2] One strand of this literature uses growth accounting to disaggregate GDP growth into factor accumulation and total factor productivity (TFP) growth. The picture that emerges from this work is that in SSA, average TFP growth has been negative in recent decades. Across all developing countries, the TFP share in GDP growth varies, but may typically be 33–50 percent. Recent research suggests that TFP growth may be of increasing importance and now accounts for the bulk of cross-country growth gaps. At a more disaggregated level, TFP growth has in recent decades been faster for agriculture than manufacturing in countries in all regions, including SSA.

The econometric literature on growth determinants constitutes a second strand. This literature has tried to unravel the determinants of growth, typically relying on single-equation cross-country regressions of a measure of GDP on a set of potential determinants selected in light of modern growth theory. In recent years, this literature has in some cases been extended to time-series analysis, analysis at the single-country level, and estimation of simultaneous-equation systems. The major growth determinants have been divided into accumulation of factors (physical capital, labor, and human capital), public policy, economic openness, and miscellaneous other conditions, often including aspects related to politics or geography.

Although this body of work has suffered from econometric problems and theoretical shortcomings (in addition to the data problems that hamper most lines of analysis), it is nevertheless possible to extract some general findings. In general, the results indicate that accumulation of labor and physical capital has a robust, positive impact on growth. When physical capital has been disaggregated into private and public capital, the growth effect has been more consistently positive for private capital. This may reflect the fact that, due to corruption and other factors, a large share of public investment has not generated public capital, as well as the fact that, in addition to growth-enhancing invest-

---

1. Supplementary information on the database is available on request from the authors.
2. This section is a synopsis of Lofgren and Robinson (2004), available on request from the authors. This document includes a full set of references. The major general references are Dumont (1996), Temple (1999), and O'Connell and Ndulu (2000).

ments that complement private sector production, public investment also has included growth-retarding investments that compete with more efficient private sector investments.

For human capital, the evidence is less clear and differs widely across studies. Theoretical growth models with human capital permit increases in human capital per worker to increase labor productivity. On balance, the empirical evidence suggests that education (typically proxied by a measure of average level of schooling) has a positive growth effect, whereas the macro-level links between health indicators and growth are less clear.

From a policy perspective, it would be useful if the analysis could be more disaggregated and if the analysis of human capital could be extended to consider the impact of public spending as opposed to indicators of education and health status. The analysis of Fan and Rao (2003), which we will draw on in the model-based analysis in this study, responds to these demands (albeit with caveats related to data and methodological problems discussed by Fan and Rao). They estimate Cobb-Douglas production functions for Africa, Asia, and Latin America with country-level GDP as the dependent variable, and, as independent variables, labor, private capital, and public capital stocks. The latter are disaggregated into agriculture, education, health, transportation and telecommunication, social security, and defense. These government capital stock variables were constructed from past government spending (both current and capital) in each functional area. With the exception of defense, the signs for the coefficients (which may be interpreted as representing elasticities) were expected to be positive. For the most part, the coefficient estimates had the expected signs, and most were significant at the 10 percent level. For Africa, the only coefficient with the "wrong" sign was for education. However, the combined marginal impact of human capital (education and health) spending was positive. The strongest positive effect was for health spending, followed by agriculture, while defense spending had a strong negative effect (Fan and Rao 2003). In other studies that have used a disaggregated approach, very strong growth effects have been identified for investments in transportation and communications infrastructure. For agriculture, the impact of infrastructure investments may be particularly strong given that transportation costs often represent a large share of output prices.

The growth literature has also addressed aspects of policy and economic performance that are not readily summarized on the basis of government budget data. There is considerable agreement that macroeconomic stability, often proxied by low inflation or a low budget deficit relative to GDP, has a positive impact on growth. Although the role of trade has become contentious, it seems that, on balance, an open trade policy and a strong involvement in foreign trade promote growth. This does not mean that the specific mechanisms are well understood or that openness invariably is growth promoting. On the contrary, economic structure and domestic policies are likely to have a strong conditioning impact on the effects of trade liberalization and economic openness.[3]

The fact that many cross-country analyses found a negative and significant SSA dummy has stimulated a search for additional growth determinants with special relevance for this region. The addition of variables indicative of geography ("landlockedness"), demographics (age dependency and the gap between growth in labor force and population), and external factors (terms-of-trade shocks and trading partner growth) has eliminated the negative dummy. Findings also suggest that once these additional growth determinants are accounted for, the marginal responses of countries in SSA to changes in their economic environment are no different from those of countries in other regions.

The cross-country regression literature strongly suggests that, on average, more rapid GDP growth is associated with more rapid poverty reduction— "growth is good for the poor." In fact, the elasticity of the head-count poverty rate with respect to mean per capita consumption (or income) is an identity that depends on the poverty line, mean per capita consumption, and income distribution (Bourguignon 2003, 5–11). Given differences across countries in these respects, poverty elasticities do also differ across countries, with averages that tend to be between –2 and –3 (Bourguignon 2003, 3–5). For example, for a sample of developing countries, Ravallion and Chen (1997) estimate an average of –3 (between –1 and –5 for the 95 percent confidence interval). Empirical findings suggest that the effectiveness of growth in reducing poverty often is higher if growth is biased in favor of rural areas, if initial inequality is lower, and/or if the initial state of rural development and human resource development is more favorable. Pro-poor public expenditures and land tenure reform can play a role in skewing the growth benefits in favor of the poor. In general, these findings confirm the notion that there may be synergies between different policies and structural characteristics; the consequences of any given policy on economic indicators depend on the nature of other policies and structural characteristics.

In sum, the literature on growth in developing countries suggests a number of desiderata for simulation models of developing countries. Such models should be able to capture a set of stylized facts concerning the relationships between poverty reduction and GDP, including the roles of labor force growth, accumulation of private capital, economic openness, productivity-enhancing public spending (on both agriculture and human development, that is, education and health), and physical infrastructure (especially transportation and communications). In addition, simulation models should permit the government to influence economic performance via policies that contribute to economic openness and enhance private capital accumulation (e.g., by raising the

---

3. For example, see case studies of Tanzania (Wobst 2001), Mozambique (Tarp et al. 2002), and Zimbabwe (Bautista et al. 2003).

incomes of agents with high savings). Models should also be able to address the trade-offs that are involved in economic development, among other things between private capital accumulation and government spending.

Finally, the literature includes a wide range of estimates of the impact of different types of government intervention and economic openness on growth and poverty. Given that it primarily is based on reduced-form models, underlying structural mechanisms are typically left out. Thus builders of simulation models face the challenge of exploring the consequences of alternative estimates of and channels for the links that have been identified in the econometric literature.

Dynamic Poverty Analysis: Model Structure and Database

In this section we present a dynamic CGE model and a database that is representative of an archetype SSA country. The model is an extension of the static standard CGE model in Lofgren et al. (2002). Its formulation incorporates insights from the literature on the potential channels through which different kinds of government spending influence productivity and economic performance.

We first situate our model in the literature on dynamic economywide policy models, then describe the model structure and its database. The appendix to this chapter presents additional information on the database.

Background

There have been two bursts of work on dynamic models in the postwar period. The first work program concerned neoclassical growth models—starting from the "Solow–Swan" model—and ran from the mid-1950s until the late 1960s.[4] This literature focused on the mathematical properties of a variety of optimal growth models, with little empirical work. This program died out in the 1970s, largely, as Barro and Sala-i-Martin (1995, 12) argue, because of its "lack of empirical relevance."

The second burst of work, which started in the mid-1980s, was based on "endogenous growth" models. Considerable progress has been made in developing analytic dynamic models that seek to incorporate the stylized facts of long-run growth as it has occurred in the past in the currently developed countries and as it is unfolding in the less developed countries in the postwar period.[5] In particular, the new approach has sought to "endogenize" the process of technical

---

4. For an extensive survey of the neoclassical growth literature in this program see Burmeister and Dobell (1970).

5. A major part of this new work program, at least as practiced by Barro and various coauthors, has involved cross-country empirical analysis to keep the theoretical models grounded in historical experience.

change in the models, linking productivity growth to factors such as R&D investment, capital growth (human and physical), and international linkages through trade.[6] The standard approach is to assume that the economy maximizes some kind of intertemporal utility function and makes choices regarding variables such as the rate of savings, investment in various kinds of physical or human capital, and investment in "research" or "knowledge creation" that affect "technical change" or "TFP growth"—where research or knowledge have elements of being public goods. These theoretical models, and their empirical counterparts, rely heavily on the mathematics of dynamic optimization and the analysis of alternative steady-state growth paths, with limited discussion of "adjustment processes" by which the steady-state path is reached.[7]

In these models, agents are assumed to optimize with perfect foresight and correct knowledge about the forces at work; these models all implicitly or explicitly embody a "rational expectations" notion of dynamic equilibrium. Agents generally operate in perfectly competitive markets. However, the models are also characterized by knowledge diffusion, spillovers, and externalities, which leads to the failure of competitive markets to achieve optimality. These market failures affect the behavior of agents; hence government policy can play a significant role in determining long-run growth.

While the work program on endogenous growth models has paid appropriate attention to the linking of theory and empirical cross-country analysis, the mathematics of dynamic optimization models constrains the "domain of applicability" of the analytic growth models. These models must, of necessity, focus on a very few driving forces and make very strong assumptions about agent behavior and the working of markets in order to remain mathematically tractable. Developing countries, on the other hand, are characterized by great heterogeneity in initial conditions, market structures, the degree of market integration, the nature of constraints on agent behavior, and the role of government.

Since the emergence of the growth literature, there has been a considerable, although narrowing, gap between growth theorists and development economists. In the words of Barro and Sala-i-Martin, "Development economists . . . retained an applied perspective and tended to use models that were technically unsophisticated but empirically useful." In development economics, CGE models have become a commonly used economywide approach. They build on and generalize earlier generations of programming and input-output models, most importantly by incorporating endogenous prices and using formulations that permit a detailed treatment of households and income distribution. The CGE literature has incorporated features from and contributed to the growth literature.

---

6. A textbook treatment of this literature is that of Aghion and Howitt (1998).

7. For a notable exception see the work of Diao, Yeldan, and Roe (1998), who focus on adjustment paths to steady states.

The dynamic CGE literature includes two strands, dynamic-recursive models and optimal growth models.[8] In recursive models, all agents (private and public) make their decisions on the basis of past and current conditions, with no role for forward-looking expectations about the future. Agents are either myopic, so they do not care about the future, or ignorant—nobody can or does know anything about the future, so all behavior must be based on information from the past. Alternatively, one can assume that the economy is on a stable (balanced) growth path; hence agents can simply assume that the future will be "like" the present, and need no other information to behave rationally.

A recursive dynamic model can be divided into a "within-period" module (in essence a static CGE model) and a "between-period" module that links the within-period modules by updating selected parameters (typically including factor supplies, population, and factor productivity) on the basis of exogenous trends and past endogenous variables. Information from past solutions can also be used in the between-period modules to generate expectations about the future, which might be used to affect agent behavior in later within-period modules. Dynamic-recursive models can be, and often are, solved recursively; the within-period modules are solved separately in sequence, and the between-period modules are solved to provide parameters needed for the within-period model in the succeeding period.

The second strand of empirical dynamic analysis is performed with optimal growth models. These may be viewed as an applied counterpart to the theoretical neoclassical optimal growth models used in the endogenous growth literature. All agents have "rational expectations" and make intertemporally optimal decisions; everybody knows everything about the future, and they use that information in making decisions. Empirical models in this tradition solve simultaneously for all variables in all time periods, often looking for infinite-horizon, steady-state, balanced growth paths.

Recursive models are used extensively in empirical policy analysis, while intertemporally optimal growth models that can be solved analytically are more important in the theoretical literature. Both modeling traditions (as well as many static models) have incorporated features highlighted by the growth literature, including endogenous determinants of productivity growth. Because they are too complex to solve analytically, CGE models in both traditions have to be solved empirically and are used in simulation analysis.

In its current formulation, our model belongs to the class of dynamic-recursive models: agents have no knowledge about the future. In the absence of empirical support for the assumption that private agents act on the basis of perfect foresight, a dynamic-recursive formulation is certainly plausible for simulation analysis. We do not explicitly specify the factors that prevent private

---

8. Dervis, de Melo, and Robinson (1982, 169–181) and Diao, Yelden, and Roe (1998) explain the structure of recursive and intertemporal dynamic models, respectively.

agents from realizing intertemporally optimal patterns of savings and investment (e.g., market imperfections, credit constraints, and/or the belief that any knowledge about the future is too uncertain to act on), but we do explore the potential gains from different policy strategies, given that agents do not have perfect foresight. The model is solved for a finite horizon and is used to explore the properties of a "growth episode" characterized by initial conditions, particular dynamic forces at work, growth linkages, agent behavior, institutional constraints, and the length of the time period.[9]

We integrate the within-period and between-period modules in one set of simultaneous equations, making it possible to solve the full model in a single pass for the planning horizon. Apart from being efficient computationally, this approach supports implementation of non-recursive-dynamic models, either by adding an objective function or by reformulating the first-order conditions of selected agents to incorporate forward-looking behavior. As an example, an objective function can be specified measuring discounted intertemporal social welfare. In the constraint set (the rest of the model), some government policies could be endogenized.[10] Maximization of the objective with respect to the choice of values for the free policy variables would generate a general-equilibrium solution with perfect foresight on the part of the government, with or without perfect foresight or freedom of action on the part of private agents. It would also be feasible to reformulate the first-order conditions of private agents to incorporate more knowledge about future periods, with perfect foresight as a special case.

Our model is designed to analyze the links between government policies, growth, and poverty reduction in SSA. Synthesizing the empirical and theoretical literature, we incorporate causal links between factor productivity and different types of government spending and openness to foreign trade. We use and extend formulations that have appeared in other CGE models, both static and dynamic. Other model features, which are of particular importance in an SSA setting, include household consumption of nonmarketed (or "home") commodities and an explicit treatment of transaction costs for commodities that enter the market sphere.

Model Structure

The model is formulated as a simultaneous-equations system, including both linear and nonlinear equations. The equations are divided into a within-period mod-

---

9. Our notion of a "growth episode" has much in common with Kuznets's (1966) notion of an "economic epoch," which he characterized as a long period whose dynamics were driven by the working out of what he called an "epochal innovation." Our episodes, however, are shorter, characterized by medium-run "drivers" or "engines" of growth.

10. If no policy choices are endogenized, the model is "square" and there is only one feasible solution. In this case, the addition of the objective function does not influence the model solution.

TABLE 6.1 Model disaggregation

Account category	Disaggregation
Activities (14)[a]	Agriculture (6): Large-scale export crop, small-scale export crop, large-scale nonexport crop, small-scale nonexport crop, large-scale livestock, small-scale livestock
	Industry (4): Mining, food and fiber, domestic manufacturing, import-substituting manufacturing
	Services (4): Construction, trade and transportation, public services, other services
Factors (5)	Labor (2): Unskilled, skilled
	Capital
	Land (2): Large-scale, small-scale
Institutions and related accounts (12)	Households: Rural upper-income, rural lower-income, urban upper-income, urban lower-income
	Government
	Auxiliary government accounts: Interest payments, tax accounts (direct taxes, export taxes, import tariffs, other indirect taxes)
	Rest of the world
	Savings–investment account (consolidated)

NOTE: The model also includes commodities, one for each activity except for large-scale export crop and small-scale export crop activities, which produce the same commodity.

[a]The numbers in parentheses indicate the number of items in the various account categories.

ule, which defines the decisions in each time period, and a between-period module, which updates the stocks of different endowments over time. This disaggregation of the model is shown in Table 6.1.

In any given time period, the equations capture the full circular flow of payments, including production (activities producing outputs using factors and intermediate inputs), consumption (by households and the government), investment (private and public), trade (both domestic and foreign), and other government revenue and spending activities, as well as the market equilibrium conditions, macro balances, and dynamic updating equations under which the agents operate.

THE WITHIN-PERIOD MODULE. In essence, the within-period module defines a one-period, static CGE model.[11] It includes the first-order conditions for optimal production and consumption decisions, given available technology and preferences. The technology is defined by a nested, two-level structure with, at

---

11. Apart from the fact that variables are time indexed, the "within-period" module is very similar to the standard static CGE model developed by researchers at the International Food Policy Research Institute (IFPRI). We keep the discussion of these features brief, focusing our attention on new features. The reader may refer to Lofgren et al. (2002) for more details on model features.

the top, a Leontief aggregation of value added and an aggregate intermediate and, at the bottom, a constant-elasticity-of-substitution (CES) aggregation of primary factors and a Leontief aggregation of intermediate inputs. Consumer demand is given by the linear expenditure system, which is derived from a maximization of a Stone–Geary utility function subject to a spending constraint. Both producers and consumers behave myopically, considering only current conditions when making their decisions. They take relevant prices (of outputs, factors, and intermediate inputs) as given, and markets are assumed to be competitive.

For primary factors, demanded by production activities, aggregate supplies are fixed. For each factor, an economywide wage variable adjusts endogenously to clear the market, equating the quantity demanded with the quantity supplied. Each activity pays an activity-specific wage that is the product of the economywide wage and a fixed, activity-specific wage (distortion) term.

The bulk of household incomes comes from factors; each household group receives factor incomes in proportion to the share of each factor stock that it controls.[12] The main items on the household spending side are direct taxes, savings, and consumption. Taxes and savings are determined on the basis of simple rules.

The government earns most of its income from direct and indirect taxes and spends it on consumption, investment, and interest payments (on its foreign and domestic debt). Real government demand (consumption and investment) is exogenous, disaggregated by function. According to the aggregate investment function of the model, private investment is a fixed share of nominal absorption (i.e., nominal domestic final demand or the sum of private and government consumption and investment spending).

All commodities (domestic output and imports) enter markets. For marketed output, the ratio between the quantities of exports and domestic sales is positively related to the ratio between the corresponding supply prices. The price received by domestic suppliers for exports depends on the world price, the exchange rate, transaction costs (to the border), and export taxes (if any). The supply price for domestic sales is equal to the price paid by domestic demanders minus the transaction cost of domestic marketing (from the supplier to the demander) per unit of domestic sales. If the commodity is not exported, total output goes to the domestic market.

Domestic market demand is the sum of demands for household market consumption, government consumption, private and public investment, intermediate inputs, and transaction (trade and transportation) inputs. Typically, domestic market demands are for a composite commodity that is made up of imports and domestic output. The ratio between the demand quantities for im-

---

12. Note that the model has no separate account for or modeling of firms (enterprises). Their savings and tax payments are allocated to the household sector, which directly receives capital incomes that, in the real world, at least in part pass through enterprises.

ports and domestic output is a function of the ratio of their demand prices. Total market demand is directed to imports for commodities that lack domestic
production and to domestic output for nonimported commodities. Import prices
paid by domestic demanders are determined by world prices, the exchange rate,
import tariffs, and the cost of a fixed quantity of transaction services per import
unit (which covers the cost of moving the commodity from the border to the
demander).[13] Prices paid by demanders for domestic output include the cost of
transaction services (in this case reflecting that the commodity was moved from
the domestic supplier to the domestic demander). Prices received by domestic
suppliers are net of this transaction cost. Flexible prices equilibrate demands
for and supplies of domestically marketed domestic output. In international
markets, the small-country assumption is followed: export demands and import
supplies are infinitely elastic at exogenous world prices.

　　In its balance of payments, the country receives foreign exchange in the
form of export revenue, net transfers to domestic institutions, foreign borrowing by the government (which may be negative if the government is repaying
debt), foreign grants, and foreign direct investment. These earnings are allocated to imports, interest payments on foreign debt, and repatriation of profits
to foreign investors. Among these components, exports, imports, interest payments, and profit repatriation are endogenous, while the rest is exogenous—in
effect imposing a fixed current account deficit.

　　For the three macroeconomic balances of the model—the government balance, savings-investment balance, and balance of payments—macro closure rules
are required for the model.[14] This model incorporates a simple set of assumptions
about how macro adjustments operate. For the government balance, government
savings is the flexible, balancing variable. For the balance of payments, endogenous adjustments in the real exchange rate (influencing the trade balance) ensure
equality between flows (including net foreign borrowing and grants) and outflows
of foreign exchange. In the savings-investment balance, real government investment is exogenous while private investment is a fixed share of absorption. Endogenous uniform percentage point adjustments in household savings rates ensure that total savings is sufficient to finance investment. As pointed out in the
simulation section, we deviate from these assumptions in a subset of the simulations for which household savings rates are fixed while the adjusting variable is
either private investment (determined by the level of available resources after the
allocation of required financing to government investment) or foreign grants (set
at a level sufficient to finance both government and private investments).

---

　　13. Note that these transaction costs are not ad valorem; the rates (the ratio between the margin and the price without the margin) change when there are changes in the prices of transaction
services and/or the commodities that are marketed.
　　14. For a discussion of macro closures in the context of the standard CGE model, see Lofgren et al. (2002, 13–17).

The CGE model determines only relative prices, and a numéraire is needed to anchor the aggregate price level. The consumer price index (CPI) is the numéraire price index, so all changes in nominal prices and incomes in simulations are relative to a fixed CPI.

Finally, the within-period block also includes relationships defining TFP by activity and individual factor productivity by factor and activity. For each activity, two sources of endogenous change in TFP are covered: (1) changes in the economywide trade-GDP ratio relative to the base year ratio[15] and (2) changes in government capital stocks, defined by functional spending area. These relationships are captured by various constant-elasticity functions linking TFP or the productivity of a specific factor to different types of government expenditure and trade. The elasticity parameters are activity-, factor-, and function-specific, making it possible to specify different channels and magnitudes for the productivity effects of different types of government spending. This type of relationship tends to be focused on the link between TFP and public capital stocks in infrastructure (or, more simply, the aggregate stock of government capital). However, in this application, we go beyond this by linking TFP to a wider range of government capital stocks (as indicated by our functional disaggregation of the government).

THE BETWEEN-PERIOD MODULE. The between-period module covers the links between time periods. It includes equations that define the stocks of different assets: factors (land, labor, and private capital), government capital stocks, and foreign debt (held by the government). All stocks are associated with specific institutions. This information is used to define the shares of each institution in total income of each factor and the interest payments of the government to the rest of the world.

Labor and land stocks are updated on the basis of exogenous trends. The population in each time period is also exogenous. The accumulation of private and government capital stocks and foreign government debt is endogenous. For both capital categories, the stock in any given year depends on past stocks, new investment, and the depreciation rate. In the accumulation equation for government capital, real investment is broadly defined to include both current and capital spending. The stock of foreign debt depends on past stocks and new borrowing.

The model is solved annually for the period 1998–2015. Each model solution generates an extensive, economywide set of results covering sectoral, household, and macro data in each solution period. In our analysis, we summarize this information in a set of indicators, including data on macroeconomic growth, changes in the structure of production and trade, and the evolution of disaggregated household welfare and poverty.

---

15. The trade-GDP ratio is defined in real terms, using base-year prices, on the assumption that TFP is related to changes in real variables, not relevant market shares.

The poverty indicators are computed on the basis of a representative-household (RH) approach in a separate poverty module. In this module, the within-group household distribution is specified by a log-normal frequency function. The 1998 poverty lines in rural and urban areas are calibrated to exogenous poverty rates; we use a log standard error of 0.35 for all RHs (representative households in the model). In the computation of poverty indicators for each simulation, the CGE model feeds the poverty module with simulated data for mean consumption and CPI for each RH.[16]

The Database: Structural Features of an Archetype Country in Sub-Saharan Africa

The model database, which captures the structural features of an archetype country in SSA, consists of a social accounting matrix (SAM), data on the labor force and population, and various elasticity parameters for functions specifying production, import demand, export supply, consumer expenditures, and links between government investment, trade, and sectoral TFP.

The SAM was constructed on the basis of a database extracted from the *World Development Indicators* that covered most countries in SSA (World Bank 2001) and a disaggregated SAM for Zimbabwe drawing on information in other SSA SAMs.[17] As a first step, the World Bank database was used to build a macro SAM for SSA, excluding South Africa (Table 6.2). Table 6.3 summarizes part of the information in the macro SAM in a more familiar table format, including some additional items, and compares the figures for SSA to those for all developing countries.

In the construction of the macro SAM, data for the different countries in the region were weighted by GDP share. Each entry was normalized to shares of GDP at market prices. Tables 6.2 and 6.3 indicate that on the spending side, private consumption is the main item—75.5 percent of GDP; out of this, 4.5 percent of GDP is home consumption. Absorption (the sum of private and government consumption plus investment) is 109 percent of GDP, which implies a trade deficit of 9 percent. Total foreign trade (the sum of exports and imports) accounts for close to 70 percent of GDP.

Investment (20 percent of GDP) is financed in roughly equal shares by private, government, and foreign savings (the current-account deficit). Due to a surplus in nontrade items in the current account, the current-account deficit is smaller than the trade deficit. Current government operations represent 21 per-

16. For further details and a discussion of alternative approaches to poverty and inequality analysis in a CGE framework, see Lofgren, Robinson, and El-Said (2003).

17. IFPRI research projects have generated SAM data for a number of SSA countries, including Malawi, Mozambique, South Africa, Tanzania, Uganda, Zambia, and Zimbabwe. See www.ifpri.org. The Zimbabwe SAM is described by Thomas and Bautista (1999).

TABLE 6.2 Macro social accounting matrix for an archetype country in Sub-Saharan Africa, 1998 (percent of GDP at market prices)

	1	2	3	4	5	6	7	8	9	10	11	Total
1 Activities		159.4		4.5								164.0
2 Commodities	72.0	18.9		70.3	13.9	30.2	20.1					225.5
3 Factors	91.1											91.1
4 Households			85.4	1.3		4.5						91.1
5 Government				2.9		4.1		5.3	6.6	1.4	0.8	21.1
6 Rest of the world		39.1	5.8		1.0							45.9
7 Savings-investment				6.9	6.2	7.0						20.1
8 Direct taxes				5.3								5.3
9 Import taxes		6.6										6.6
10 Export taxes		1.4										1.4
11 Activity taxes	0.8											0.8
Total	164.0	225.5	91.1	91.1	21.1	45.9	20.1	5.3	6.6	1.4	0.8	

SOURCE: World Bank (2001) and authors' calculations.

TABLE 6.3 Macro aggregates for Sub-Saharan Africa and all developing countries, 1998 (percent of GDP at market prices)

Item	SSA	All developing countries
Private consumption (C)	74.9	61.8
Investment (I)	20.1	23.5
Government consumption (G)	13.9	14.0
Exports (X)	30.2	27.1
Imports (M)	39.1	26.5
Absorption ($= C + I + G$)	108.9	99.3
GDP at market prices ($\text{GDP} = C + I + G + X - M$)	100.0	100.0
Net indirect taxes (T)	8.9	0.4
GDP at factor cost ($= \text{GDP} - T$)	91.1	99.6

SOURCE: World Bank (2001) and authors' calculations.

cent of GDP. On the spending side, consumption is the main item (14 percent of GDP). The major financing sources are import taxes (7 percent of GDP), direct taxes (on households and enterprises; 5 percent), and transfers from abroad (4 percent). Table 6.3 shows that, compared to the broader group of all developing countries, SSA is characterized by the allocation of a smaller GDP share to investment, a larger share to consumption, and a large trade deficit (as opposed to a slightly positive trade balance). For the full micro SAM, see Lofgren (2004); the appendix to this chapter includes tables that show the key parts of the database that are related to income distribution. The micro SAM was built by disaggregating the information in the macro SAM, starting from information in a Zimbabwe micro SAM. In addition to the information in the macro SAM, SSA averages for the shares of agriculture in value added, exports, and imports were also imposed, using World Bank data.[18]

Tables 6.4–6.6 summarize the sectoral structure, household income sources, living standards, and the rural-urban dichotomy of our stylized SSA economy. Table 6.4 indicates that the agricultural sector dominates employment and accounts for roughly half of total exports but only a small part of imports. A large part of agricultural output is exported, while the share of imports in its final demand is minuscule; agriculture produces a mix of traded and nontraded goods. Table 6.5 shows how the different representative household groups make their living: in both rural and urban regions, upper-income households earn incomes from skilled labor and rely more strongly on capital income. Rural households earn income from large-scale and small-scale land, respectively. The income sources of urban households are less diversified, especially for low-income groups who earn almost all of their income from unskilled labor. Rural low-income households have a diversified income profile, with unskilled labor dominating but also with substantial shares for capital and land. According to Table 6.6, the national head-count poverty rate is 42.3 percent. Rural areas, which account for some two-thirds of the population, have lower per capita incomes and constitute a large share of the poor. Table 6.7 shows the TFP linkage elasticity parameters, extracted from Fan and Rao (2003), and the channels through which they operate in the model.

Tables 6A.1 and 6A.2 show the central-case values of the elasticities for trade, production, and consumption. In the process of selecting these values, we consulted econometric and other model-based studies of SSA. Here we analyze the sensitivity of simulated results to changes in trade elasticities. Tables 6A.3–6A.5 provide base-year information from the model database on factor value shares within and across sectors as well as factor income distribution across households.

The model replicates major stylized facts and empirical regularities reported in the literature review in the second section of this chapter: GDP growth is negatively correlated with national, urban, and rural head-count poverty rates,

---

18. The archetype SAM was balanced using a cross-entropy estimation technique. See Robinson, Cattañeo, and El-Said (2001).

TABLE 6.4 Economic structure in base year (percent)

Sector	Value added	Output	Employment	Exports	Export/ output	Imports	Import/final demand
Export crops	18.4	11.4	15.2	46.4	62.6	0.1	1.2
Other crops	8.0	4.9	21.1	1.4	6.7	0.3	2.7
Livestock	5.5	4.3	20.7	0.4	1.6	—	—
Mining	4.0	3.9	1.1	9.3	35.8	1.1	11.5
Food and fiber	8.6	12.4	3.0	3.2	3.6	4.7	9.7
Domestic manufacturing	4.9	6.3	5.0	1.6	3.7	4.4	17.7
Import-substituting manufacturing	9.1	12.8	2.9	13.0	15.6	65.4	63.5
Construction	2.4	6.2	2.2	—	—	—	—
Trade and transportation	13.8	15.9	11.3	—	—	—	—
Public services	10.4	8.5	5.8	—	—	—	—
Other services	14.9	13.4	11.7	24.7	33.9	23.9	39.6
Total	100.0	100.0	100.0	100.0	16.3	100.0	26.2
Agriculture	32.0	20.5	57.0	48.2	40.4	0.4	1.3
Nonagriculture	68.0	79.5	43.0	51.8	10.9	99.6	28.9
Total	100.0	100.0	100.0	100.0	16.3	100.0	26.2

SOURCE: Model database constructed by the authors for this chapter.

NOTE: —indicates a value of zero.

TABLE 6.5 Household income sources in base year (percent)

Households	Unskilled labor	Skilled labor	Capital	Large-scale land	Small-scale land	Rest of the world	Net domestic transfers	Total
Rural								
Upper-income		29.6	48.6	18.7		3.1		100.0
Lower-income	59.1		17.4		10.3	12.3	0.9	100.0
Urban								
Upper-income		51.4	43.4	2.5		2.8		100.0
Lower-income	78.9		6.0			15.2		100.0

SOURCE: Lofgren (2004).

NOTES: Net domestic transfers are net transfer receipts from other households and the government. The value is shown in the table (as income) only if the net is positive.

TABLE 6.6 Household poverty and population data (percent)

	Per capita income	Head-count poverty rates	Population shares	Poor popluation shares
Rural				
Upper-income	224.3	0.0	16.4	0.0
Lower-income	21.9	72.5	49.3	84.4
Urban				
Upper-income	315.3	0.0	13.7	0.0
Lower-income	44.3	32.0	20.6	15.6
Total	100.0	42.3	100.0	100.0
Rural	72.5	54.4	65.7	84.7
Urban	152.7	19.2	34.3	15.6

SOURCE: Model database constructed by the authors for this chapter.

NOTE: Per capita income is indexed so that the economywide average is 100 percent.

TABLE 6.7 TFP linkage elasticity parameters

Government expenditure category	TFP link elasticity value	Standard error of estimated elasticity	Linkage channel
Agriculture	0.052	0.024	TFP in agriculture
Human capital	0.115	n.a.	Labor productivity in all nonmining sectors
Defense	−0.182	0.034	TFP in all nonmining sectors
Transportation	0.021	0.021	TFP in trade services (strong effect); TFP in other nonmining sectors (weak effect)
Other	0	n.a.	None

NOTES: Elasticity estimates and *t* statistics are based on Fan and Rao (2003). Human capital is an aggregation of education and health, with the elasticity calibrated to give the same GDP growth as when the disaggregated Fan and Rao elasticities are used. Linkage channels are incorporated in the dynamic CGE model. n.a., not available.

and positively correlated with growth in exports, imports, investment and capital stocks (both private and public), government consumption, and labor force growth. Private investment and capital stocks are more strongly correlated with growth than the corresponding public items.[19]

---

19. To verify the validity of the model for growth analysis, we computed correlation coefficients between GDP growth and the indicators listed in this paragraph, using as data inputs the results from the simulations reported in this study (treating each simulation as an observation).

Simulations

We use the model to explore the impact of alternative policies on long-run growth and poverty in SSA, especially the impact of expanded government spending in different target areas—agriculture, transportation, and human capital—in macroeconomic settings that differ in terms of changes in other areas of government spending (e.g., is nonproductive spending reduced?), the availability of foreign grants, and the behavior of private investment. Our starting point is a dynamic base simulation that provides a benchmark against which the other scenarios are compared.

The Base Simulation

In the base simulation, government demand (both consumption and investment and across all functional areas) grows by 1.9 percent per year, a rate that is calibrated to maintain the base-year absorption share for this demand category. The base-year shares are also maintained throughout the simulation period for the other parts of absorption, private investment and household consumption— for private investment given that this demand category also is fixed as a share of absorption and for household consumption as the residual demand type.

Most real macro aggregates, including real household consumption, grow at annual rates of between 1.5 and 2.0 percent. (The base columns in Tables 6.8 and 6.9 provide a summary of results; the simulations in the other columns are presented below.) This range of growth rates also holds for all aggregate production sectors except mining, for which zero growth is imposed (an assumption that may be seen as reflecting a government decision on the rate of natural resource extraction). The endogenous annual rate of TFP growth is very close to zero. Household consumption and the rest of the economy grow at a rate that is very close to the population growth rate (2 percent), leaving growth in total household per capita consumption (our aggregate welfare indicator) close to zero, with growth rates that are slightly positive in rural areas and slightly negative in urban areas. The head-count poverty rate (P0) also remains roughly the same; it registers a slight decrease, from 42.3 percent to 41.7 percent. The poverty gap and the squared poverty gap (P1 and P2) also change by little. Given little change in poverty measures and mean per capita consumption, the poverty elasticities for the base simulation contain little information.[20]

---

20. As noted in the previous section on the between-period module, we compute poverty indicators on the basis of the assumption of a constant, log-normal consumption distribution within each model household group. For the simulations that generate significant changes in mean per capita consumption and the head-count poverty rate, the (postcalculated) elasticity is typically between −1.0 and −4.0, values that are within the range observed in the literature. The elasticities for the poverty gap and the squared poverty gap are also in line with expectations. Differences in the head-count poverty elasticity across simulations are related to the pattern of relative consumption gains across different household groups.

TABLE 6.8 Scenarios for reallocation of public spending: Summary results

	1998	BASE	AGRI[a]	TRNS	HCAP	DEF	AG-TR-HC
			Annual growth rates, 1998–2015 (percent)				
Absorption	4,969.37	1.83	2.17	1.96	2.01	0.03	2.07
Household consumption	3,416.29	1.88	2.31	2.04	2.12	-0.56	2.19
Government consumption and investment	858.90	1.91	1.91	1.91	1.91	1.91	1.91
Private investment	694.19	1.49	1.79	1.57	1.61	0.11	1.66
Exports	1,377.50	1.73	2.36	1.90	1.97	-0.77	2.09
Imports	1,784.78	1.67	2.13	1.79	1.84	-0.07	1.92
Real exchange rate (index 1998 = 100)	100.00	0.05	-0.12	0.05	0.06	-0.19	0.02
Agriculcural/nonagricultural terms of trade (index 1998 = 100)	100.00	0.21	-0.55	0.23	0.28	-0.11	0.08
Total GDP (at factor cost)	4,158.39	1.90	2.27	2.04	2.12	-0.14	2.17
Agriculture	1,329.11	1.97	2.85	2.13	2.18	-0.34	2.36
Mining	166.54	0.00					
Other industry	938.18	1.69	1.91	1.80	1.84	-0.14	1.87
Government services	430.64	2.05	2.08	2.14	2.21	0.93	2.19
Other services	1,193.11	2.17	2.22	2.37	2.50	-0.44	2.46
TFP index	100.00	-0.01	0.29	0.11	0.18	-1.77	0.22

(*Continued*)

TABLE 6.8 Continued

	1998	BASE	AGRI[a]	TRNS	HCAP	DEF	AG-TR-HC
			Annual growth rates, 1998–2015 (percent)				
Total factor income	4,158.39	1.86	2.26	2.00	2.05	-0.17	2.12
Private capital	1,873.67	1.77	2.12	1.89	2.01	0.03	2.06
Land	372.87	3.44	3.92	3.69	3.92	0.19	3.96
Low-skilled labor	543.96	1.71	2.11	1.87	1.85	-0.55	1.93
High-skilled labor	1,367.90	1.53	1.99	1.66	1.56	-0.42	1.69
			Percentage point deviations from 1998 values				
Ratios to GDP							
Investment	20.11	0.30	-0.14	0.19	0.13	2.38	0.05
Government expenditure	23.26	0.10	-0.42	-0.01	-0.08	2.47	-0.17
Private saving	6.88	0.55	0.57	0.30	0.01	4.93	0.11
Government saving	6.19	-0.69	-0.51	-0.41	-0.13	-5.37	-0.18
Foreign saving	7.04	0.44	-0.20	0.29	0.25	2.82	0.12
Poverty head-count rate (P0)	42.31	-0.59	-7.56	-2.34	-3.22	19.90	-4.62

NOTES: All quantity variables are in real terms. Unless otherwise noted, data in the column headed "1998" are in base-year local currency units (only relative magnitudes matter). Income variables are deflated by the consumer price index (CPI). The real exchange rate is price-level deflated; the price index used is the CPI.
[a]See text for explanation of simulation names.

TABLE 6.9 Scenarios for reallocation of public spending: Welfare indicators

	1998	BASE	AGRI[a]	TRNS	HCAP	DEF	AG-TR-HC
			Annual growth rates, 1998–2015 (percent)				
Household consumption per capita							
Rural upper-income	552.30	0.14	0.54	0.32	0.45	-2.52	0.50
Rural lower-income	60.18	0.21	0.83	0.37	0.49	-2.05	0.59
Urban upper-income	804.78	-0.29	0.09	-0.14	-0.11	-2.55	-0.04
Urban lower-income	113.57	-0.31	0.11	-0.17	-0.19	-2.38	-0.09
Average, all households	254.16	-0.08	0.34	0.09	0.16	-2.46	0.23
Rural	183.21	0.15	0.61	0.33	0.46	-2.40	0.52
Urban	390.06	-0.30	0.09	-0.15	-0.12	-2.52	-0.05
			Percentage point deviations from 1998 values				
Poverty head count rate (P0)							
Total	42.31	-0.59	-7.56	-2.34	-3.22	19.90	-4.62
Rural	54.37	-2.62	-10.87	-4.50	-6.00	16.50	-7.50
Urban	19.20	3.30	-1.20	1.80	2.10	26.40	0.90
Elasticity		1.05	-2.96	-3.75	-2.79	-1.36	-2.77
Poverty gap (P1)							
Total	11.52	-0.50	-3.27	-1.29	-1.74	12.97	-2.23
Rural	15.62	-1.23	-4.82	-2.22	-2.93	14.50	-3.53
Urban	3.66	0.90	-0.29	0.48	0.54	10.04	0.26
Elasticity		3.26	-4.71	-7.61	-5.53	-3.26	-4.91
Squared poverty gap (P2)							
Total	4.27	-0.29	-1.51	-0.65	-0.86	7.37	-1.07
Rural	5.95	-0.61	-2.25	-1.08	-1.40	8.95	-1.68
Urban	1.05	0.31	-0.10	0.17	0.18	4.33	0.09
Elasticity		5.12	-5.87	-10.33	-7.37	-4.99	-6.37

NOTES: Household consumption is real per capita consumption; data in the column headed "1998" are in base-year local currency units (only relative magnitudes matter). The elasticities for P0, P1, and P2 are the ratios between the percentage of change in the poverty indicator and the percentage of change in aggregate per capita consumption.

Public Spending Simulations: Reallocation to Target Areas

The assumptions for the nonbase simulations are presented in Tables 6.8 and 6.10. The results for the first set of nonbase simulations are summarized, along with results for the base simulation, in Tables 6.8 and 6.9. These simulations all involve reallocating government demand into alternative priority areas while keeping the real growth of total government demand constant. Unless otherwise noted, in the second year (1999), 10 percent of total government spending is moved from what is classified as "other" (which has no productivity effects) into one or more priority areas, that is, a reallocation that in the base year corresponds to 1.9 percent of GDP, or 10 percent of government demand. After this, government demands in all functional areas grow at the same annual rate across all government functions (1.9 percent). In the first experiment, AGRI, government spending is reallocated to agriculture, in 1999 raising its share of GDP 0.9 to 2.8 percent. This intervention has a positive impact on overall economic performance and poverty reduction. Annual growth in most macro aggregates increases by around 0.3–0.6 percent. As expected, annual agricultural GDP growth increases more rapidly (by 0.9 percent), while the terms of trade for agriculture relative to nonagriculture deteriorate. The terminal-year poverty head-count rate is 7 percentage points lower than in the base scenario. This scenario reinforces the pro-rural trends of the base scenario. In rural areas, per capita consumption growth improves, especially for low-income households. Accordingly, the rural poverty head-count rate declines significantly compared to 1998.[21]

In 1998, government spending on transportation and communication was similar in volume to agricultural spending. In the second experiment, TRNS, spending in this area in 1999 increases from 0.8 to 2.6 percent of GDP. Given a lower elasticity, the aggregate effect of expanding government spending in this area is weaker, inducing an overall growth expansion and a decline in head-count poverty that is around one-third as strong as in AGRI. Compared to AGRI, the sectoral pattern of gains is more even, including a considerably smaller growth gain for agriculture. Performance according to per capita consumption and the different poverty indicators is more positive than under the base scenario, but much less positive than in AGRI.

In the HCAP simulation, the GDP share of government expenditures on health and education expands from 3.9 percent to 5.8 percent (that is, there is a much smaller relative increase in spending in the targeted area relative to the simulations AGRI and TRNS). The growth rate of GDP goes from 1.9 percent in the base run to 2.1 percent, a moderate increase. The poverty head count falls by 2.6 percentage points relative to the terminal-year value in the base simulation, with the largest percentage point decline in rural areas. However, com-

---

21. In this scenario, neither poverty nor per capita consumption changes much compared to 1998. As a result, the recorded poverty elasticities are not informative.

TABLE 6.10 Assumptions for nonbase simulations

Simulation name[a]	Description
AGRI	Shift in government spending from "other" to agriculture
TRNS	Shift in government spending from "other" to transportation
HCAP	Shift in government spending from "other" to human capital
DEF	Shift in government spending from "other" to defense
AG-TR-HC	Shift in government spending from "other" to agriculture, transportation, and human capital
AGRI+	Expansion in government spending on agriculture at the expense of private investment
TRNS+	Expansion in government spending on transportation at the expense of private investment
HCAP+	Expansion in government spending on human capital at the expense of private investment
AGRI+F	Expansion in government spending on agriculture with foreign grant financing
TRNS+F	Expansion in government spending on transportation with foreign grant financing
HCAP+F	Expansion in government spending on human capital with foreign grant financing
TRNS-EL	Shift in government spending from "other" to transportation with aggregate TFP elasticity of agriculture
HCAP-EL	Shift in government spending from "other" to human capital with entire productivity gain to unskilled labor
DEPR-03	Reduction of public capital stock depreciation rate from 5 percent to 3 percent
AGRI-HI	Same as in AGRI, but with high (doubled) trade elasticities
AGRI-LO	Same as in AGRI, but with low (halved) trade elasticities

NOTES: In all public spending simulations, expansion or reallocation refers to a change in 1999 corresponding to 10 percent of 1998 government demand (or 1.9 percent of GDP). Starting in 1999, all government demand areas have grown at a uniform annual real rate of 1.9 percent. Unless otherwise noted, we use the elasticities in Table 6.7.

[a]See text for explanation of simulation names.

pared to the scenario AGRI, poverty indicators perform less strongly in both rural and urban areas.

According to the empirical estimates of the TFP linkage elasticities, the impact of defense spending on GDP is very negative. This relationship should be viewed as capturing not only the opportunity cost of the resources allocated to defense but also other factors that are associated with high defense spending, such as wars, civil strife, and an unfavorable business climate. The scenario DEF assumes an increased allocation of government expenditures to defense, amounting to about 1.8 percent of GDP (from 0.6 percent to 2.4 percent). The results are very detrimental for growth and poverty reduction. The GDP growth rate turns negative, changing from 1.9 percent in the base run to –0.1 percent, and the terminal-year poverty head-count rate is 20 percentage points higher than in the base simulation, almost a 50 percent increase in poverty. Avoiding civil strife and the disruptions associated with higher defense expenditures is clearly very important.

The final simulation, AG-TR-HC, tests the impact of a simultaneous increase in the three areas of government spending for which positive effects were reported earlier—agriculture, transportation, and human capital. In each area, spending is set to increase by around 1.9 percent of GDP in the base year at the expense of the area of "other" government spending, for which spending declines drastically between 1998 and 1999, from 10.7 to 5.1 percent of GDP. The outcomes in terms of GDP growth, household consumption, and poverty are weaker than when reallocated spending is channeled exclusively to agriculture (AGRI), but stronger than in the base simulation. Compared to the base, the gains in consumption and poverty reduction are shared across rural and urban households.

Public Spending Simulations: Expansion in Target Areas

The preceding set of public expenditure simulations all assumed that the government reallocated spending from nonproductive areas. Alternatively, the government may increase spending. If so, the source of the additional resources needed must be specified. We explore the impact of two alternatives, domestic (with the resources freed up by means of reduced private investment) and foreign (with the resources provided as grants). The second set of simulations involves expanded spending of the same magnitude and in the same three areas—agriculture, transportation, and human capital—as in the preceding simulations, but without accompanying cuts in spending on other, unproductive areas. The results are summarized in Tables 6.11 and 6.12.[22]

In the first three simulations (AGRI+, TRNS+, and HCAP+), this spending expansion is made possible by reducing spending on private investment. A comparison between the results in Tables 6.11 and those in Table 6.9 for all three simulations shows that private investment declines strongly (most of the growth is wiped out), whereas private consumption (both aggregate and by household type), exports, imports, and GDP growth decline to a more moderate extent.

22. Technically, we introduce two new closure rules for the savings investment balance. Under both, household savings rates are fixed. For the first three simulations in Table 6.11 (AGRI+, TRNS+, and HCAP+), private investment is flexible, determined by the amount of residual financing. For the following three simulations (AGRI+F, TRNS+F, and HCAP+F), we reinstate the assumption of a fixed absorption share for private investment while flexing the amount of foreign grants to ensure that available savings is sufficient to finance private investment at the required level. Throughout the simulations, the other components of foreign savings—net foreign borrowing and net foreign investment—are fixed in foreign currency units.

The only exception is government demand (consumption and investment), which increases as part of the policy change. Accordingly, poverty rates increase relative to the scenarios with spending reallocation. From a different perspective, when the comparison is made to the base simulation, the effects are also mostly negative when the spending increase is directed to transportation and human capital (TRNS+ and HCAP+). On the contrary, when agriculture is targeted (AGRI+), overall poverty declines compared to the base (due to a positive impact on rural, low-income households), whereas other changes are minor.

The results point to the importance of links between government spending and private investment: if government spending crowds in (out) private investment, the overall impact of government expansion on growth and poverty is considerably more positive, ceteris paribus. Empirically, the relative strengths of crowding in and crowding out are likely to vary across countries and time periods; on balance, model specifications under which private investment grows in response to more public investment may be more relevant empirically.[23] The results also point to the importance of ensuring that government spending is productive. Finally, they indicate that spending to enhance productivity in agriculture can be very important to the poor. In these simulations, the impact is positive due to the fact that the poor (both rural and urban) primarily rely on unskilled labor (not land) for their incomes and benefit from a productivity-driven decline in the agricultural terms of trade (as food prices decline).

In the next three simulations (AGRI+F, TRNS+F, and HCAP+F), this spending expansion is accompanied by an expansion in foreign grants that maintains total savings at a level sufficient to finance an unchanged absorption share for private investment. In 1999, the year of the spending expansion, foreign grants jump by 2.3 percentage points of GDP (from 3 percent to 5.3 percent). After this, they decline gradually, in the final year exceeding the base-year value by some 1.5–2.0 percent of GDP. This increased inflow of foreign resources generates a slight appreciation of the real exchange rate, for the period as a whole at an annual rate of 0.1 percent. A comparison between the results across the different scenarios in Table 6.11 shows that the availability of foreign financing has a salutary impact on macro aggregates and poverty reduction. For each scenario, a comparison to the relevant preceding scenario (identical in terms of government expansion) shows that the annual growth rate for total absorption increases by 0.4–0.6 percentage points, with the strongest

---

23. Agénor, Bayraktar, and Aynaoui (2005, 5–7, 22, and 29–30) discuss links between public and private investment and survey evidence indicating that public investment crowds in private investment. Their econometric estimates for Ethiopia suggest the presence of a mild crowd-in effect and a positive link between GDP growth and private investment. If so, among our scenarios, those with a fixed absorption share for private investment—AGRI, TRNS, HCAP, AGRI+F, TRNS+F, and HCAP+F—are most relevant empirically because they permit growth, including growth induced by larger public capital stocks, to have a positive impact on private investment growth.

TABLE 6.11 Scenarios for expanding public spending: Summary results

	BASE	AGRI+[a]	TRNS+	HCAP+	AGRI+F	TRNS+F	HCAP+F
			Annual growth rates, 1998–2015 (percent)				
Absorption	1.83	1.79	1.64	1.73	2.35	2.11	2.14
Household consumption	1.88	1.87	1.64	1.73	2.39	2.10	2.14
Government consumption and investment	1.91	2.48	2.48	2.48	2.48	2.48	2.48
Private investment	1.49	0.37	0.38	0.64	1.97	1.72	1.73
Exports	1.73	2.04	1.61	1.71	2.22	1.79	1.89
Imports	1.67	1.74	1.45	1.53	2.36	2.00	2.00
Real exchange rate	0.05	-0.17	0.04	0.06	-0.24	-0.05	-0.03
Agricultural/nonagricultural terms of trade	0.21	-0.82	0.01	0.09	-0.64	0.15	0.21
Total GDP (at factor cost)	1.90	1.90	1.73	1.84	2.33	2.10	2.17
Agriculture	1.97	2.57	1.89	1.96	2.81	2.09	2.15
Mining	0.00	0.00	0.00	0.00	0.00	0.00	0.00
Other industry	1.69	1.49	1.45	1.53	1.96	1.84	1.86
Government services	2.05	2.14	2.21	2.30	2.44	2.48	2.55
Other services	2.17	1.65	1.84	2.03	2.30	2.42	2.55
TFP index	-0.01	0.30	0.12	0.18	0.28	0.11	0.18

Total factor income	1.86	1.88	1.67	1.76	2.34	2.07	2.11
Private capital	1.77	1.96	1.76	1.89	2.20	1.96	2.07
Land	3.44	3.00	2.90	3.22	3.76	3.56	3.82
Low-skilled labor	1.71	1.56	1.40	1.42	2.20	1.94	1.90
High-skilled labor	1.53	1.54	1.29	1.24	2.16	1.81	1.70
				Percentage point deviations from 1998 values			
Ratios to GDP (percent)							
Investment	0.30	-2.42	-1.66	-1.27	0.58	0.89	0.79
Government expenditure	0.10	0.01	0.49	0.45	-0.08	0.37	0.35
Private saving	0.55	0.50	0.50	0.51	0.57	0.56	0.56
Government saving	-0.69	-2.98	-2.72	-2.26	-1.79	-1.69	-1.38
Foreign saving	0.44	0.05	0.55	0.48	1.80	2.02	1.61
Poverty head-count rate (P0)	-0.59	-2.21	2.16	1.07	-8.36	-2.79	-3.32

NOTES: All quantity variables are in real terms. Income variables are deflated by the consumer price index (CPI). The real exchange rate is price level deflated; the price index used is the CPI.

[a]See text for explanation of simulation names.

TABLE 6.12 Scenarios for expanding public spending: Welfare indicators

	BASE	AGRI+[a]	TRNS+	HCAP+	AGRI+F	TRNS+F	HCAP+F
Household consumption per capita			Annual growth rates, 1998–2015 (percent)				
Rural upper-income	0.14	0.04	-0.14	0.00	0.58	0.34	0.43
Rural lower-income	0.21	0.43	0.00	0.14	0.88	0.39	0.48
Urban upper-income	-0.29	-0.29	-0.49	-0.44	0.22	-0.04	-0.05
Urban lower-income	-0.31	-0.34	-0.56	-0.55	0.20	-0.12	-0.16
Average, all households	-0.08	-0.09	-0.31	-0.22	0.43	0.14	0.18
Rural	0.15	0.14	-0.10	0.04	0.66	0.35	0.44
Urban	-0.30	-0.30	-0.50	-0.46	0.22	-0.06	-0.07
Poverty head-count rate (P0)			Percentage point deviations from 1998 values				
Total	-0.59	-2.21	2.16	1.07	-8.36	-2.79	-3.32
Rural	-2.62	-5.25	0.00	-1.50	-11.62	-4.87	-6.00
Urban	3.30	3.60	6.30	6.00	-2.10	1.20	1.80
Elasticity	1.05	3.51	-0.99	-0.69	-2.62	-2.76	-2.52
Poverty gap (P1)							
Total	-0.50	-1.30	0.65	0.09	-3.54	-1.43	-1.75
Rural	-1.23	-2.48	0.09	-0.73	-5.13	-2.35	-2.89
Urban	0.90	0.97	1.71	1.67	-0.49	0.33	0.44
Elasticity	3.26	7.54	-1.10	-0.22	-4.07	-5.19	-4.87
Squared poverty gap (P2)							
Total	-0.29	-0.67	0.24	-0.04	-1.62	-0.71	-0.86
Rural	-0.61	-1.20	0.05	-0.36	-2.38	-1.14	-1.39
Urban	0.31	0.34	0.61	0.59	-0.16	0.11	0.15
Elasticity	5.12	10.53	-1.09	0.23	-5.03	-6.94	-6.46

NOTES: Household consumption is real per capita consumption. The elasticities for P0, P1, and P2 are the ratios between the percentage of change in the poverty indicator and the percentage of change in aggregate per capita consumption.

[a]See text for explanation of simulation names.

increase for private investment. The increase in GDP growth is smaller, 0.3–0.4 percentage points. At the end of the period, poverty rates (both rural and urban) are 4–6 percentage points lower. The outcome is also more positive (although by a much smaller margin) than for the corresponding preceding scenarios with spending reallocation. These outcomes are expected because, at a given rate of GDP growth, larger foreign grants permit the country to enjoy larger trade deficits and higher levels of absorption. In addition, the fact that both government spending and private investment expand permits GDP to grow more rapidly, further boosting absorption.[24]

Sensitivity Analysis

The final set of simulations explores the sensitivity of the results to alternative values for model parameters that are particularly uncertain and may be important in the context of the current set of simulations: productivity elasticities and linkages, depreciation rates for public capital stocks, and trade elasticities. The results are summarized in Tables 6.13 and 6.14.

The first two simulations analyze the sensitivity of the results to changes in public expenditure elasticities. The estimated TFP linkage elasticity for public expenditure on transportation is modest relative to some other empirical findings (cf. Easterly and Rebelo 1993, 2 and 14, and Hulten 1996). In the simulation TRNS-EL, we set the transportation elasticity at the level of the agricultural elasticity (an increase that corresponds to around 1.5 standard deviations). Apart from this, the simulation is identical to the earlier transportation scenario (TRNS). Compared to the base simulation, the impact is a modest acceleration in aggregate GDP growth (by 0.3 percentage points, with stronger gains within services and agriculture), and a strong gain in poverty reduction as the final-year rate is 6.3 percentage points below the 1998 level. Compared to the scenario in which spending is reallocated to agriculture (AGRI), aggregate growth is very similar (but slightly stronger). As opposed to the agricultural scenario, under this new scenario terms of trade shift in favor of agriculture, while the distribution of factor incomes shifts in favor of land and, to a lesser extent, unskilled labor. Given that low-income households consume a large share of agricultural and food products, the AGRI scenario, under which the prices of these products fall, is slightly more pro-poor.

---

24. In addition, we carried out a third set of simulations in which public spending is expanded in a setting in which private investment is a fixed share of absorption (i.e., the same savings-investment closure rule as for the reallocation simulations). A comparison to the scenarios with spending reallocation shows that aggregate spending expansion leads to smaller increases in aggregate household consumption and final-year poverty head-count rates that are around 2 percentage points higher. Compared to the base, final-year poverty is still lower when spending on agriculture or human capital expands (by 4.9 and 0.8 percentage points, respectively), but unaffected when transportation spending is increased.

TABLE 6.13 Sensitivity analysis: Summary results

	BASE	TRNS-EL[a]	HCAP-EL	DEPR-03	AGRI	BASE-HI	AGRI-HI
			Annual growth rates, 1998–2015 (percent)				
Absorption	1.83	2.22	1.99	2.06	2.17	1.86	2.21
Household consumption	1.88	2.39	2.10	2.17	2.31	1.88	2.32
Government consumption							
and investment	1.91	1.91	1.91	1.91	1.91	1.92	1.92
Private investment	1.49	1.73	1.51	1.65	1.79	1.69	2.02
Exports	1.73	2.26	1.84	2.07	2.36	1.72	2.41
Imports	1.67	2.06	1.74	1.91	2.13	1.65	2.17
Real exchange rate	0.05	0.05	0.10	0.02	-0.12	0.09	-0.01
Agricultural/nonagricultural							
terms of trade	0.21	0.26	-0.06	0.09	-0.55	0.23	-0.33
Total GDP (at factor cost)	1.90	2.34	2.14	2.16	2.27	1.93	2.30
Agriculture	1.97	2.46	2.47	2.35	2.85	1.85	2.84
Mining	0.00	0.00				0.00	
Other industry	1.69	2.03	1.74	1.87	1.91	1.80	1.99
Government services	2.05	2.33	2.11	2.19	2.08	2.10	2.10
Other services	2.17	2.76	2.36	2.45	2.22	2.31	2.26

TFP index	-0.01	0.37	0.22	0.21	0.29	-0.01	0.29
Total factor income	1.86	2.30	2.01	2.11	2.26	1.89	2.28
Private capital	1.77	2.16	1.99	2.05	2.12	1.82	2.06
Land	3.44	4.20	3.47	3.94	3.92	3.07	4.00
Low-skilled labor	1.71	2.18	1.17	1.92	2.11	1.82	2.19
High-skilled labor	1.53	1.93	1.91	1.68	1.99	1.65	2.07

Percentage point deviations from 1998 values

Ratios to GDP (percent)							
Investment	0.30	-0.02	0.25	0.06	-0.14	0.11	-0.31
Government expenditure	0.10	-0.24	0.06	-0.16	-0.42	-0.28	-0.63
Private saving	0.55	-0.19	0.76	0.13	0.57	0.80	0.54
Government saving	-0.69	0.16	-0.87	-0.20	-0.51	-1.03	-0.60
Foreign saving	0.44	0.00	0.36	0.14	-0.20	0.33	-0.25
Poverty head-count rate (P0)	-0.59	-6.32	-6.05	-4.52	-7.56	-0.66	-7.66

NOTES: All quantity variables are in real terms. Income variables are deflated by the consumer price index (CPI). The real exchange rate is price level deflated; the price index used is the CPI.

[a]See text for explanation of simulation names.

TABLE 6.14 Sensitivity analysis: Welfare indicators

	BASE	TRNS-EL[a]	HCAP-EL	DEPR-03	AGRI	BASE-HI	AGRI-HI
			Annual growth rates, 1998–2015 (percent)				
Household consumption per capita							
Rural upper income	0.14	0.71	0.23	0.48	0.54	0.06	0.55
Rural lower income	0.21	0.70	1.08	0.58	0.83	0.19	0.83
Urban upper income	−0.29	0.17	−0.04	−0.05	0.09	−0.23	0.11
Urban lower income	−0.31	0.12	−0.67	−0.10	0.11	−0.23	0.15
Average, all households	−0.08	0.43	0.14	0.21	0.34	−0.08	0.36
Rural	0.15	0.71	0.45	0.50	0.61	0.09	0.62
Urban	−0.30	0.16	−0.15	−0.06	0.09	−0.23	0.12
			Percentage point deviations from 1998 values				
Poverty head-count rate (P0)							
Total	−0.59	−6.32	−6.05	−4.52	−7.56	−0.66	−7.66
Rural	−2.62	−9.00	−13.12	−7.50	−10.87	−2.25	−10.87
Urban	3.30	−1.20	7.50	1.20	−1.20	2.40	−1.50
Elasticity	1.05	−1.99	−5.80	−2.88	−2.96	1.22	−2.86
Poverty gap (P1)							
Total	−0.50	−2.84	−3.03	−2.16	−3.27	−0.55	−3.32
Rural	−1.23	−4.17	−5.71	−3.43	−4.82	−1.17	−4.86
Urban	0.90	−0.29	2.10	0.29	−0.29	0.65	−0.38
Elasticity	3.26	−3.29	−10.68	−5.06	−4.71	3.74	−4.56
Squared poverty gap (P2)							
Total	−0.29	−1.32	−1.47	−1.04	−1.51	−0.30	−1.53
Rural	−0.61	−1.96	−2.62	−1.63	−2.25	−0.58	−2.26
Urban	0.31	−0.10	0.75	0.10	−0.10	0.22	−0.13
Elasticity	5.12	−4.13	−13.93	−6.58	−5.87	5.59	−5.67

NOTES: Household consumption is real per capita consumption. The elasticities for P0, P1, and P2 are the ratios between the percentage of change in the poverty indicator and the percentage of change in aggregate per capita consumption.

[a]See text for explanation of simulation names.

The second simulation in Tables 6.13 and 6.14, HCAP-EL, repeats the re-allocation of spending in favor of human capital (as for the simulation HCAP) with an adjustment in the productivity elasticities to reflect the assumption that the aggregate productivity gain is channeled solely through a productivity gain for unskilled labor (as opposed to both skilled and unskilled labor in HCAP and all other simulations) without any change in the aggregate impact. Compared to the base scenario, the impact on growth and poverty reduction is still positive. Aggregate GDP growth is very similar to that in the HCAP scenario, but the results reveal a strong slow-down in income growth for the targeted unskilled labor factor (indicative of an inelastic demand for this factor) and, to a lesser extent, for land.

Production expansion in agriculture switches terms of trade against this sector. The final-year poverty rate is 2.8 percentage points lower. These results reflect the role of the demand side in determining the distribution of gains from higher productivity.

Finally, economic performance is strongly influenced by the efficiency with which public spending is managed, an aspect that, inter alia, is reflected in the rate at which public capital depreciates. In the literature, assumptions about depreciation rates vary widely.[25] In the scenario DEPR-03, we reduced the depreciation rate for public capital from 5 percent to 3 percent. Compared to the base scenario, GDP growth goes up by around 0.3 percent, and final-year poverty is 3.9 percentage points lower. In orders of magnitude, these gains are similar to those of the preceding scenarios in which public spending was switched to different target areas.

Finally, we carried out the full set of simulations with three alternative sets of trade (Armington and constant elasticity of transformation, or CET) elasticities: in addition to the central case (which was reported earlier), a high and a low case for which every elasticity was doubled and halved, respectively.[26] To illustrate the impact of changing elasticity assumptions, the last two columns of Tables 6.13 and 6.14 show the summary and welfare results for two scenarios with high trade elasticities, the base (BASE-HI) and a high-elasticity version of AGRI, the scenario with a reallocation of public spending in favor of agriculture (AGRI-HI). To facilitate comparison, the preceding column repeats the (central-elasticity-case) results for AGRI that were reported earlier, in Tables 6.9 and 6.10. It is evident that the results are very close for BASE-HI relative

---

25. For example, in the literature on developing countries, the rates used by Dessus and Herrera (1996, 14) and Arndt, Robinson, and Tarp (2001, 12–13) are 4 percent and 7.5 percent, respectively.

26. For commodities with both imports and domestic use of domestic output, the Armington elasticity indicates the degree of substitutability in domestic market use between these two sources. For domestic outputs with both exports and domestic sales, the CET elasticity indicates the ease with which output can shift between these two destinations.

to BASE, for AGRI-HI relative to AGRI, and in terms of the impacts of the policy change (AGRI relative to BASE compared to AGRI-HI relative to BASE-HI), the most critical comparison. For the latter, most growth rates change by 0.1 percentage points or less. The largest differences are related to the agricultural sector (which also was subject to the largest shock: when the elasticities are higher, the terms-of-trade loss that occurs when agriculture expands is smaller (0.56 versus 0.76 percentage points), permitting a larger increase in the annual growth in land returns (by 0.92 versus 0.49 percentage points). These observations suggest that the policy-relevant messages that emerge from this analysis tend to be robust to changes in these trade elasticities. This robustness of the results was also evident for the other simulations and with low trade elasticities (not reported here). It is in sharp contrast with the relatively strong sensitivity of simulation results to changes in macro closures, as shown earlier.[27]

Conclusion

When designing strategies for SSA aimed at accelerating growth and reducing poverty, it is particularly important to understand the links between economic performance and different types of public spending. We developed a model—a dynamic-recursive CGE model—that incorporates these links and includes the minimum household detail needed to analyze distributional impacts, and applied it to an archetype SSA country for the period 1998–2015. For the impact of public spending, we rely on econometric estimates of linkages between TFP growth and public spending in different functional areas. We used the model to simulate the impact on growth and distribution of different public expenditure strategies targeting agriculture, human capital, and transportation and communication.

Our base simulation projects a continuation of past trends in factor accumulation and TFP growth, with only modest aggregate GDP growth and little change in per capita household consumption and the head-count poverty rate. The results for the other simulations indicate that, relative to the base, economic performance can be improved significantly when government resources are reallocated from unproductive areas to the different target areas, with the most positive overall effects when agriculture is targeted. For the case of agriculture, the reallocation of 10 percent of government demand (1.9 percent of GDP) from unproductive areas in the beginning of the period reduces the final-year poverty rate by 7.5 percentage points. The impact on growth and poverty is less positive (and may be negative if government productivity is low) when the government expands spending in target areas without cuts elsewhere and without any additional foreign financing, leaving fewer resources available for private con-

---

27. Similarly, in the context of a CGE model applied to Mexico, Coady and Harris (2004, 10 and 22–24) concluded that their results were extremely robust to changes in a wider range of elasticities (not only trade, but also production and consumption elasticities).

sumption and/or investment. In order to enhance long-run growth, it is important to focus on government investments that induce the private sector to invest. However, if additional foreign grants are sufficient to cover government financing needs, the scope for growth in domestic absorption is widened, with a positive impact on household welfare and poverty reduction.

The simulated impact of reducing the depreciation rates for public capital stocks suggests that the gains from raising the efficiency of public spending may be just as important as the allocation of resources to areas with high payoffs. In another simulation, we reallocated government spending to defense, using empirical estimates of the TFP linkage elasticity of defense spending. These elasticities capture not only the opportunity cost of defense spending but also the broader economic consequences of wars and civil strife. The impact was very negative, including an increase in the poverty rate by 20 percentage points and zero GDP growth, clearly pointing to the importance of conflict resolution and management as a prerequisite for successful development.

On a cautionary note, these results are very sensitive to the values of the various elasticities linking TFP growth to public expenditure. It may also well be that the econometric estimates, which are based on noisy historical data for a period in which many countries were undergoing changes in their economic and political systems and some were involved in armed conflict, do not provide parameter values that we can confidently use in projections for the next 15–20 years. There is clearly a need for much more work to understand the nature of the linkages and to provide better estimates of the parameters involved.

In terms of methodology, our findings suggest that, when designing strategies for poverty reduction, including interventions favoring agriculture and different types of human capital accumulation, it is important that the framework used consider not only aggregate returns and productivity effects but also distributional aspects manifested in relative price changes (including the terms of trade between agriculture and nonagriculture). A dynamic CGE model provides a good framework for incorporating the linkages that economic theory and empirical analysis consider important. Such models enable analysts to simulate the effects of different estimated linkage elasticities and incorporate different analytic specifications that theory indicates might be important.

Appendix 6A: Supplementary Tables.

See tables on pages 220–222.

TABLE 6A.1 Trade and production elasticities

	Value added	Export	Import
Large-scale export crop	0.4	1.6	0.6
Small-scale export crop	0.4	1.6	0.6
Large-scale other crop	0.4	1.3	0.7
Small-scale other crop	0.4	1.3	0.7
Large-scale livestock	0.4	1.3	
Small-scale livestock	0.4	1.3	
Mining	0.8	1.6	0.6
Food and fiber	0.8	1.3	0.9
Domestic manufacturing	0.8	0.9	1.3
Import-substituting manufacturing	0.8	0.9	1.3
Construction	0.8		
Trade and transportation	0.8		
Public services	0.8		
Other services	0.8	0.8	1.3

SOURCES: Literature estimates and authors' assessment.

TABLE 6A.2 Household expenditure elasticities for consumption of marketed commodities

	Rural households		Urban households	
	Upper-income	Lower-income	Upper-income	Lower-income
Other crops	0.5	0.8	0.4	0.8
Livestock	1.1	1.2		1.2
Food and fiber	0.5	0.8	0.4	0.8
Domestic manufacturing	1.3	1.2	1.2	1.2
Import-substituting manufacturing	1.3	1.2	1.2	1.2
Trade and transportation	1.3	1.2	1.2	1.2
Public services	1.3	1.2	1.2	1.2
Other services	1.3	1.2	1.2	1.2

SOURCES: Literature estimates and authors' assessment.

NOTE: Elasticities for home-consumed goods are the same as for their marketed counterparts.

TABLE 6A.3 Factor value shares within sectors (percent)

Activities	Unskilled labor	Skilled labor	Capital	Large-scale land	Small-scale land	Total
Large-scale export crop	2.3	38.7	25.9	33.1		100.0
Small-scale export crop	53.8		16.8		29.4	100.0
Large-scale nonexport crop	3.7	24.4	21.6	50.3		100.0
Small-scale nonexport crop	61.3		21.4		17.3	100.0
Large-scale livestock	4.6	37.7	57.7			100.0
Small-scale livestock	69.2		30.8			100.0
Mining	3.5	24.3	72.2			100.0
Food and fiber	6.3	15.2	78.5			100.0
Domestic manufacturing	20.9	29.8	49.3			100.0
Import-substituting manufacturing	3.3	31.8	64.9			100.0
Construction	14.9	58.3	26.8			100.0
Trade and transportation	15.7	36.9	47.4			100.0
Public services	5.9	59.8	34.3			100.0
Other services	15.4	33.4	51.2			100.0
Total	13.1	32.9	45.1	7.9	1.0	100.0
Agriculture	17.7	26.9	27.3	24.8	3.2	100.0
Nonagriculture	10.9	35.7	53.4			100.0

SOURCE: Model database constructed by the authors for this chapter.

TABLE 6A.4 Factor value shares across sectors (percent)

Activities	Factors					
	Unskilled labor	Skilled labor	Capital	Large-scale land	Small-scale land	Total
Large-scale export crop	3.0	19.9	9.7	70.5		16.9
Small-scale export crop	6.2		0.6		43.4	1.5
Large-scale nonexport crop	1.3	3.4	2.2	29.5		4.6
Small-scale nonexport crop	15.8		1.6		56.6	3.4
Large-scale livestock	0.9	2.9	3.2			2.5
Small-scale livestock	16.0		2.1			3.0
Mining	1.1	3.0	6.4			4.0
Food and fiber	4.2	4.0	15.0			8.6
Domestic manufacturing	7.8	4.4	5.3			4.9
Import-substituting manufacturing	2.3	8.8	13.1			9.1
Construction	2.8	4.3	1.4			2.4
Trade and transportation	16.5	15.5	14.5			13.8
Public services	4.7	18.8	7.9			10.4
Other services	17.5	15.1	16.9			14.9
Total	100.0	100.0	100.0	100.0	100.0	100.0
Agriculture	43.3	26.2	19.4	100.0	100.0	32.0
Nonagriculture	56.7	73.8	80.6			68.0

SOURCE: Model database constructed by the authors for this chapter.

TABLE 6A.5 Factor income distribution across households in base year (percent)

Activities	Factors					
	Unskilled labor	Skilled labor	Capital	Large-scale land	Small-scale land	Total
Rural						
Upper-income		33.1	46.2	86.7		38.1
Lower-income	45.0		4.5		100.0	9.2
Urban						
Upper-income		66.9	47.9	13.3		44.4
Lower-income	55.0		1.4			8.3
Total	100.0	100.0	100.0	100.0	100.0	

SOURCE: Model database constructed by the authors for this chapter.

References

Agénor, P. R., N. Bayraktar, and K. El Aynaoui. 2005. Roads out of poverty: Assessing the links between aid, public investment, growth, and poverty reduction. Policy Research Working Paper 3490. Washington, D.C.: World Bank.

Aghion, P. A., and P. Howitt. 1998. *Endogenous growth theory.* Cambridge, Mass.: MIT Press.

Arndt, C., S. Robinson, and F. Tarp. 2001. Parameter estimation for a computable general equilibrium model: A maximum entropy approach. Discussion Paper 40. Trade and Macroeconomics Division. Washington, D.C.: International Food Policy Research Institute.

Barro, R., and X. Sala-i-Martin. 1995. *Economic growth.* New York: McGraw-Hill.

Bautista, R. M., M. Thomas, K. Muir-Leresche, and H. Lofgren. 2003. *Macroeconomic reforms and agriculture: Towards equitable growth in Zimbabwe.* Research Report 128. Washington, D.C.: International Food Policy Research Institute.

Bourguignon, F. 2003. The growth elasticity of poverty reduction: Explaining heterogeneity across countries and time periods. In *Inequality and growth: Theory and policy implications,* ed. T. S. Eicher and S. J. Turnovsky. Cambridge, Mass.: MIT Press, pp. 3–26.

Burmeister, E., and R. Dobell. 1970. *Mathematical theories of economic growth.* New York: Macmillan.

Coady, D. P., and R. L. Harris. 2004. *Evaluating targeted cash transfer programs: A general equilibrium framework with an application to Mexico.* Research Report 137. Washington, D.C.: International Food Policy Research Institute.

Dervis, K., J. de Melo, and S. Robinson. 1982. *General equilibrium models for development policy.* New York: Cambridge University Press.

Dessus, S., and R. Herrera. 1996. *Le rôle du capital public dans la croissance des pays en développement au cours des années 80.* Documents Techniques 115. Paris: Centre de Développement de l'OCDE.

Diao, X., E. Yeldan, and T. L. Roe. 1998. A simple dynamic applied general equilibrium model of a small open economy: Transitional dynamics and trade policy. *Journal of Economic Development* 23 (1): 77–101.

Dumont, J.-C. 1996. *La contribution des facteurs humains à la croissance: Une revue de littérature des évidences empiriques.* Paris: DIAL–Université Paris IX–Dauphine.

Easterly, W., and S. Rebelo. 1993. Fiscal policy and economic growth: An empirical investigation. Working Paper 4499. Cambridge, Mass.: National Bureau for Economic Research.

Fan, S., and N. Rao. 2003. Public spending in developing countries: Trend, determination and impact. EPTD Discussion Paper 99. Washington, D.C.: International Food Policy Research Institute.

Hulten, C. R. 1996. Infrastructure capital and economic growth: How well you use it may be more important than how much you have. Working Paper 5847. Cambridge, Mass.: National Bureau for Economic Research.

Kuznets, S. 1966. *Modern economic growth: Rate, structure, and spread.* New Haven, Conn.: Yale University Press.

Lofgren, H. 2004. An archetype social accounting matrix for Sub-Saharan Africa, 1998. Mimeo, International Food Policy Research Institute, Washington, D.C.

Lofgren, H., and S. Robinson. 2004. Growth, poverty, and public policy: A selective review of the literature. Mimeo, International Food Policy Research Institute, Washington, D.C.

Lofgren, H., R. L. Harris, and S. Robinson, with assistance from M. El-Said and M. Thomas. 2002. *A standard computable general equilibrium (CGE) model in GAMS.* Microcomputers in Policy Research, Vol. 5. Washington, D.C.: International Food Policy Research Institute.

Lofgren, H., S. Robinson, and M. El-Said. 2003. Poverty and inequality analysis in a general equilibrium framework: The representative household approach. In *The impact of economic policies on poverty and income distribution: Evaluation techniques and Tools,* ed. François Bourguignon and Luiz A. Pereira da Silva. Washington, D.C., and New York: World Bank and Oxford University Press, 325–337.

O'Connell, S. A., and B. J. Ndulu. 2000. Africa's growth experience: A focus on sources of growth. Swarthmore College, Swarthmore, Pa. Mimeo. Available at <www.swarthmore.edu/SocSci/soconne1/aercgrth.html> (accessed November 2007).

Ravallion, M., and S. Chen. 1997. What can new survey data tell us about recent changes in distribution and poverty? *World Bank Economic Review* 11: 357–382.

Robinson, S., A. Cattañeo, and M. El-Said. 2001. Updating and estimating a social accounting matrix using cross entropy methods. *Economic Systems Research* 13 (1): 47–64.

Tarp, F., C. Arndt, H. Tarp Jensen, S. Robinson, and R. Heltberg. 2002. *Facing the development challenge in Mozambique: An economywide perspective.* Research Report 126. Washington, D.C.: International Food Policy Research Institute.

Temple, J. 1999. The new growth evidence. *Journal of Economic Literature* 37 (1): 112–156.

Thomas, M., and R. M. Bautista. 1999. A 1991 social accounting matrix for Zimbabwe. Trade and Macroeconomics Division Discussion Paper 36. Washington, D.C.: International Food Policy Research Institute.

Wobst, P. 2001. *Structural adjustment and intersectoral shifts in Tanzania: A computable general equilibrium analysis.* Research Report 117. Washington, D.C.: International Food Policy Research Institute.

World Bank. 2001. *World development indicators.* Washington, D.C.

7 Lessons Learned: Major Findings and Policy Implications

SHENGGEN FAN AND ANNIE WHITE

Over the past several decades, developing countries have had mixed performance in reducing poverty. While East Asia, particularly China, has achieved astonishing progress in eradicating severe poverty through strong economic growth, many African countries have experienced an increase in poverty both in absolute numbers and as a percentage of their population. Today more than one billion poor still live on less than U.S. $1 per day (Chen and Ravallion 2004).

Donor and international development agencies are evaluating these past failures and have committed themselves to concrete goals with the formulation of the Millennium Development Goals. But what strategies are needed to achieve these ambitious goals? One important pillar of such development is the creation of international "big push" strategies, led by the United Nations Millennium Project and the countries of the Organisation for Economic Co-operation and Development. These strategies call for a drastic increase in international development aid and the elimination of debts for poor countries.

Along with leading a renewed international push for eradicating world poverty and hunger, developing countries themselves have started to contribute with their own efforts. Many developing countries have begun issuing poverty reduction strategy papers (PRSPs) or equivalents to outline strategic plans and to earmark financial resources to achieve their poverty reduction goals. Common among these strategies is the promotion of public investment as a stimulus to increase private domestic savings and investments. By combining both international and domestic efforts, it is hoped that public investment will help poor countries break out of their poverty trap and ultimately meet the MDGs.

Questions that remain to be answered are these: How should these pledged resources be allocated? Can these resources be used efficiently in order to achieve the stated objectives? Are there trade-offs within and across sectoral expenditures? To answer these questions, it is crucial to investigate how these public resources contributed to development in the past.

This final chapter presents major conclusions from and policy implications of the studies completed thus far on public spending and poverty reduction in developing countries. The chapter focuses on priority challenges and strategies

225

for public spending on education, health and safety nets, infrastructure, agriculture, and agricultural research and development. The chapter also presents lessons learned and suggestions for future research, including important knowledge gaps yet to be addressed.

Major Findings

In this section we describe the major findings of this synthesis and their implications. We begin by establishing the theoretical role of government expenditures and their motivation. After outlining a hypothesis that government expenditures *can* affect growth and poverty, we summarize how they in fact do so in more than 44 countries in three separate regions. We further this analysis by using four country case studies to evaluate how government expenditures have helped promote growth, and specifically through what channels. Chapter 4 looked specifically at human capital expenditures such as those on nutrition, health, and education and focused on measuring how the benefits of such human capital expenditures are distributed across various income groups. Chapter 5 went further to illustrate the crucial safety nets that must be integrated into any pro-poor spending pattern and the overall reforms necessary to enhance public expenditures. In this chapter we incorporate information from the previous chapters and use a computable general equilibrium (CGE) model to simulate the effects of various spending scenarios on growth and poverty, using data from developing African countries. Then we summarize lessons learned along with general directions for future research.

The Rationale for Government Spending

With the recent establishment of the eight MDG, the international development community has intensified its efforts to increase and redirect resources in order to reduce world poverty and hunger. These efforts are reinforced by the adoption of strategic plans such as those presented in PRSPs in many developing countries. The partnership into which participating countries has entered serves as a commitment to development by improving governance and therefore public spending.

However, while there is a broad consensus that renewed economic growth is a necessary condition for meeting development goals, it is also widely accepted that growth alone is insufficient. In order for growth to become a sufficient condition, more direct public action is required, specifically more labor-intensive and agriculture-intensive investments. Additionally, the asset base of poor households (particularly human capital) needs to be fostered so that household members can participate in the growth process. Short-term public transfers are also required. These serve to protect and raise the level of consumption of the poorest households while providing time for the benefits from such a three-pronged strategy to accrue. Public policy has a crucial role to play in achieving these objectives. Government spending policy is the most prominent among all types of public policy. Beyond this, however, we find that it is not just the scale of government budgets that matter, but also when, where, and how governments intervene.

Any credible evaluation of the levels and composition of public expenditures must start with a clear understanding of the underlying rationale or motivation for government intervention. The answer to the question regarding when governments should intervene depends sensitively on the perspective from which one approaches the issue. In Chapter 1 the welfarist approach was outlined as the main lens through which economists justify public intervention, particularly when there is market failure and a problem with income distribution. Two other approaches have gained prominence over the past three decades—the *basic need*s approach (focusing on human needs) and the *capabilities approach* (focusing on individual accomplishments and potential). Both of these approaches distinguish income as a "means" or as an "end," often highlighting the commonly observed lack of a strong correlation between income and other outcomes that enter into one's concept of development.

It is also important to recognize that trade-offs between equity and efficiency are not always present. The poor are often poor because they are disproportionately affected by market failures. This leads to "win-win" possibilities, because government intervention can lead to both a more efficient and a more equitable allocation of resources. The evidence from Chapter 3 clearly confirms this. When government increases its investment in agricultural research, rural education, and infrastructure, particularly in less favored areas, both growth and poverty reduction goals are likely to be achieved simultaneously. It is crucial, therefore, to avoid excessive pessimism regarding a negative trade-off between equity and efficiency objectives.

It is extremely important that the role of public policy be understood within the existing set of economic, social, and political *institutions*. We find that if public policies are to be capable of delivering more broad-based growth, there is a need to develop more effective institutions, particularly for providing social safety nets and social insurance. It is widely accepted that the establishment of secure and stable property rights has played a crucial role in modern economic growth.

Each country has different motivations to invest in certain geographic areas and sectors. Government should invest in physical infrastructure because it has characteristics of public goods. Typically, the market fails to provide these goods, especially in rural areas. Furthermore, returns to public investments vary, depending on the type of investment and the particular region, even within the same country. If public resources can be allocated optimally, this implies that there is great potential for more growth and poverty reduction, even with the same amount of investment. Therefore, as demonstrated specifically in Chapter 2, it is important to include all (or most) types of public investment when assessing their impact on growth and poverty reduction.

Cross-Country Analysis of Spending Patterns and Factors

Although it has been established that government spending can affect growth and poverty reduction, it is crucial to understand how the patterns of public spending have changed over time and the factors that have affected these changes. This background was presented in Chapter 2 by compiling and analyzing government expenditures, by type, across 44 developing countries, between 1980 and 2002.

Across all three regions, total government expenditures increased from U.S. $993 billion in 1980 to $1,595 billion in 1990. By 2002, this spending had increased to $3,347 billion, with Asia accounting for 67 percent of total expenditures in 2002. Asia had the most rapid growth, at a rate of 7 percent per annum. This staggering rate of growth was followed at a slower pace by that of Africa, where expenditures grew at 4.2 percent over two decades, after a brief contraction in the early 1980s. Latin America experienced the slowest overall growth in expenditures (3.7 percent per annum) between 1980 and 2002, suffering an 18 percent reduction in spending during the mid-1980s. Most of the expenditure growth in Latin America occurred during the 1990s, in response to the two earlier contractions. Overall, total government expenditures as a percentage of GDP also increased across all regions in the study, albeit more erratically.

Studying the composition of government expenditures is useful in order to assess government spending priorities over time, and we have found that the composition of government also varied dramatically across all regions. In 2002 the top three areas of expenditure for Africa were education, defense, and health. A discouraging trend in Africa is that spending on agriculture, transportation, and communications has gradually declined. Asia has seen a steady increase in education spending and social security, but a decrease in agriculture spending by roughly half. Governments in Asia have also reduced their spending on health as a share of total government spending, which indicates that the economy is continuing to recover from the 1997 Asian financial crisis. In Latin America, social security ranks at the top of all government expenditure items, while agriculture accounts for a small fraction of total expenditures. This is mainly due to the small share of agriculture in national GDP.

Agriculture expenditure as a percentage of agriculture GDP measures government spending on agriculture relative to the size of the sector. This measurement is very important, because agriculture remains the largest sector in rural, developing regions. Compared to developed countries, in developing countries this percentage is extremely low. In the former it is usually more than 20 percent, while in the latter it averages less than 10 percent. In Africa, the percentage remained at roughly 7 percent throughout 1980–2002. Asia's performance was better than that of Africa; its percentage remained constant at 8–10 percent. Latin America saw more of a dramatic increase, with its agriculture spending moving to 13 percent from just 6 percent over two decades. Again, though spending on agriculture research across all developing regions was low compared to that in developing countries, it increased at relatively stable rates. These various types of agricultural spending remain one of the most crucial instruments for promoting growth and alleviating poverty.

Roads, electricity, telecommunications, and other infrastructure services are also important to stimulate growth in agriculture and in rural areas in addition to enhancing food security and reducing poverty. Infrastructure scarcity is partly due to the high per capita costs of serving dispersed populations, but also due to an urban bias in the allocation of public investments. There have been major differences in total infrastructure expenditures between regions. Africa's total spending increased between 1980 and 2002. Conversely, Asia's decreased, mainly due to a rapid decline in China's government spending on infrastructure. Latin America experienced a contraction in its spending during the 1980s but recovered during the 1990s. For government spending on infrastructure as a percentage of total expenditures, the trend is more discouraging. In Africa, the share of infrastructure investment in total spending declined only slightly, from 6.5 percent in 1980 to 3.8 percent in 2002, while Asia's share dropped more than half, from 12 percent to 5 percent. In Latin America, the share declined from 6.7 percent to 2.0 percent in the same period.

Several factors have contributed to the spending patterns in many developing countries for the past two decades. Most obviously, government spending priorities may change depending on the stage of a country's development. In a largely agrarian society, government may spend more on agriculture as a share of total government spending. As a country advances through the various stages of development, the share of agricultural spending declines, but as a percentage of agricultural GDP it increases. Public spending is also affected by a country's political process. Voters' preferences, interest groups, and the sophistication of political institutions all play key roles. In many cases, the middle and upper classes have a much stronger influence on the final allocation than does the lower class. Rarely are the results of such persuasion pro-poor.

The structural adjustment programs (SAPs) implemented beginning in the 1980s have had a profound impact on government spending patterns. They were designed and implemented to correct short-term balance-of-payments problems. The most important element of SAPs is cutbacks in government spending. Fiscal restraint is one of the key contentious issues that every country faces with respect to the macroeconomic adjustments needed in the event of fiscal crises. The agricultural sector, together with infrastructure, has been particularly hard hit.

The performance of government spending relative to economic growth is mixed. In Africa and Asia, government spending on agriculture and education were particularly strong in promoting economic growth. In Latin America, spending on agriculture, infrastructure, and social security had positive growth-promoting effects. SAPs had a negative effect on growth in Africa, but no statistically significant effects in Asia or Latin America.

Several lessons can be drawn from this study. First, various types of government spending have differential impacts on economic growth, implying that there is a greater potential to improve the efficiency of government spending by reallocating it among sectors. Second, governments should reduce their spending in unproductive sectors such as defense and curtail excessive subsidies for fertilizer, irrigation, power, and pesticides. Third, all regions should increase their spending in agriculture, particularly on production-enhancing investments such as those in agricultural R&D. This type of spending not only yields high returns in agricultural production, but also has a large impact on poverty reduction, because most of the poor still reside in rural areas and their main source of livelihood is agriculture.

Country Case Studies on Rural Investment

Chapter 3 uses four case studies to analyze how government spending patterns have helped to promote economic growth and poverty reduction. This was done by collecting detailed regional evidence of government expenditures over time and by estimating econometric equation systems. This approach can help to reduce the estimation bias by controlling for omitted variables and the endogeneity of government spending variables. It can also help to track the different effects of government spending on poverty reduction through different channels. The major findings from this synthesis show that the trickle-down effect of agricultural growth, stimulated by public investment, is still the dominant pathway in alleviating rural poverty. Therefore, any investment that can lead to a high rate of agricultural growth will also have a large impact on poverty reduction. However, nonfarm employment and rural wages have become increasingly important in helping the poor during the post–green revolution period in many Asian countries.

Cross-country analyses combined with detailed case studies show that agricultural research, education, and rural infrastructure are the three most effective areas for public spending in promoting agricultural growth and poverty reduction. Agricultural research has the greatest impact in developing countries in mitigating poverty and productivity concerns. For example, agricultural research has the second-largest impact on poverty reduction in rural India, next to road investment. In China, agricultural research has the largest productivity effect on agricultural production. Agricultural research also has the second-largest impact on overall poverty in China, after rural education.

Education investment has high returns in both economic growth and poverty reduction. In rural areas, its poverty reduction effects are often greater than its effects on productivity growth. In addition to having trickle-down effects on poverty reduction, education often helps the rural poor to improve their nonfarm wages, employment, and rural–urban migration, leading to an increased impact on rural poverty reduction. However, it is important to note that different kinds of education have differential impacts on rural poverty. Rural primary education has a substantially greater impact than do secondary and tertiary education. For example, Thailand has invested heavily in primary education and has attained one of the highest rural literacy rates in the developing world. Enhancing expenditures on agriculture and education, government investments in infrastructure are key to long-term economic growth and poverty reduction. For example, government spending on rural roads has the greatest impact on the reduction of poverty in India.

The trade-off between agricultural growth and poverty reduction is generally small among different types of investment. Expenditures on agricultural research, education, and infrastructure development have a great impact on growth as well as poverty reduction. Regional analyses conducted for China and India suggest that more investment in many less developed areas not only offers the largest amount of poverty reduction per unit of spending, but also leads to the highest economic returns.

Government spending on antipoverty programs generally has a small impact on poverty reduction, mainly due to inefficient targeting and a misuse of funds. Government spending on irrigation has played an important role in promoting agricultural growth and poverty reduction. But today this type of spending has smaller marginal returns in both growth and poverty reduction.

These questions remain: Why do certain investments have higher returns than others? And why does the sector in which growth can have both large economic returns and poverty reduction effects not receive government investment priority?

Health and Nutrition Interventions

As shown in Chapter 2, most developing countries allocate a substantial portion of their public expenditures to their social sectors (education and health budgets). Therefore, Chapter 4 looked specifically at human capital expenditures such as those on nutrition, health, and education and their effects on the poor. With an emphasis on program design, this chapter focused on measuring how the benefits of human capital expenditures are distributed across various income groups. Additionally, we identified particular types of expenditure within these sectors that are more pro-poor. The chapter emphasized that returns from a given total level of public health expenditures depend simultaneously on the composition of these expenditures, the delivery of health services, and the use of services by individuals. Although there is some evidence that health expenditures decreased in the early 1980s, in many cases these have recovered, so that by the late 1990s they were at or above 1980 levels. It may be that the problem is an inappropriate composition of health expenditures.

Within the health community and among donors, there is agreement that primary healthcare investments can efficiently and effectively improve the health status of people in developing countries. However, there is some evidence that the emphasis on providing and subsidizing inexpensive curative care through the primary health network is likely to have a significant "crowding-out" impact on private provision. This may result in a substantially smaller net health impact. However, there is also strong evidence that reducing subsidies will result in even less equal access to health services. Therefore, the introduction of fees needs to be selective; for example, they should be applied only to better-off households and to inexpensive curative care.

Improving health status requires the provision of quality care. This issue is now beginning to receive much attention. The lack of quality healthcare is particularly a problem for poor households without access to affordable private provision. There is therefore a need to find ways to deliver quality services to poor populations, first by recognizing the capacity-intensive nature of such services and then by finding cost-effective solutions. Community actors may have a potentially beneficial impact here.

Improving the quality of healthcare is unlikely to have any substantial impact on health outcomes unless ways are found to improve access to such care for poor households. Improving the distributional impact of health expenditures therefore requires both a reallocation of resources toward primary healthcare and an increase of access to quality health services for the poor. This may be done partly through enhanced resource allocation and mobilization.

While there may be some role for the introduction of fees for some services and income groups, such an approach may not be consistent with improving the nutrition and health status of poor households. However, recent experience with targeted health subsidies suggests that conditioned transfers can be very effective in increasing the access of the poor to health services as well as addressing poverty and malnutrition. The results from Mexico's Oportunidades program suggest that an integrated approach that addresses access, information, quality, and poverty provides great potential. But the design of these programs needs to reflect the health and administrative realities of the targeted countries.

Education Interventions

There is still much debate about how best to allocate scarce public resources across competing uses within the education sector. What constitutes an appropriate distribution of scarce resources across these competing uses will depend on the precise policy objectives, for example, increasing average enrollment or performance versus ensuring more equal access. However, available evidence, outlined in Chapter 4, points to some significant findings on the importance of education investments in developing countries.

Public expenditures on education in developing countries are typically regressive, reflecting the large budget share of expenditures going to tertiary-level education. But even expenditures on primary education are at best only slightly progressive, reflecting the inequality of access. Extensive expansion is worthwhile only if basic quality is maintained (e.g., access to basic infrastructure and instructional resources, including teachers or instructors who turn up and are motivated to teach). Although extensive expansion, such as building more schools and providing facilities, is likely to be more progressive on the margin, when initial enrollment levels are relatively high, it is unlikely to be a cost-effective way of improving the equality of access relative to better-targeted expenditures. Further increasing enrollments from already high levels tends to be extremely difficult and often costly, partly reflecting the preferences and constraints facing extremely poor households. In such circumstances, targeted education subsidies can be a very cost-effective way of making education more accessible to children from the poorest households. Once a basic level of quality is attained, intensive expansion is more likely to have an effect on improving student performance than on increasing enrollment and is thus likely to be only slightly progressive even if confined to primary education.

Social Safety Net Spending

Chapter 5 expands the discussion in Chapter 4 by arguing that food subsidies, human capital (nutrition, health, and education) subsidies, and public works are crucial safety nets for the poor and must be integrated into any pro-poor spending pattern. The main findings are presented here.

Empirical evidence clearly shows that universal food subsidies are not very effective ways of transferring resources to the poor. This reflects the fact that they are very rarely progressive and often involve large consumption and production efficiency costs. Bureaucracy and leakages will obviously increase the transaction costs and thus efficiency costs. For this reason, universal food subsidies are often viewed as stopgap policies in developing countries, to be used until more cost-effective transfer instruments can be developed.

Although targeted food subsidies (e.g., those provided through ration shops) can greatly increase their benefit incidence and reduce associated efficiencies, in practice their performance has not always been great, reflecting both high amounts of leakage to the non-poor and high costs associated with distributing food and with corruption. Empirical evidence highlights the high costs often associated with such transfers.

Public works are particularly effective in addressing the issue of vulnerability to poverty and in crisis situations. Although well-designed and -implemented public works programs appear to have great potential for targeting poor households, they also appear to be a relatively expensive way of dealing with current poverty; high nonwage costs and forgone earnings make the cost per unit (net) of income transferred to poor households relatively high.

There is evidence that community participation in selecting assets and implementing programs may have high returns. However, there is also some evidence that community involvement works well only when there are good governance structures and active participation of civil society in these structures. For instance, social funds put more emphasis on asset creation and community involvement in designing, proposing, and implementing projects in order to take advantage of high returns.

Many countries in Latin America have recently introduced a program innovation whereby targeted transfers are linked with a condition that households invest in their children's nutrition, health, and education. These new human capital programs are attractive because they address many of the shortcomings of existing social safety nets. Evidence shows that these programs are very well targeted, using a combination of geographic, demographic, proxy means, and community targeting methods. Rigorous evaluations have also shown that targeted human capital subsidies have a substantial impact on nutrition, health, and education outcomes.

Pro-Poor Spending: A Macroeconomic Perspective

Although Chapter 3 considered possible pathways by which government spending affects the poor, certain general-equilibrium effects were assumed to be small or nonexistent. To relax this assumption, in Chapter 6 a dynamic CGE model was developed to simulate the effects of various spending scenarios on growth as well as on poverty, using the data from developing African countries and estimated parameters from Fan and Rao (2003). The results are by and large consistent with the findings in Chapters 2 and 3, but with more quantitative assessment with regard to opportunity costs and trade-offs, therefore offering new policy insights.

Economic performance can be improved when government resources are reallocated from unproductive areas to the different target areas. The most positive overall effects are realized when agriculture is targeted. For example, the reallocation of 10 percent of government demand (1.9 percent of GDP) from unproductive areas in the beginning of the study period reduces the final-year poverty rate by 7.5 percentage points. The impact is less positive (and may be negative) when the government expands spending in the target areas without cuts elsewhere and without any additional foreign financing. This leaves fewer resources available for private consumption and investment. However, if additional foreign grants are sufficient to cover government financing needs, the scope for growth in domestic absorption is widened, with a positive impact on household welfare and poverty reduction.

The impact of reducing the depreciation rates for public capital stocks suggests that the gains from increasing the efficiency of public spending may be as important as the allocation of resources to areas with large payoffs. In another simulation, using empirical estimates of the total factor productivity linkage elasticity of defense spending, government spending was reallocated to defense. Such elasticities capture not only the opportunity cost of defense spending but also the broader economic consequences of wars and civil strife. In all, the impact of defense spending was negative, showing an increase in the poverty rate by 20 percentage points and zero GDP growth. This clearly points to the importance of conflict resolution and management as prerequisites for successful development.

What We Have Learned: Implications for Policy

This section summarizes what we have learned from the synthesis exercise presented in this book. There are many lessons one could draw from such rich information. We limit our findings to the objectives of the proposed outline of this book.

Agricultural Spending Is Crucial for Economic Growth and Poverty Reduction

Agricultural spending is one of the most important government instruments for promoting economic growth and alleviating poverty in rural areas of developing countries for the following reasons: (1) the majority of the world's poor earn a large share of their income from agriculture, (2) growth in agriculture contributes to poverty reduction indirectly through increased rural wages and both farm and nonfarm employment, and (3) agricultural growth may also contribute to poverty reduction in urban areas by lowering food prices for urban residents and helping national economic growth.

Agricultural spending has been declining in many developed countries. However, compared to developed countries, developing countries have extremely low agricultural spending as a percentage of agricultural GDP. The former usually have more than 20 percent such spending, while the latter average less than 10 percent. More important, agricultural spending has been further reduced under the structural adjustment programs. The share of agricultural spending in total government spending gradually declined from 12 percent in 1980 to 6 percent in 2002.

Disaggregating total agricultural expenditures into research and non-research spending reveals that research (or productivity-enhancing) spending has a larger impact than nonresearch (or non-productivity-enhancing) spending. This is particularly the case for agricultural R&D, which not only yields high returns to agricultural production, but also has a large impact on poverty reduction. While governments in developing countries should increase their overall spending on agriculture, agricultural R&D deserves special treatment.

Broader Types of Investment in Rural Areas Are Needed, Such as in Education and Health

One of the main conclusions of this book is that there is a need to bolster the education and health sectors in developing countries. Human capital services are crucial, particularly in countries where SAPs have been implemented. In Africa, governments reduced their shares of spending for education and social security, while education also suffered from reduction in government expenditures in Latin America.

The contribution of education and health spending to economic growth is also a significant factor in reducing poverty in the developing world. In regions such as Africa, government spending in health was particularly strong in promoting economic growth. Only education spending contributed positively to economic growth in Asia. In Latin America, education and health spending had a positive growth-promoting effect. Both these types of spending have positive spillover effects. Therefore, governments should reduce their spending in unproductive sectors such as defense and reallocate public monies to education and health.

An important conclusion with regard to health expenditures is that the reduction of public subsidies, and the consequent introduction of user fees, needs to be selective in that it should apply only to better-off households and to inexpensive curative healthcare. This is necessary because there is strong evidence that reducing subsidies can result in more inequity in access to health services and in health outcomes.

Public education expenditures in developing countries are typically regressive in that a large share of expenditures go to tertiary-level education. Even those countries that spend more on primary education experience inequality of access. Our conclusion is that primary education needs substantially more investment. The logic here is that once a basic level of education is attained, intensive expansion is more likely to have an effect on improving student performance than on increasing enrollment and is thus likely to be only slightly progressive even if confined to primary education.

To improve the distributional impact of public health expenditures, governments need to reallocate public monies toward primary healthcare and increasing access to quality health services for the poor. Hospitals need to target poor people for access to services, and health facilities need to be made available in sparsely populated areas where the poor reside. In addition, the poor should be made aware of the benefits of preventive healthcare. It is also important to understand the potential role of community actors in such a scenario. This is one of the alternative expansion strategies that governments can use to create better synergies between scarce healthcare resources and access to services by the poor.

It is clear that the non-poor have captured most of the benefits from public education expenditures in developing countries. One of the main conclusions for the education sector is that targeted education subsidies relative to extensive expansion can be a very cost-effective way of making education more accessible to children from the poorest households. For example, subsidies targeted at poor households should meet the extra private costs of education but also provide an additional increment of increasing consumption.

Social Safety Nets Must Be Targeted to the Poorest of the Poor

Social safety nets in the form of food subsides and public works are crucial in times of crises and for poverty reduction. Empirical evidence shows that universal food subsidies are not very effective in transferring resources to the poor because they are regressive and incur high consumption and production efficiency costs. They are therefore used as stopgap measures. Targeted food subsidies in theory increase the benefits derived by the poor and reduce inefficiency, but in practice perform badly due to leakages to the non-poor and incur high distribution and corruption costs.

When addressing the *vulnerability* of the poor, public works are important, particularly in crises such as postconflict situations or in seasonal changes in employment. Therefore, we conclude that labor-intensive public works that require few management skills and pay relatively low wages are preconditions to effectively address both current poverty and vulnerability. This narrow targeting of public works programs is crucial as a coping mechanism for the poorest of the poor in times of need.

Community participation in selecting assets and implementing programs is fundamental to asset creation, because community involvement may bring high returns. However, these communities must have good governance structures and the active participation of civil society. In addition, social funds are probably better at addressing structural poverty through community asset creation. However, good geographic targeting of these programs and active promotion of demand for them in the poorest communities is necessary for them to have a substantial impact on poverty.

An important conclusion is that increasing human capital in poor households can contribute significantly to breaking the intergenerational transmission of poverty in the longer term. Targeted government transfers conditioned on households' investment in children's nutrition, health, and education promote this accumulation of human capital.

The fact that human capital programs have been successful in some poor countries suggests that they have the potential for success elsewhere. However, the design of these programs will need to evolve in the local context for them to be successful. Other economic policies must also be conducive to generating broad-based growth capable of productively absorbing the more skilled labor force required for such programs. These programs are no panacea for development. However, we conclude that their proven performance justifies serious consideration of such programs as an important component of an overall poverty alleviation system in a developing country.

Knowledge Gaps and Directions for Future Research

Despite the existing literature on public spending and poverty reduction, much research needs to be done in the future. This section summarizes the knowledge gaps and points out directions for future research, which should not only serve as a guide for future work by the International Food Policy Research Institute, but also have implications for public spending in relation to poverty reduction in general. Our suggestions are as follows.

1. Developing countries must pay greater attention to systematically compiling public investment data in rural areas. Various international agencies, such as the World Bank, the Food and Agriculture Organization, and the International Monetary Fund, have made efforts to help developing countries establish national statistical systems to collect, compile, and monitor development indicators related to agriculture production and inputs, income, employment, wages, and poverty. But these efforts seldom include information on rural infrastructure, technology, education, and related government investment. Without such information, it is difficult to assess the potential holistic impacts of government intervention on agricultural growth and poverty reduction.

2. A general-equilibrium analysis is needed to show how government investment in rural areas affects not only the agricultural sector and rural areas, but also other sectors and cities. To date, most of the studies conducted have been single-sector, partial-equilibrium analyses, which do not have the ability to track general-equilibrium and societal effects. Ignoring these impacts results in severe underestimation of the overall impact of public investment on poverty.

3. How to finance needed public investment in rural areas deserves more attention. There are two major means of financing expenditures for public goods—general government financing (for example, taxes) and cost recovery (for example, user fees) for service provision. The financing of public expenditures has important implications for efficiency and equity.

4. An analysis of the political and institutional context of public investments and conditions for the efficient provision of public goods and services is also much needed to improve the efficiency of public investments. In particular, how governments can design mechanisms (policies, regulations, and fiscal systems) to mobilize public resources to invest in rural areas deserves much more research attention in the future. How to reform public institutions by improving incentives, accountability, human capital, and management is also an important issue for research.

    Past assessments of the impact of public investment assumed that institutional and political constraints were exogenous to the model. Research on how governance affects the efficacy of public investment needs more attention. There is a vast literature of empirical studies on the relationship between various governance indicators and development outcomes. However, these studies have been done primarily at the cross-country level. It is important to examine the relationship between governance and development outcomes at the sector level in the context of specific countries.

5. Research also needs to be done on the role of traditional and indigenous organizations, as well as local community involvement, in infrastructure provision. The political economy of the devolution and decentralization of power in infrastructure provision, along with problems of common property rights, also needs empirical analysis. In addition, the theory of new institutional economics suggests that pricing policies and subsidies in infrastructure need further research.

References

Chen, S., and M. Ravallion. 2004. How have the world's poorest fared since the early 1980s? *World Bank Research Observer* 19 (1): 141–169.

Fan, S., and N. Rao. 2003. Public spending in developing countries: Trend, determination and impact. EPTD Discussion Paper 99. Washington, D.C.: International Food Policy Research Institute.

Contributors

David Coady is technical assistance adviser to the International Monetary Fund, Washington, D.C.

Shenggen Fan is director of the Development Strategy and Governance Division of the International Food Policy Research Institute, Washington, D.C.

Hans Lofgren is a senior economist at the World Bank, Washington, D.C.

Neetha Rao was formerly a senior research assistant in the Development Strategy and Governance Division of the International Food Policy Research Institute, Washington, D.C.

Sherman Robinson is a professor at Sussex University, U.K.

Anuja Saurkar is a research analyst in the Development Strategy and Governance Division of the International Food Policy Research Institute, Washington, D.C.

Annie White was formerly a research assistant in the Development Strategy and Governance Division of the International Food Policy Research Institute, Washington, D.C.

Bingxin Yu is a postdoctoral fellow in the Development Strategy and Governance Division of the International Food Policy Research Institute, Washington, D.C.

241

Index

Page numbers for entries occurring in figures are followed by an *f;* those for entries in notes, by an *n;* and those for entries in tables, by a *t.*

Adato, M., 168–69

Africa: agricultural spending in, 27, 27t, 28, 33, 228; foreign aid in, 30; health care in, 120; public spending allocations in, 24, 25t, 26, 228; public spending trends in, 21, 22, 23t, 24, 228; public works programs in, 165; women's nonfarm activities in, 63–64. *See also* Sub-Saharan Africa; *individual countries*

agricultural growth: determinants of, 38–39, 40t; economic growth contribution of, 59; land distribution and, 60, 65; poverty reduction effects of, 58–61, 81, 230, 231; productivity increases, 58, 59, 62, 71, 74, 76, 81; public spending effects on, 20, 38–39, 40t, 41, 71, 76, 78, 84–85, 231; regional differences in, 61, 64

agricultural research spending: agricultural growth effects of, 39, 231; poverty reduction effects of, 78, 80–81, 82–83, 230, 235; productivity increases from, 58, 76, 230; trends in, 27–28, 229

agriculture: employment, 59, 62; green revolution, 59, 62, 64–65; indigenous knowledge of, 67. *See also* food

agriculture, public spending on: agricultural growth effects of, 20, 38–39, 40t, 41, 71, 76, 78, 84–85; economic growth and, 38, 41, 186, 206, 208–9, 213, 217–18; geographic allocation of, 73; increasing, 230, 235; in India, 76–78; as percentage of agricultural GDP, 27, 228–29, 235; poverty reduction effects of, 209, 217–18, 235; proportion of public spending, 26, 33, 41;

trends in, 26–28, 27t. *See also* agricultural research spending

Ahluwalia, M. S., 59

Ahmed, A., 135, 175

Ahmed, R., 156

Alston, J., 11

Angrist, J., 134

Argentina, Trabajar program, 167–68

Arrellano, M., 36

Aschauer, D., 20

Asia: agricultural spending in, 27, 27t, 28, 228–29; economic development and public spending, 23–24; public spending allocations in, 24–26, 25t, 228; public spending trends in, 21, 22, 23t, 228. *See also* green revolution; *individual countries*

Bamako initiative, 120

Bangladesh, 117, 121; Food for Education program, 135, 170, 174–76, 178; Food for Work program, 163, 164, 165

Barro, R., 188, 189

basic needs approach, 5–6, 227

Beintema, N., 27–28

benefit incidence approach, 115–16, 124–26, 137–39

Besley, Tim, 73

Bidani, B., 119

Binswanger, Hans, 73

Blair, Tony, 2

Blundell, Richard, 36

Bolivia, education in, 133

Bond, S., 36

Brazil, BA program, 128, 170

246   *Index*